TROUBLE IN OUR BACKYARD

TROUBLE IN OUR BACKYARD

CENTRAL AMERICA AND THE UNITED STATES IN THE EIGHTIES

EDITED BY

MARTIN DISKIN

With a Foreword by JOHN WOMACK, Jr.
And an Epilogue by GÜNTER GRASS

PANTHEON BOOKS, NEW YORK

Grateful acknowledgment is made to the following for permission to reprint or adapt from previously published material:
Monthly Review Press for "The Nicaraguan Crisis," *Monthly Review* 34:6 (November 1982), pp. 1–16. Copyright © 1982 by Monthly Review Inc. By permission of Monthly Review Press.
NACLA for a complete version of Steven Volk's "Honduras: On the Border of War," *NACLA Report on the Americas* 15:6 (November–December 1981).
Socialist Review for "Revolution and Transition in Nicaragua," *Socialist Review,* no. 59 (September–October 1981).

Library of Congress Cataloging in Publication Data
Main entry under title:

Trouble in our backyard.

Includes index.
    1. Central America—Foreign relations—United States—Addresses, essays, lectures. 2. United States—Foreign relations—Central America—Addresses, essays, lectures. 3. Central America—Politics and government—1979– —Addresses, essays, lectures. 4. United States—Foreign relations —1981– —Addresses, essays, lectures. I. Diskin, Martin, 1934–
F1436.8.U6T76 1984   327.728073   83–42810
ISBN 0-394-52295-8
ISBN 0-394-71589-6 (pbk.)

Manufactured in the United States of America

9 8 7 6 5 4 3

Design by Robert Bull

To the long-postponed dream of a united Central America

ACKNOWLEDGMENTS

It is obvious that at this moment books of this sort are sorely needed if the national debate about Central America is to be founded in fact and reason. André Schiffrin, the publisher of Pantheon Books, has actively supported this effort since its inception. For that I am deeply grateful. Wendy Wolf, my editor, has been a constructive participant. Her critical reactions have always been on the mark, and her gentle nudging, when needed, has kept this book as close to schedule as it has been. Stephen Ault translated the essays by Torres and Maira. His work was supplemented by that of Eric Schultz, who did further translation and helped edit several other essays as well. Both of them were sounding boards who helped me better to understand the texts and often suggested clearer ways to express the authors' intentions. Karen Chaney typed and retyped several articles and generally kept track of the various intermediate versions of the manuscript. Finally, I wish to express my deep gratitude to all the contributors, who not only taught me a great deal about contemporary Central America but strengthened my commitment to social justice in that region. Through books such as this, we hope to activate the American people to ensure that the United States will become part of the solution and not, as at present, part of the problem.

CONTENTS

FOREWORD
John Womack, Jr.

Mon centre cède, ma droite recule,
situation excellente. J'attaque!
—MARSHAL FOCH

There never has been a center in Central America. The land is an isthmus, narrow, without a core. It lies along 800 miles of green volcanoes, the Guatemala trench, fractured across the middle by the Nicaragua rift. It is a country of eruptions and earthquakes. Since the founding of San Salvador in 1528, seismic shocks have knocked the town down nine times. The people of Central America have never acted together or felt united. When the Spaniards first went conquering there in the 1520s, they found nearly a score of different kinds of folk—Quiché, Cakchiquel, Tzendal, Tzotzil, Tzutujil, Ixil, Kekchi, Mam, Potomam, Pipil, Lenca, Chorotega, Jicaque, Nicarao, Paya, Huetar, and others. And more numerous than the varieties of people were their chiefdoms. Over 450 years later the region remains "a nation divided," five nominally sovereign states, de facto a confederacy of maybe twenty-five localized and contentious societies, which during the last 100 years capitalist development has only in part and tenuously organized into a struggle between classes. There the center is a dream, or a nightmare, or a lie of artificially sweet reason to justify an establishment for screwing the poor.

In the Spanish Empire the isthmian provinces were a distant colonial frontier between Mexico City and Bogotá. Their high court in Guatemala City held faint sway over them. Their Caribbean coasts harbored Dutch pirates as early as the 1580s, runaway African slaves from the West Indies after 1630, English pirates and merchants by 1650, English settlers, loggers, by 1660. A stretch of the Honduran-Nicaraguan Caribbean coast, La Mosquitia, came under Charles II's sovereign claim in 1670. Spanish expeditions now and then descended to expel the intruders, in vain. The English on the coast now and then raided up into the interior, to force respect for their settlements, in vain. Throughout the eighteenth and into the nineteenth century, power in Central America did not balance or tilt on a pivot, but further fragmented, thinned toward a vacuum.

In the 1830s, a few years after Spain lost all its mainland colonies to independence, Americans began seriously to challenge Englishmen as the chief merchants in Mexico and Central America. They did not seek grounds for production. They wanted a short way for trade between the Atlantic and Pacific oceans, a way quicker than the trip across the North American continent or around Cape Horn. They eventually focused on three passages. The first and for long the most attractive was the Isthmus of Tehuantepec, in Mexico. The second was a cut through Nicaragua. The third was a canal across the Colombian province of Panama. The substantiation of Mexican sovereignty in the 1850s and 1860s drew into official U.S.–Mexican relations the question of a passage through Tehuantepec. The American entrepreneurs in rivalry with the English refocused then on Nicaragua and Panama. They concentrated on Nicaragua once a French company commenced construction of a canal across Panama in 1880. But the rooting of American transport, land, and tropical-fruit companies in the region in the 1880s consolidated its political fragmentation; the companies, later combined in United Fruit, could deal more profitably with five separate than with five united Central American states. U.S. Marines expelled the English from Nicaragua's Caribbean coast in 1894 and protected the Nicaraguan claim to rule La Mosquitia, in defense of persistent American plans for a Nicaraguan canal. But Americans newly interested in Panama succeeded in rigging Panamanian independence and a U.S.–Panamanian treaty for a canal in 1903, the U.S. purchase of the (incomplete) French works in 1904, and a U.S. commitment to build a Panamanian canal in 1906. This turn established Central American division, since it based U.S. geopolitical concerns in the satellite to the south.

No more coherent were the social and political conflicts within each state. Before the 1880s they were usually about who controlled surplus produce. On the surge of the new businesses, they were increasingly about who owned the very forces of production. Old or new, they carried the fury of blood feuds and often burst into violence. After the turn of the century, these fights not only disturbed United Fruit but also irritated Brown Brothers and Company, which had loans out in the region. Besides, they worried the U.S. government as opportunities for English (or German or even Japanese) intrigue in the isthmus, dangerously close to the Panamanian canal works.

Since no center would emerge by itself in Central America, the United States in 1909 sent the marines back into Nicaragua to install a faction promising to become a force for general moderation. The marines fulfilled their mission. But when they left in 1910, the feuding immediately resumed. The marines returned to Nicaragua in 1912 on a broader mission, to make themselves the force to hold the entire region still for United Fruit, New York banks, and the Canal Zone to the south. They succeeded. But they solved nothing basic. And when they withdrew in 1925, class war and partisan strife in Nicaragua blew up in the nationalist revolt led by Augusto Sandino—with deep reverberations in the other states.

The marines returned again to Nicaragua in 1926, on instructions this time not only to reimpose a pro-American order in Central America but also to create a local force to maintain the order indefinitely. They took seven years to crush the Sandinista guerrillas. In the struggle they organized and trained a tough new army, the Nicaraguan National Guard, just what was called for, although somewhat misnamed, less a Nicaraguan guard than an American guard manned by Nicaraguans. When the last marines pulled out in 1933, the U.S. minister to Nicaragua made sure that command of the National Guard went to the most American Nicaraguan politico he knew, a character who, having taken a business course in Philadelphia, sold cars, refereed boxing, umpired baseball, read meters, and inspected toilets in his fatherland, had become the Nicaraguan consul in Costa Rica, deputy foreign minister, and lately minister of foreign affairs, a hustler, a heavy charmer, and a real killer, Anastasio Somoza. "He's a sonofabitch," FDR later allowed, "but he's ours."

This solution—banana fascism—prospered. For forty-six years, thanks to U.S. sponsorship, the Nicaraguan National Guard and the Somozas who commanded it compensated for the lack of a center in Central America. Through the guard, Somoza stabilized the region, not by developing an order, but by terrorizing Nicaraguans of all classes and parties and enforcing U.S. constraints on other states that drifted too far out of line. His only slippage occurred in 1946–47, when the U.S. encouraged leftist social reforms in the region, particularly in Guatemala and Costa Rica. But the United States' favorite son of a bitch proved his mettle, endured the American lapse, and in the ensuing cold war provided the base for U.S. subversion of Guatemala's reforms and confinement of Costa Rica's to Costa Rica. He went to his reward by virtue of assassination in 1956, but his sons perpetuated his memory in their more or less flagrant dictatorship of Nicaragua and their intimidation of governments elsewhere in the region. After the Cuban revolution, the Somozas often led their American sponsors in deciding what was desirable and what was intolerable in Central America and the Caribbean. They promoted the formation of the Central American Common Market in 1960. They urged and materially backed the invasion of Cuba in 1961. They (with Trujillo) initiated the mocking of the Alliance for Progress's democratic aspects. They were the keystone in the building of the Central American Defense Council in 1964. Once they ran serious deficits in regional trade, they encouraged the Salvadoran war against Honduras in 1969, which wrecked the common market. And they bought sufficient U.S. congressmen in the 1970s to make the State Department stake American strategic interests in the isthmus not just on Nicaragua but on their family's fortunes.

All this went to historic hell in the revolution of 1979. That summer the National Guard was defeated in the field by the armed forces of the leftist Frente Sandinista de Liberación Nacional. The guard disintegrated and disbanded. The Somozas fled to Florida, then to Paraguay. And an FSLN junta took charge of Nicaragua, bound to establish the Sandinista forces as the new Nicaraguan army, determined to carry out leftist reforms in their state, intent on reasserting sovereignty in foreign relations, hoping for revolutions like theirs among their neighbors.

Since that summer two struggles have racked Central America.

One is the mounting conflict between right and left—the con-
catenation of a U.S.–directed siege of the Sandinistas in Nicaragua,
a civil war in El Salvador, official terrorism and guerrilla resistance
in Guatemala, and intrigue and underground organization in Honduras and Costa Rica. The other struggle is the frantic U.S. effort
to find a basis for restoring the old order. This flailing endeavor
U.S. officials dignify as a search for the center. But in fact it is no
more than the U.S. government's shocked, if not stupefied, reaction to the loss of its geopolitical stakes in Nicaragua, that is,
various bungling attempts to get back the venerable American
position there. Evidently the U.S. government would declare a
Central American Hitler to be a man of the center, if the lie
facilitated the recovery of old American confidence in the region.

Unless a world war happens, the political directions practically
possible in Central America in the next ten years are these:

(1) A victory of the right, which the U.S. government would
call the center. It would occur upon a U.S.–sponsored destruction
of the Sandinista government in Nicaragua, a consequently coordinated civil war throughout the isthmus, the collapse of the
Guatemalan, Salvadoran, and Honduran armies, and finally a U.S.
occupation of the region. In American bitterness John Prine might
then sing, "It's hello California. Hello, Dad and Mama. Ship ahoy,
your baby boy is home from Guatemala."

(2) A victory of the left, which the U.S. government now refers
to as Soviet agents. It would occur upon U.S. sponsorship of
negotiations to end the war in El Salvador, a leftist revolution in
Guatemala, a leftist coup in Honduras, reorganization of the Salvadoran, Guatemalan, and Honduran armies, and the constitution
of a new Central American common market and defense council.
This would not amount to socialism, which no major force on the
Central American Left now has or in calculable circumstances will
soon have on its agenda. It would mean the commencement of a
serious civic culture in the region. In American pride Pete Seeger
might then sing, "Last night I had the strangest dream . . ."

(3) The present prolonged, ten more years of U.S.–subsidized
rightist survival and U.S.–condemned leftist rebellion. It would
occur if the U.S. government continued to search for a center. It
would mean ever-deepening American delusion, shame, and deca-

dence, and Central American torment as gruesome as perdition, the present agony simply repeated over the years, the uniformed and civilian dead disfigured and dismembered in futile sacrifice. God only knows what an American might then sing. "I'm always chasing rainbows"? Or, "Yes, we have no bananas"? If this is what happens, there will be no words in Central American songs, for on the isthmus words will not be enough to tell the grief.

1 February 1983

INTRODUCTION
Martin Diskin

*"You'd be surprised
—they are all individual countries."*

When Ronald Reagan said this on his junket in Latin America in November 1982 most listeners interpreted the "you" to be Reagan speaking for himself. Such explosions of insight by our chief executive may ignite optimism in those who believe that knowledge informs policy, but the pessimists can point to the enormous body of good scholarship concerning Latin and Central America that should already have laid bare the ignorance that underlies (and the falsehoods used to express) our official policy. The gap between reality and policy can be linked in large part to the fact that official American understanding of the Southern Hemisphere is based not on careful academic analysis but on the historical residue of realpolitik that divides the world into areas of significant—and insignificant—turf. An incident involving Henry Kissinger, the classic practitioner of realpolitik, illustrates this neatly: after a June 1969 speech in which the Chilean foreign minister described the difficulties of dealing with the United States, Kissinger set the minister straight about how the world was really structured. He told him, at lunch at the Chilean embassy the next day, "Nothing important can come from the South. The axis of history starts in Moscow, goes to Bonn, crosses over to Washington, and then goes on to Tokyo. What happens in the South is of no importance. You're wasting your time."[1]

The arrogance of this perspective is evident in the more intimate metaphor by which Central America[2] has lately been described— the "backyard," a piece of property not just adjacent to but in our domain itself, close and manageable. The corollary to Kissinger's statement—that any social change must necessarily reflect the hand of the Soviets—is equally patronizing. It is in part due to just such arrogant myths and to the indifference of those in power that we find ourselves with a critically distorted notion of what Latin and Central America are, with a fiction that impedes the establishment of informed, let alone respectful, relations.

The elements that make up this mythic image of Latin America, and particularly of Central America, include the assertion that Central American countries are, at heart, city-states, not larger (and more complex) nations; that political life in them is intimate and even tribal; and that a guiding principle in politics is the fear of (and need for) order, discipline, and authority.[3] Thus, when we look at their strong cultural differences and their apparent classic inability to manage for themselves, we can seize an opening for U.S. "guidance."

The justifications for U.S. control were, earlier in this century, more directly stated: the governments of Central America could not survive without our support.[4] In recent years, authorities have turned to indirect needs, invoking the Communist menace in the Dominican Republic in 1965 and in Guatemala in 1954, or vaguely referring to the "real will" of the people, as in Chile in 1973. The direct hegemonic impulse, whose benevolent implications were automatically assumed from the inherent and unassailable morality of the United States, has given way to more complicated arguments of national security. Although the United States for decades virtually ignored the domestic problems of these countries, the defeat of the red enemy is suddenly being identified with (or as) the true path toward modern national development.

Something is changing, though. The subterranean turmoil that has always accompanied the misery and injustice of the region has surfaced in direct hostility. Aimed in the first instance against the autocratic and oligarchic systems that have ruled, these movements have also increasingly identified the United States as the overwhelming, imperial power of the region, whose interests are not compatible with genuine liberation. Thus, although the United States had no substantial direct capital investment in Nicaragua, our foreign policy doggedly supported Somoza until the final Sandinista triumph. After half a century of backing one bloody dictator after another in El Salvador (quaintly characterized as a "moderately authoritarian rule tempered by paternalism and populism",[5] even Salvadorans like Major D'Aubuisson who owe their political existence to U.S. policy regard the United States as imperialist and its ambassador as a "proconsul." The revolutionary activity that is sweeping through Central America is assuming a dual goal—to rid each country of its indigenous ruling classes and to reduce the dependency on the United States, which has meant only unhappiness in the past.

The anti-American tone of Central American revolutionaries is an inevitable by-product of American policy. Our loyalty to the dreary succession of Guatemalan dictators, from Castillo Armas in 1954 to Ríos Montt in 1982, has demonstrated a rigidity of purpose unmodified by learning. Our relations with the military election thieves of El Salvador is another example. After a reformist military coup was itself replaced by military hardliners, John F. Kennedy said that "governments of the civil-military type of El Salvador are the most effective in containing Communist penetration in Latin America."[6]

U.S. policy in Central America has been directed largely toward the preservation of the status quo. This meant preserving an economic relation in which the U.S. was the strongest (and most profiting) partner of each country in the region. Political non-change, termed "normalcy," had as its most significant feature the absence of Communist influence. Maintaining the status quo was usually guaranteed by the local military with strong support from the United States. To get the local proxies started in their mission, we showed them the way in the first decades of the century, through a series of invasions and military occupations, in which we seized control of the customshouses as escrow. Fifty years later, however, our well-laid plans are erupting in a manner we never expected.

The military, whose job it is to kill—whether for the coffee planters of Guatemela or El Salvador, for United Fruit in Honduras, or for Somoza in Nicaragua—has done its work with such thoroughness that it has become the main mode for political expression (the historic interclass "dialogue") in these countries. What several decades ago was the solution to the problem of installing agro-export industries and eliminating annoyances like unions and opposition parties is now itself the problem. Accustomed to the efficiency of murder as a form of political discourse, the military-economic elites are reluctant, perhaps unable, to contemplate any other form. The central role of the military has been rationalized as the "strong authority and discipline" needed in countries where "Western civilization has been only weakly established and is woefully underinstitutionalized."[7] The projection of U.S. military power has also been strongly approved by one of the palace theorists as a promoter of freedom. For Huntington, the U.S. Marines' invasions and occupations of Nicaragua, Haiti, the Dominican Republic, and other countries in the period 1900–33 "often bore striking resemblances to the interventions by federal marshals in the conduct of elections in the American south in the 1960s; registering voters, protecting against electoral violence, ensuring a free vote and an honest count."[8] These invasions left in their wake the Somozas, the Duvaliers, and the Trujillos, apprentice dictators who quickly became masters and who endured into the 1960s, 1970s, and 1980s, a point Huntington chooses not to dwell upon.

The legacy of military domination that exists today is in part of our own making. The installation of military regimes friendly to the United States was a conscious policy as early as 1954. A recently declassified National Security Council document entitled "U.S. Policy toward Latin America" argued for "the ultimate standardization of Latin American military organization, training, doctrine, and equipment along U.S. lines" to accomplish the "understanding of, and orientation toward, U.S. objectives on the part of the Latin American military." The same document includes a general discussion of U.S. priorities in Latin America. After advocating that there be "adequate protection in Latin America of and access by the United States to raw materials essential to U.S. security," it goes on to urge that the United States encourage Latin American governments "to base their economies on a system of private enterprise and, as essential thereto, to create a political and economic climate conducive to private investment, of both domestic and foreign capital, including . . . opportunity to earn and in the case of foreign capital, to repatriate a reasonable return."[9]

As the military is increasingly unable to contain indigenous revolutionary movements, our response is to blame the Soviet

Union for creating "unrest," a point of view that neatly bolsters the policy thrusts of an overall national-security posture. As we invoke the Soviet threat, we continually reinforce the goal of keeping the Soviets out at any costs—that is, of securing the region against penetration. Although administration officials occasionally discuss domestic reasons for conflict, they hasten to add that our response to the dislocation must be twofold: to promote improvements in human welfare and to eliminate injustice, but at the same time to defeat the Soviet-backed insurgency in the wars in Guatemala, El Salvador, and Nicaragua.[10]

Only one of these efforts—the military effort—is being seriously prosecuted. The economies of these three countries are desperately troubled, a situation only exacerbated by the military activity, and our influence continues to be expressed almost exclusively through that military force. Although Honduras elected a civilian president in November 1981, U.S. relations have been pursued principally through contact with General Alvarez, thus strengthening the military over the civilian force. In Guatemala, we recognized the military coup of Ríos Montt with indecent haste and exert no pressure on his government to hold elections. In El Salvador the ritual of presidential certification has had the effect of demonstrating the obsessive interest of the United States in supporting the military despite the abundant documentation of its moral unsuitability. Even in Costa Rica, a nation that abolished its military in 1948, we are urging the acceptance of military training and arms rather than the more important economic stabilization that is required.

We have thrown our weight behind a policy that is leading to a collision course with the populations of Central America. This policy holds a double appeal for Washington. First, for Reagan and like ideologues, this is the perfect arena in which to demonstrate how to handle the evil of communism. No coddling or dialoguing with people who "lie and cheat." Furthermore, a victory has seemed attainable at a relatively low cost. It has appeared until recently that the steady increase of military assistance would be the sensible route toward exterminating the insurgency. That has not proven to be as obvious as it once seemed. The reasons for this go well beyond strategic considerations. They lie in the social fabric of the region, and they lead to the conclusion that our present policy can "succeed" only in the sense that it may buy a bit of time.[11]

U.S.-Soviet relations have evolved since the height of Cold War tension. Containment, with its military and economic elements, generally gave way to détente, with a greater emphasis on diplomatic means. When the Third World is the arena for U.S.-Soviet contention however, the arguments for limiting Soviet power, and therefore the threat to U.S. security, become more diffuse and rely on traditional sphere of influence notions. If, as some theorists would suggest, national security can be linked to national needs, many measures are justified to squelch social change. Thus, if strategic metals (copper, bauxite) are involved or geopolitical balances are in jeopardy, the most convenient argument for the U.S. to make will center around possible Soviet penetration. Some would go beyond the protection of national needs and include "wants" to insure security. Tucker writes in *Foreign Affairs,* "In Central America there are no vital raw materials or minerals," but the region "bears geographical proximity to the U.S. and historically it has long been regarded as falling within our sphere of influence" and we "have regularly played a determining role in making and unmaking governments, and we have defined what we have considered to be the acceptable behavior of governments. So, in Central America our pride is engaged as it cannot possibly be engaged in Africa or in Southeast Asia." Furthermore, "we enjoy clear military superiority and may expect to retain such superiority in the future."[12] The above argument explains the reason and the means to reassert domination over Central America in the context of a "resurgent America." Tucker is specific about the projection of U.S. power, that is, the commitment of military force to the region.

This position, reflecting a nostalgia for an imperial United States, is based on a notion that the distinction between needs and wants must fail if the impression of weakness or an incomplete hegemony is projected. Therefore, policy must be fashioned so that supremacy is constant. The realpolitik of the Tucker article makes no mention of any indigenous cause of the present crisis, or of any steps that would alleviate the crisis by affecting the root causes. It clearly opts, however, for propping up a right-wing dictatorship with American military force. The Reagan administration has been particularly creative in its search for ways to justify a policy obviously not in the best interest of the majority of the population in Central America. The most startling example of this inventive scholarship has been the new distinction between authoritarian and totalitarian regimes, neatly discriminating between regimes we like and those we disapprove of. Proposed by Jeane Kirkpatrick in the pages of *Commentary,* these definitions, though short on facts, reflect a good deal of pragmatism. After recognizing that regimes like those of Somoza or of the shah of Iran offer a kind of stability we find convenient, she terms these "authoritarian" and, by implication, acceptable, thus ratifying the recent direction of foreign policy. In this new nomenclature, the southern-cone national-security regimes (Argentina, Chile, and Uruguay) are said to be authoritarian (that is, good), and countries such as Cuba, Grenada, and Nicaragua are criticized as totalitarian—that is, bad. A remarkable degree of discipline has been imposed on members of the administration to include in every mention of countries from the latter group epithets like *totalitarian, Marxist-Leninist, foreign-supplied,* and *Cuban- or Soviet-dominated.*

Kirkpatrick's scheme does not withstand the slightest scrutiny. The authoritarians' alleged capacity for change has not been borne out by the tyrannical dynastic rules of Somoza, Batista, or Pinochet, who has provided himself with a life tenure, as have Stroessner, of Paraguay, and Duvalier, of Haiti. The fact that the regimes are "indigenous" has not meant they are any milder as a result. The records of human-rights abuses range from the direct elimination of political opposition to genocide, and they do not seem to respond significantly (or at least positively) either to internal opposition or to the general impulses contained in the messages the United States has sent them.

Kirkpatrick's definition of totalitarianism rings equally false; in fact, the criteria of "acceptability" shift utterly when she turns unsympathetically to these countries. For example, to satisfy her standards for Cuba or Nicaragua, U.S.–style democracy would have to prevail, complete with periodic elections and a press much freer than exists in El Salvador, Chile, or Paraguay. The epithet *totalitarian* effectively sanctions the full inventory of invective and of forms of economic and now military aggression—not unlike the way the term *subversive* is used in El Salvador or Guatemala, as a license to hunt all critics of the regime in power.

For a historian or political scientist, the Kirkpatrick formula—apart from its simplistic and shaky logic—fails to connect to the basic definitions that are in standard usage in analyses of Central American history and politics.

Authoritarianism, particularly bureaucratic authoritarianism, is a well-developed notion, studied by leading Latin Americanists; it refers to the complete control exercised by the military and to the formal, institutional expression of this control (the bureaucracy). It takes into account the high toll exacted in human-rights abuses necessary to stifle any civil response to militarization. It particularly focuses on the question of the relation between modernization and democracy, because it has appeared in the most advanced Latin American societies—Argentina, Uruguay, Chile, and, in a nonmilitarized form, Mexico.[13]

Totalitarianism, a concept most prominent in discussions of the Nazi regime, has not been an important theme in Latin American analysis. If it had been, it would probably have applied to those long-standing regimes characterized by total control, not necessarily through a military institution but through a rigid chain of command that reports to one center—the leader. Perhaps this is closer to the sense intended by Arendt in her discussion of totalitarianism. In any event, Kirkpatrick's polemic was avidly snapped up by the Reagan administration, given how it fit so neatly—if simplistically—the doctrine of "supporting our friends and punishing our enemies." The Communist specter haunting Central America needs constant reinforcement through the periodic injection of information favorable to the administration. The administration has regularly built its case—ultimately a case for greater military involvement—on allegations that Soviet involvement is great, that the Salvadorans are gaining control over their abusive elements, that Nicaraguan military preparations are aggressive in nature and intent, and that domestic repression is worse in Nicaragua than in neighboring countries. At the same time, it regularly ignores evidence concerning the nature of the Salvadoran extreme Right and its relation to death squads and terrorism, accurate investigations of the conduct of the Salvadoran armed forces, and realistic assessments of the land-reform program. A September 1982 report from the House Intelligence Committee addresses all these difficulties in intelligence gathering and points to the policy implications of the slanted data used. One example should suffice. A set of documents was captured on the occasion of the arrest of Major D'Aubuisson in May 1980. These documents "included a log of meetings, expenditures, arms lists with references to silencers and other special equipment, names, addresses and phone numbers of rightist Salvadoran businessmen, and various propaganda flyers discrediting U.S. policy in El Salvador and urging support for a coup." From that time until the committee report in September 1982, "these documents had been virtually ignored not only by policymakers, who felt they had no immediate use for them, but more importantly, by the intelligence community."[14] The burying of these important data concerning the man who ultimately became the leading figure in the constituent assembly after the March 1982 elections contrasts very strongly with the indecent haste to issue a white paper entitled "Communist Interference in El Salvador in February 1981," whose accuracy has been shown to be so questionable as to render the paper useless. In June 1983, a defecting member of the Nicaraguan state-security apparatus was, after extensive debriefing, presented to certain members of the press at Heritage House, a right-wing research organization. His remarks received wide press coverage, although his allegations concerning the Nicaraguan reception of the pope, the nature of the charges against the U.S. consular officials expelled from Nicaragua, and other matters were not verified in the usual manner. The works of Kirkpatrick, Tucker, and Huntington come from a whole body of scholarship about Central America that regards the task of the production of knowledge to be supportive of existing and past policy, or at least to present arguments in the voice of the friendly policymaker. Many of these works are synoptic, broad historic pictures rather than concrete and detailed analyses of specific events. The essays and statements of these scholars are really messages to the regime urging greater resolve in maintaining the present direction; their "think pieces" neither allude to past research nor justify their generalizations through existing literature.

The Reagan administration recently began to institutionalize this source of confirmation when it suggested the creation of a research apparatus controlled by the National Security Council.[15] Enough money would be appropriated—a sum in the range of $15 million to $20 million has been discussed—to instantly make this the major source of funding for the study of international affairs, this at a time when the National Science Foundation is operating with a frozen budget.

There is, however, a second world of scholarship, almost wholly separate from that upon which the administration draws, which has studied Central America much as any other problem or region is handled within the bounds of the social-science canon. In emphasizing analysis—as opposed to cheerleading—it has developed a consensus about the region that, not surprisingly, differs considerably from the administration's picture.

This book comes from that scholarly world and looks beyond (or behind) current administration descriptions and rhetoric concerning Central America to provide an image of the region as something more substantial than a manipulable backyard. The authors present the historical, social, political, and economic background needed to appreciate the developments in the region, not as a new and sudden set of disasters, but as a historic process in which the solutions to ancient problems have been repeatedly postponed and aborted.

The interference with the development and liberation of the population of this region has involved U.S. support for its military and civilian dictators all too anxious to serve themselves by serving the U.S. The final act of disrespect for the people of Central America is to blame the victim through slogans such as "banana republic" or to infantilize them and declare their nations immature. Any serious scrutiny of the record points out how self-serving these attitudes are. This book, along with other recent works, is an effort to correct these false impressions and to promote public awareness so that perhaps policy may, in time, reflect knowledge rather than convenience or arrogance.

We begin with an overview by Edelberto Torres-Rivas, perhaps the most distinguished Central American scholar working today, tracing in broad strokes the history of the region since the Spanish conquest. He shows how the dependent position of the region, engendered and fostered by its definition as a raw material source for industrial and powerful nations, particularly the United States, has stifled its social and economic development. This sort of development without progress—that is, the use of countries in such a way that their production of wealth is unrelated to the benefit of the local population—ultimately leads to a dead end where new social forces arise with nothing left to lose. They find themselves talking to the same indifferent and cruel elites who have always counted on U.S. support and complicity to quell "disturbances" such as the reformism of Arbenz, ended in 1954.

Torres's dynamic vision shows a complex process of growth without development, enrichment without distribution, and production without social benefit. This stalemate has increased social tension and provided the powder for an explosion. The impressive increases in the GDP over the period 1960–79, about 5 percent a year, fit into Torres's analysis as he traces the social class consequences and the population shifts toward the cities with the growth of service activities and the reproduction of poverty. Torres's rich, contextualized account helps us appreciate how this sort of "development" itself fosters rebellion.[16] It also suggests how the present calls for a new "Marshall Plan" for the region could drive up the GDP without providing social justice.

The image of U.S. foreign policy in the essay by Luis Maira is a glimpse of ourselves as many people in the world see us. A Chilean with direct knowledge of the consequences of U.S. foreign policy, Maira is nevertheless optimistic. His country-by-country review indicates the logical outcomes of the rigid ideological position of the Reagan administration. He shows, too, how international political groupings such as the Christian Democratic Union and the Socialist International have assumed a stance often quite divergent from that of Washington. Major Latin American countries like Mexico and Brazil have publicly expressed reluctance to support the Reagan view of Communist interference, and Mexico has not played the role of domino assigned to it by Washington. His analysis of how the foreign policies of other Latin American countries are affected by regional events (economic or military, such as the Falklands/Malvinas episode) makes prediction difficult, but he clearly accords them weight in the formation of international opinion, in strong contrast to the previously cited view of Kissinger. His conclusion, though, is not that international groups and regional actors may block the Reagan policy toward Central America but that alliances, regrouping in response to Reagan, may actually transform the nature of the international power structure. If Reagan is projecting onto Central America a new pattern for relations between the U.S. and the Third World, he may be shoring up the U.S. sphere of influence, which has been shrinking for the past twenty-five or so years. Whether this interpretation comes from a fractured lens or a crystal ball remains to be seen.

Lars Schöultz's essay on Guatemala simultaneously traces the impact of U.S. policy and the conduct of Guatemalan politics. In his words, a U.S. posture based on denying inroads to the "Communists" by the support of "right-wing tyrannies" has led to "the defense of the existing structure of socioeconomic privilege and the demobilization of emerging social sectors." Since the last period of reformism, that of the Arévalo and Arbenz regimes (1945–54), abruptly ended with the active help of the United States,[17] both U.S. policy and Guatemalan politics have reflected the above. The results, which tally with Torres's account, have been steady rises in the GDP through the development of agro-export industries and manufacturing, with a simultaneous erosion of the level of welfare of the bulk of the population. Shelton Davis documents the deterioration of the conditions of life for the Guatemalan peasantry. This process seems to require the repression of dissidence, some of which is caused by the very changes initiated by the regime. Thus, population increase leads to an urban-migration pattern, bringing more workers to the cities, and gives rise to forms of worker organizations that become targeted for repression, or, in Schöultz's term, *demobilization*. Davis shows how, in the countryside, a cooperative movement, financed in good measure by U.S. funds (AID), resulted in some improvement in peasants' welfare and encouraged incipient organization. Because of that, in places where new cooperatives were set up, land values increased and local bosses and military chiefs began preying on these peasants. Sometimes their leaders were eliminated because of the perceived threat to the system of labor procurement for the cotton and sugar plantations.

One of the real difficulties with such closed systems is that in them even a bit of reformist change is seen as a total threat.

El Salvador, with its "reactionary despotism," is quite similar in this regard. Here, Enrique Baloyra points out, there is an oligarchic rule, whose contours involve control by a reactionary sector—the imposition of an exclusionary political regime denying citizenship to its opponents and striving to impose co-optation and obedience in place of the consent of the governed. The role of the military in this reactionary alliance became more prominent as the need for repression increased. At present, 4 years after a military-inspired coup on 15 October 1979, some would argue that oligarchic rule has broken down. Pure oligarchic rule has perhaps given way to an oligarchic-military alliance that had worked well to support agrarian development and stifle opposition. This alliance, once again, has been so refined and dominant in defining the terms of national debate that it is now incapable of political participation in anything resembling a democratic mode. The U.S. support for elections in El Salvador assumes continuous control by this alliance, because the military-oligarchic union has the capacity to stage a right-wing coup, and thereby render elections meaningless. Thus, the wealth of information supplied by Baloyra concerning the class beneficiaries of the shifting terms of the alliance really serves to underline its flexibility and adaptability in the face of popular challenges. Shamefully, Washington's present policy panders to the economic interests of the agrarian financial oligarchy and supports militarily the traditional mechanisms of repression, thus encouraging this alliance to simply adopt new coloration without substantially altering its age-old project. The reformist portion of U.S. aid, the land-reform program for example, has foundered on the usual violent domination of the peasantry, as rising numbers of land-reform beneficiaries are evicted with the sanction and help of the armed forces.[18] The economic portion of the aid package is designed to shore up the crumbling national economy so that it might begin again to produce for its traditional beneficiaries. The new face of the reactionary despotism has shown itself to be as influential as ever.

One of the most important recent influences in stimulating change has been the popular Catholic Church—or, more precisely, the work of parish priests and nuns, the formation and activities of Christian Base Communities, and the labors of lay preachers and catechists. Tommie Sue Montgomery's essay on Christianity as subversion shows the steps that have led some portions of the church to advocate liberation, while other sectors within the ecclesiastic hierarchy have continued to support existing regimes. In El Salvador and Nicaragua, progressive church people have themselves tasted state repression and discovered that their traditional pastoral mission was tolerated only insofar as it was an ideological tool for promoting quiescence among exploited populations. When Archbishop Romero began to preach that submission to an unjust state was not a religious obligation, he was immediately branded a Communist and was ultimately killed. Bishops may bless helicopters but must not involve themselves in "politics"!

This important change in the definition of the religious office has raised two interesting points. First, as an institution, Catholicism is deeply involved in reflection and debate over its proper role. On the one hand, the pope has requested the resignations of Catholic clergy in the Sandinista government; on the other, he has openly preached against the Polish state and in favor of organized labor. This debate is far from over; it is actually gaining momentum with the large public role the Catholic bishops have played in the United States because of their pastoral letter regarding nuclear disarmament. It will probably lead either to a bifurcation and polarization within the church, a condition the Vatican seeks to avoid, much like Maira's prediction about polarization within world capitalism, or to a strengthened commitment to the conservative or progressive positions. Since the first possibility is too full of schismatic overtones to be permitted, it might be expected that a new form of church activism will be defined and that the papal office will sum up the debate once it concludes.

The second point is that, independently of the internal church debate, political partisanship about Central America, and other regions, is increasingly expressed in terms of religious behavior.

The Sandinistas and supporters of liberation theology regard Nicaragua as a crucible in which a new, revivified pattern of Christian behavior is being formed, one that enjoys much sympathy elsewhere in Latin America. Others regard the Sandinista posture as a demonic deviation from the traditional role of the church. Given Reagan's characterization of the Soviet Union as the "Empire of Evil," the vigorous debate the pope encountered on his recent visit to Nicaragua is evidence of how things are going to hell, literally. Part of this debate involves the contrast between Protestantism, especially of the evangelical sort, and Catholicism. In Guatemala today, with its born-again evangelical leader Ríos Montt, popular Catholicism, has been charged with subversion. Adherence to the vigorously proselytizing fundamentalism of the Verbo church of Ríos Montt has been pushed as part of a definition of legitimate citizenship where religious affiliation is equated with support of the government. It is well worth watching to see whether this struggle is projected into the United States, a Protestant country.

Much of what now lends a sense of danger and high stakes in Central America involves Nicaragua. The Sandinista state was the first revolutionary separation from the U.S. orbit since the Cuban revolution in 1959, and its continued existence has become a challenge to the Reagan administration. Richard Fagen discusses two important elements of the present Nicaraguan situation. One issue of great importance for any developing and liberating country is the tension between the decisive leadership necessary to consolidate the gains won in the overthrow of the dictator (Somoza) and the planning to launch a genuinely democratic society, where the real involvement and the consent of the governed will be the motor of politics. The tension between a vanguard party and popular participation, only theoretical while there is obvious massive support for government policy, is nevertheless a problem to be resolved. National elections have been scheduled for 1985, when enough public discussion and enlightenment will presumably have taken place to permit the use of constitutional and electoral means.

The second issue, related to the first, is the recognition of the pressure that the United States has placed on this system. Beginning with the economic isolation of Nicaragua, the cessation of U.S. aid, and the influencing of international lenders to do the same, U.S. pressure has increased to its present level of the direct financing of armed intervention by troops loyal to the preceding regime. Given the delicate process of emerging from an insurrectionary war and trying to evolve a democratic state, this pressure influences all the efforts at domestic openness and responsiveness that the Sandinistas are trying to maintain. Simultaneous with the covert and illegal actions against Nicaragua is the effort to create a negative image, through the selective use of intelligence and deliberate shading of the facts and selective emphases on certain questions.[19] While events are moving very quickly, Fagen's analysis is a reminder that there are real problems in the effort to create a new society. Unfortunately, U.S. intervention seems to be one of them.

The last place in the backyard, the one with perhaps the least-flattering image is Honduras, supposedly the classic "banana republic." In Steven Volk's essay, we see how early Honduras was used as a locus for foreign investment and control, where *la bananera* could create a situation in which its interests took precedence over those of the nation. Here the social and productive structure of Honduras permitted two distinct forms of internal organization to coexist. On the north coast, banana country, an enclave developed with the help of foreign capital, complete with its own labor force and productive infrastructure. It looked toward its American market and suffered barely any interference from the central government. The rest of the country, sparsely populated, was divided into peasant smallholdings, occasional ranches, and haciendas. There was no massive displacement of peasants from the land, because they were not needed on the coast for harvesting, as they were in the annual rhythms in El Salvador and Guatemala. Thus, Honduras lived in a state of tranquil underdevelopment, *la bananera* prospering, much like a mosquito engorging itself quietly on its host's blood. However, the host must ultimately weaken and grow sick, and Honduras, to date the most static of Central American countries, is slowly being drawn into the maelstrom, in Volk's phrase, of the region. Unionism, a social awakening engendered on the banana plantations, has taken on an increasingly threatening dimension as it appeals to more varied sectors of the population as a route to social change. How far into the convulsive events of the isthmus Honduras is being carried remains to be seen.

History moves too rapidly for any book to report events; we have therefore tried to provide an outline and background without which an understanding of the swiftly changing currents in Central America is impossible. At this moment, late June 1983, the pace appears to have quickened and public discussion takes place over a substratum of imminent war. U.S. financing of military aggression against Nicaragua, long suspected through leaks, has now been admitted by the Reagan administration. When the training of somocistas in Florida was criticized, the former secretary Thomas Enders characterized them as "harmless weekend warriors" and refused to see such activity as a violation of the Neutrality Act.[20] This refusal, and the open support for what Reagan has called "freedom fighters," points out what Washington favors as a solution to the regional problem. Although there is no longer a Haig to trumpet that we will "go to the source," the provocation we are financing in Nicaragua seems designed to promote armed engagement between Honduras and Nicaragua, or perhaps to entice Cuba to enter the arena. Honduras has been heavily fortified with considerable amounts of American equipment and arms left after various military exercises, and the possibility that a Tonkin Gulf incident will ignite a war seems high. In that event, the U.S. would perhaps enter massively on the side of Honduras in order to definitively erase the Nicaraguans. Coincident with this high-profile taunting of Nicaragua, while our mercenaries kill its peasantry, is a systematic refusal to enter any direct conversations with any of the adversary parties in the region. The United States has also tried to undermine the efforts of the Contadora group (Mexico, Venezuela, Colombia, and Panama) in its efforts to promote regional negotiations to effect a political settlement in the region. Guatemala, meanwhile, is the testing ground for rural pacification involving the massive killing of the rural indigenous population. Far from criticizing this policy, Reagan has stated that Ríos Montt has gotten a "bum rap," and he has launched efforts to restore military aid to that regime. In a rather insulting response to a congressional suggestion that negotiation be a condition for military aid to El Salvador, the administration appointed as a special envoy the former senator Richard Stone, also an ex-lobbyist on behalf of the Lucas García government, the military dictatorship preceding Ríos Montt's regime. Stone's job as administrator-negotiator is to fail in such a way that the military solution will seem to be the only option left.[21] Honduras, converted from a country trying to effect a democratic transition from military to civilian rule into a staging ground for a U.S. show of force toward Nicaragua and a training field for the Salvadoran military, has been transformed once again into a dependent of the United States. Its importance lies in its strategic location as well as in the absence of congressional limitations on the number of military advisers or on the scope and nature of covert operations. As the argument continues in Congress about the "legality" of U.S. actions—that is, about the adherence to or violation of the Boland amendment—the greater discussion of the international criminality under UN and OAS provisions recedes into the background.

The latest effort to prevail in El Salvador is a mélange of plans that have emerged at various times during the last few months. They involve the restructuring of the military in the direction of a meritocratic form, and stepped-up action against the guerrillas in their zones of control. A "civic action" program reminiscent of the CORDS program in Vietnam will then aid in the reconstruction of bridges, highways, and schools and in the creation of employment in the countryside. This plan, nothing short of a radical change in the conduct of the war in El Salvador, is to be the prelude—the "shield," in Shultz's words, behind which an election will be held in December 1983. The announcement of the election was made by President Magaña in March during the pope's visit to El Salvador after instructions from Reagan were brought by Richard Stone before he became special envoy. Once again, the timing and the enormousness of the task, the general lack of purpose of this administration to attack the problem at its social roots, suggests that this plan is also supposed to fail in order to clear the decks for war.

The panorama is generally bleak. Reagan has had good luck in obtaining appropriations from Congress for military activities in Central America. The mood now seems one of expectation that the heavy air will be ignited by an induced spark.

Will this show Kissinger to have been right? The United States can overwhelm small countries but it can not stop or reverse history. The United States can, and probably will, rain death on innocent people in Central America, as it did in Southeast Asia some years ago, but the impulses that Guatemalan Indians, Salvadoran peasants, and Nicaraguan workers are now expressing through their lives and deaths are meaningful. Roque Dalton said it this way:

Todos juntos
tenemos más muerte que ellos
pero todos juntos
tenemos más vida que ellos

All of us together
have more death than they have
but all of us together
have more life than they have[22]

NOTES

1. Seymour M. Hersh, *The Price of Power: Kissinger in the Nixon White House* (New York: Summit Books, 1983), 263.
2. Central America here refers to Guatemala, Honduras, El Salvador, Nicaragua, and Costa Rica; Panama is often included, although neither it nor Costa Rica is represented in this volume, because their participation in the "trouble" has not been crucial. In the last two years the Reagan administration has increasingly used the term *Caribbean basin* to include "the islands of the Caribbean as well as the mainland nations of the circum-Caribbean." (Howard J. Wiarda, "The Central American Crisis: A Framework for Understanding," *American Enterprise Institute Foreign Policy and Defense Review* 4, no. 2 [1982]: 4–6.) This goes beyond some definitions that include the Caribbean portion of those countries. It invokes the East-West dimension (i.e., the presence of Cuba) as well as a domino theory (the region as a funnel toward the Panama Canal with increased jeopardy of supply routes, the "falling" from south to north of countries until Mexico goes, the mixing of countries we have had diplomatic influence over, e.g., Jamaica and Puerto Rico, with countries we have "guided," e.g., Guatemala). Failing any compelling reason to use this novel geopolitical idea, we continue to discuss Central America in the usual fashion—to refer to those countries situated in the isthmus that connects North and South America.
3. Wiarda, "Central American Crisis," 4–6.

4. The under-secretary of state Robert Olds wrote in a 1927 State Department memorandum:

> Our ministers accredited to the five little republics, stretching from the Mexican border to Panama . . . have been advisers whose advice has been accepted virtually as law in the capitals where they respectively reside. . . . We do control the destinies of Central America and we do so for the simple reason that the national interest absolutely dictates such a course. . . . Until now Central America has always understood that governments which we recognize and support stay in power, while those we do not recognize and support fail.

Quoted in Jenny Pearce, *Under the Eagle: U.S. Intervention in Central America and the Caribbean* (London: Latin American Bureau, 1981), 19.

5. Wiarda, "Central American Crisis," 4.

6. Thomas Anderson, *Matanza,* El Salvador's Communist Revolt of 1932 (Lincoln: University of Nebraska Press, 1971), 157.

7. Wiarda, "Central American Crisis," 5.

8. Samuel P. Huntington, "American Ideals versus American Institutions," *Political Science Quarterly* 97 (1982): 27.

9. Gordon L. Bowen, "U.S. Foreign Policy toward Radical Change: Covert Operations in Guatemala, 1950–1954," *Latin American Perspectives* 10, no. 1 (1983): 98–99.

10. This two-track policy has been derailed with the replacement of Thomas O. Enders as assistant secretary of state for inter-American affairs.

11. Recently, General Myeral of the Joint Chiefs of Staff commented on the inadvisability of committing U.S. troops to Central America, mostly because of the lack of public acceptance and clear understanding of their purpose. In the same interview, however, he expressed the opinion that after the next election in El Salvador, it might be necessary to commit troops. See *New York Times,* 10 June 1983.

12. Robert W. Tucker, "The Purposes of American Power," *Foreign Affairs* 59 (1980–81): 270–71. Also Noam Chomsky, "Resurgent America" in *Towards a New Cold War* (New York: Pantheon Books, 1981), pp. 216–229.

13. See David Collier, ed., *The New Authoritarianism in Latin America* (Princeton: Princeton University Press, 1979); Alfred Stepan, ed., *Authoritarian Brazil* (New Haven: Yale University Press, 1973).

14. House Permanent Select Committee on Intelligence, Subcommittee on Oversight and Evaluation, *U.S. Intelligence Performance on Central America: Achievements and Selected Instances of Concern: Staff Report* (Washington, D.C.: GPO, 1982), 12, 13.

15. Andrew Kopkind, "A Diller, a Dollar, an N.S.C. Scholar," *Nation,* 25 June 1983, 797.

16. For a case study, showing that growth in the GDP and impoverishment in the countryside in El Salvador are parallel and mutually interdependent

processes, see Carmen Diana Deere and Martin Diskin, "Rural Poverty in El Salvador: Causes, Dimensions, and Trends," *International Labour Organization* (forthcoming).

17. See note 13 in Lars Schöultz's essay.

18. Lurence R. Simon, James C. Stephens, Jr., and Martin Diskin, *El Salvador Land Reform, 1980–1981: Impact Audit* (Boston: Oxfam-America, 1982); Lydia Chavez, "Salvadoran Plan for Land Changes Suffers Setbacks," *New York Times,* 5 June 1983.

19. House Permanent Select Committee on Intelligence, *Report,* 20–21.

20. Quoted in Wiarda, "Central American Crisis," p. 7.

21. Frank Brodhead, "Stoned Again in the Caribbean," *Resist Newsletter,* June-July 1983.

22. Verse from Roque Dalton's poem "Todos," in *Las historias prohibidas del pulgarcito* (Mexico: Siglo Veintiuno, 1980), 129.

Central America Today

A STUDY IN REGIONAL DEPENDENCY

Edelberto Torres-Rivas

To many foreign observers it seems incomprehensible that the Central American isthmus, with an area of only 431,000 square kilometers, could have produced such a diversity of national histories, providing examples of utterly opposed political, cultural, and social experiences. No doubt there exists a shared situation of underdevelopment and, to that extent, all Central America experiences a condition of basic, structural homogeneity. By underdevelopment we mean both the *function* that an agrarian economy fulfills in its relations with the industrialized world market, and the resulting internal political and social *structure*. Thus, our similarities come from the manner in which the region was articulated to the great currents of international commerce, and from the ways in which capitalism was here implanted, all of which occurred in the nineteenth century. Our differences correspond to our varied precolonial situations, to dissimilar colonial experiences during which the present political and cultural tradition was shaped, to the particular forms that social and economic structure adopted as the export economy developed, and to the relations and conflicts between social groups and classes. All of this dates from the beginning of the sixteenth century.

Similarities and differences must be explained if one is to understand diversity in unity. This is the situation with which Central America presents us and, in general outline, it is what we are going to present in this essay.

THE COLONIAL HERITAGE, 1524–1838

The activities of the European conquerors varied in the places that became the present countries of Central America. In what became Costa Rica and Honduras, colonists tended to settle and work the land. Guatemala, on the other hand, became a commercial center. A bit of both were found in what is today El Salvador and Nicaragua. The Central American region then, was not the object of a unified European conquest. These separate outcomes were the result of different attempts at conquest, sometimes quite bloody, that originated in Mexico, Santo Domingo, and Panama. Only after 1560 was a rough border drawn for what was called the Kingdom of Guatemala, covering most of contemporary Central America. Until 1743, this area was also under a unified religious command as well.

The history of the Central American region begins not in 1524, when Guatemala City was founded, but many centuries earlier. The heirs of Mayan culture, bearers of an extraordinarily rich tradition, endured; they conditioned the long colonial period and have appeared again and again throughout the republican phase and up to the present day. The strength of the indigenous culture was not uniform. The physical and human locus of that culture— what is called Mesoamerica—reached only as far as Guatemala and part of Honduras. In Costa Rica the indigenous population was smaller and resisted more, and was as a result decimated and then pushed into a marginal corner. In Guatemala the indigenous population still constitutes a demographic majority. The process of *mestizaje* (racial mixing) was intense in the other countries, especially in El Salvador and Honduras, where racial homogeneity was produced through *mestizaje*. Subsequently, an African aggregate of some importance formed along the Atlantic coast of Honduras, Nicaragua, and Costa Rica.

The isthmus has been poor in mineral wealth and other economic resources; its geographical position is what has bequeathed it a geopolitical destiny that it has still not overcome. As a result, the colony had only administrative and political significance, but this was particularly strong in Guatemala, headquarters of the captaincy-general of the Kingdom of Guatemala and seat of the colonial authorities. Here settled a ponderous civil, ecclesiastical, and military bureaucracy, and here the *encomienda* prospered beyond its legal limits.[1] In the rest of what is today Central America, the colony functioned more weakly, and autarchical forms of economic and political life developed.

Accordingly, the colonial experience marked out different destinies for the five provinces. The characteristic feature of the period was not permanent stagnation but cycles of boom and depression alternating inexorably. Ephemeral successes for a mining economy (gold and silver) were replaced by the modest agricultural production of tobacco, cacao, and indigo. Only a select minority of Spaniards and *criollos* [2] profited from agricultural production in this region, and the export-import trade was restricted to those who lived in Guatemala City. The monopoly exercised by the principal families of Guatemala through the Consulado de Comercio (Consulate of Commerce) gave them legal control over the flow of trade from all the other provinces after 1790. The prosperity of an aristocratic elite in Guatemala has always contrasted with the permanent difficulties endured by the small groups of landholders and businessmen in the provinces.

FEDERATION AND ANARCHY, 1838–1840[3]

Civil war did not precede independence but was instead a consequence of it. In Central America, breaking the colonial tie was a bureaucratic operation, hurriedly carried out by Guatemala City *criollos*. When the news reached the various provinces, the solidity of the supposed Kingdom of Guatemala was put to the test,[4] through a conflict in which the disintegrative forces shaped during the colonial period were decisive.

The federation project—the Federal Republic of Central America, which the Guatemala liberals supported to fill the vacuum of authority left by the rupture of the colonial link—did nothing except unleash an atrocious civil war. Known in Latin American political literature as the "period of anarchy" (1823–40) in Central America, it broke loose with such homicidal fury that the federalist program failed. Although the conservatives upheld the unitary ideal, they also lacked the power to impose it. Indeed, once Spanish authority had been broken, this became a revolt against Guatemala and then, within each country, a rivalry between liberals and conservatives, a conflict sometimes complicated by local loyalties. This struggle—which lasted months in Costa Rica, years in Guatemala and El Salvador, and decades in Honduras and Nicaragua—yielded multiple results. The Central American nation that was being formed fell apart, and from it came five projects for nation-states, which foundered in stagnation for over half a century, were subject to foreign rapine,[5] and were each to experience from that time on a difficult individual history.

THE EXPORT ECONOMY

In this introductory summary we must pause at the moment when, through external action and local political conditions, Central American society succeeded in building an export economy. The region thus became permanently linked to the world economy, expanding from the impact of the industrial revolution; internally, commercial agriculture with coffee and then bananas as its focus permitted the establishment of an increasingly important economic structure. Between 1850 and 1870 Central America exported on the average 11 percent of the world's coffee; in 1916 it accounted for 58 percent of the world's banana production.

The experience of forming agro-export structures was different for each of the national societies. These differences express precisely the particular character of economic growth, and political domination that was adopted as a solution in each setting. This provides a good example of how the "colonial past" conditioned later local history. For instance, Costa Rica established its coffee-plantation economy on the basis of the family plot. The peasant smallholding, peacefully and gradually established through the relative independence of the direct producer, fulfills the egalitarian dream of the *campesino* (peasant). Here the concentration of wealth was organized through the monopoly on coffee processing and marketing rather than on production.

At the extreme opposite from this unique experience appears the rest of Central America, particularly El Salvador and Guatemala. Agrarian capitalism developed on the basis of large landholding property, and the accumulation of land was carried out to the direct detriment of the indigenous communal lands *(ejidos)*. Political violence presided over this operation in the name of progress.

In one case after another, the "civilizing mission of coffee" brought about an opportunity for consolidating for the first time a stable, consensual sort of political power. In the context of Central America, what we call "oligarchic domination" was the social predominance of the agrarian classes: the owners of the large coffee plantations and the merchants, who monopolized coffee processing *("beneficio")*[6] and foreign trade. The authority of this class grew along with the expansion of the export economy, and it afforded an opportunity for advances in the building of the nation-state. Obviously, this opportunity was not the same for everyone. Costa Rica again presents an extraordinary example of political stability and slow but sure economic consolidation. A tiny oligarchy was able to control the power of the state and then, to create a structure of domination based on hegemonic manipulation. This system remained stable until the 1940s.

In Guatemala, however, political violence was required to break down the social and political privileges of the *criollos*. The heirs of the colonial tradition, they clung to the old order centered on the political power of the church, economic control through the Consulate of Commerce, and rent generated by relatively unproductive plantations *(latifundios)* of the dye economy.* Beginning in 1871 the so-called liberal revolution unleashed extraordinary energy and forcibly created conditions for developing commercial export agriculture.

In El Salvador, liberal reformism had a similar vigor but did not confront a *criollo* sector by force, and the separation of the church from the state was not a painful operation. The coffee planters' predominance, mounted on a peculiar form of agrarian capitalism, was based upon opposing forms of land ownership: *latifundios* burgeoned, forcing the mass of the rural population into a family subsistence economy linked to the new landowning class through archaic forms of rent expropriation. This fact is fundamental for understanding the particular situations of both Guatemala and El Salvador.

From this moment on, coffee becomes the symbol of progress,

---

*See Torres-Rivas, "Guatemala: Medio siglo de historia política," in *América Latina: Historia de medio siglo,* ed. Pablo González Casanova (Mexico: Siglo Veintiuno, 1981), 139–46.

the opportunity for establishing the authority of a social class and for modifying, belatedly, the old colonial order. Agro-export interests become the national interest. This was true in Costa Rica, El Salvador, and Guatemala. In Honduras and Nicaragua, mono-crop production and its articulation with the world market encountered violent calamities.

Even greater social and economic backwardness in these two countries delayed the appearance of class forces able to exploit the opportunities for international trade. The best opportunity occurred in Honduras with banana exporting, but national efforts were quickly (1890) supplanted by the modern, capitalist, foreign-owned plantation. Agricultural production for the local market and commerce both remained in the hands of Honduran owners, but in a rudimentary form. The efforts of the liberal generation of 1880 proved inadequate to make the country into a prosperous, integrated nation. Under such conditions, and with an adverse geography as well, the creation of the national state was slow and difficult.

The period of anarchy lasted in Nicaragua for more than a century; to be specific, the struggle between liberals and conservatives was the cause of William Walker's filibustering adventure (1854), the failure of the liberal revolution, and U.S. intervention (1911), which lasted, with a brief pause, until 1933. Those rivalries explain in part the Somoza family dictatorship, which is the direct result and immediate extension of foreign military intervention. Nicaragua was not a stranger to the modernizing cycle of coffee, after 1870, but the accompanying productive structure did not attain sufficient stature to become the axis of social and political change. The magnificent conditions the country offers for an interocean passageway—still undeveloped—may constitute its true "wealth."

Honduras and Nicaragua entered into the world market haphazardly, and largely by way of forms of the foreign "enclave," in the paradigmatic examples of the banana in one case and gold and silver mining in the other. In Nicaragua a true export economy was built on the basis of the cotton plantation only in the early 1950s.

ECONOMIC GROWTH SINCE 1945

Putting aside the individual characteristics of development in each of the Central American countries—the product of a specific earlier history—we find common situations in their current pattern of economic growth. The most important features of the period that we are interested in—from the end of the fifties, when the Common Market mechanisms began to operate, until the end of the sixties, when that project went into a crisis—are the subject of this section.

Toward the end of the fifties, that is, more than ten years after the end of the Second World War, the Central American agrarian matrix continued to be the most important. Most savings originated in export agriculture and in the commercialization of its products, the most dynamic demand factors rested upon it, and it was the principal source of income for the state. As a result, the foreign sector retained its leading role—one that, since the time of its insertion into the world market, had been the most dynamic factor in Central American development.[7] Nevertheless, although the raw-material exporting model had since the thirties shown a definite structural incapacity to serve as the focus for the development of these societies, growth continued to rest on declining opportunities for agricultural production and export.

The Central American productive system, organized to perform in the old international division of labor, received occasional stimuli in the postwar inflationary period. This encouraged the coffee-plantation oligarchy to retain confidence in a development model that revolved around the increased planting of coffee, without diversifying production.

Even at a stage in which traditional growth opportunities for coffee were being exhausted, the oligarchy's "colonial" vision changed only when the international market was drastically altered by falling prices and a rigid quota policy. Brief, and thus artificial, recoveries have continued to provide a stimulus for coffee exports (1964–65 and 1972–73) so that Central America has been the only Latin American region that has continued to expand coffee cultivation, thereby modifying its agrarian structure only slightly. In order to compensate for the low prices, the absolute volume of sales had to be increased, to the point that in the sixties alone Honduras doubled its production and Costa Rica's increased by 50 percent.[8]

Central America's international function as an agricultural appendix is being reinforced in the current decade. Once again foreign needs introduce new demands for raw materials: cotton, sugar, and meat.[9] Such products gain momentum only when external factors push them, in such a manner that their increase in no way corresponds to an organic internal diversification that is planned and attempted by the agencies managing the national economy.

What we see, therefore, is a partial modification of the agro-export matrix, which does nothing but emphasize our internal structural weakness in the face of foreign markets. The relative modernization of agriculture caused by the introduction of cotton, cattle, and sugar cane has reinforced our dependent articulation with the U.S. market. The sugar boom is so much a reflection of the U.S. economy that it occurred only under the shelter of the redistribution of the Cuban sugar quota after 1961, and cotton began to gain importance only once the traditional suppliers in the Middle East had redirected their trade toward the U.S.S.R.

Another important partial modification in the region's productive structure derives from the impact of the inappropriately named Common Market. In fact, it was a free-trade zone whose uniform tariff with respect to the rest of the world and lowering of customs barriers, along with other regional-policy measures, created an important focus of growth.

It is not our purpose to analyze in detail this now semiparalyzed effort to establish a common market in the region; during that process important changes in production and trade did certainly occur. Indeed, intraregional commerce did grow rapidly in the first few years, from $8 million in 1950 to more than $850 million in 1980.[10] Between 1960 and 1970 trade within the region attained such an importance that it represented more than 28 percent of the transactions with the rest of the world. Between 1970 and 1980 it declined to 23 percent, but totaled more than a billion dollars.

The establishment of a free-trade zone and the set of measures that accompanied it brought the curtain down on the traditional crafts industry, which was viewed as idle productive capacity. But it also created conditions for setting up "final touch" industries. This policy has been called "import substitution," which turns out to be a euphemism, since it has not meant development of an endogenous capacity to use local raw materials to manufacture goods previously imported from abroad. "Import substitution" here means the replacement of finished products by their semifinished components, which has made possible the introduction of industries whose basic productive process is carried out in the industrial metropolis. The "industrial" plants that grow under the privileged shelter of industrial development laws, tax exemptions, and other benefits perform only such simple tasks as packaging, labeling, or final assembly. This has increased imports from the United States from $210 million in 1961 to $365 million in 1968 and $675 million in 1976.

With the replacement of finished products by their component parts, not only do the industrialized economies retain an important share of industrial value added but the result for the local consumer market is a rise in prices and a decline in product quality. The social base of the internal consumer markets expands very slowly. This is definitely not the industrialization that will help change all Central American society or the factor that will be able to absorb the increasingly abundant labor force, nor will it raise the standard of living for most sectors of the population. Furthermore, it is not along this path of capitalist "modernization," without social change, that some form of national autonomy can be attained.

The composition of intraregional trade and its variations during the decade illustrate clearly the nature of dependent industrialization. The products that the region exchanges are no longer unprocessed agricultural products, but nondurable consumer goods, processed foods, and chemical products—that is, they fall under the headings of light or intermediate industry, the production of durable consumer goods or capital goods being almost nonexistent. It is interesting to note that in 1979, on the average, 84.4 percent of the region's manufactures were sold within the Common Market, the remaining 16 percent going to industrialized countries.[11] Approximately three-quarters of the "Central American" products traded are produced in factories that are under U.S. ownership or in which the majority capital is North American. The laws that protect U.S. investment in the national arena assure it the free repatriation of capital, which by the end of the sixties totaled approximately $120 million.[12] Thus, the Central American market is further subordinated to the U.S. market through the implanting of an industrial sector that depends, moreover, on importing semifinished parts and technology.

Despite these limitations, the "common market" has created conditions facilitating the introduction of an industrial base that has contributed to economic-social differentiation. The secondary sector's participation in the gross domestic product can serve as an index to exemplify the degree of this change.[13] In relation to the growth of the GDP or of agricultural-livestock production, the rates of industrial expansion are undoubtedly important, particularly for El Salvador and Costa Rica, where they reach a level of almost 20 percent of that total.[14]

In Latin American countries with delayed industrialization, as in those in Central America—that is, those that began the process when the effects of the postwar boom had weakened considerably —the introduction of a manufacturing base was carried out under conditions even more unfavorable to national control of the productive processes. The governmental policies of "import substitution" were not enacted under conditions of crisis in the international market and relative loosening of the commercial and financial ties to the industrialized North, which prevailed in the more developed Latin American societies. In Central America, where the process of industrialization had barely begun at the end of the fifties, the substitution practices were carried out within the framework of a restructured and reinvigorated international market system, one in which the hegemony of the major U.S. corporations was consolidated.

The political effects of such a structure of domination are no less important than the economic ones. Under these conditions the transfer of certain limited productive processes to the periphery, authorized and promoted from the metropolitan centers, was related not to endogenous factors or to the needs of Central American development but simply to the expansionist interests of the large transnational corporations.

Under these international conditions, the Central American Common Market presented a favorable moment for the reorientation of traditional foreign investment in the region, and/or for its entry into new sectors, taking advantage of the possibilities for profit in the new economic opening. Total foreign capital investment has grown from $65 million in 1946 and $527 million in 1965 to almost $1 billion in 1975.[15] The change in U.S. direct investment is noteworthy, although it follows the same tendency already indicated by numerous analysts for the rest of Latin America. Until 1959 almost 60 percent of such investment was located in export agriculture, railroads, harbors, and electric power; investment in manufacturing has gone from $21 million (1961) to $232 million (1969)[16]—an amount that means that all new industry starting after 1961 was predominantly North American. One cannot properly call this the denationalization of traditional industry, through the displacement of local entrepreneurs, although that has occurred in such relatively unsophisticated sectors as the dairy industry and the manufacture of chocolates, shoes, and other items. The manufacture of consumer goods for nonimmediate consumption (tires, textiles, glass, pulp and paper, plastics, pharmaceuticals, chemical and electrical products, and so on) has always been largely in the hands of U.S. and, to a lesser extent, Canadian, Japanese, and Mexican capital.

It is worth underscoring the growing interest of Mexican investors in the Central American market; at the end of 1971 fifty-five Mexican firms had established themselves in the region, with investments totaling $90 million, and the Common Market's trade with Mexico grew from $7.8 million in 1960 to $24.1 million in 1970 and to around $40 million in 1980.[17] The trade advantage for Mexico in this exchange is in a ratio of eight to one. Some Mexican entrepreneurs are associated with Central American capitalists, but there exists the suspicion that many nominally Mexican firms conceal U.S. interests.

Still, it should not be forgotten that Central America does not represent an important industrial market and will not for many years. The "modernization" of imperialist investment is only a relative, momentary variation. Thus, while on the one hand the typical foreign enclave remains vigorous only in Honduras and, in a modified form, in Costa Rica, and the vertical integration of the banana industry has disappeared—less because of nationalist measures than for the convenience of transnational interests[18]—on the other hand, investment in extractive industry is appearing in the region for the first time: petroleum and nickel in Guatemala, iron in Honduras, aluminum and sulfur in Costa Rica. The political significance and the volume of these investments have not been adequately studied, but they will be more important in the immediate future than the capital invested in the manufacturing sector.

For this brief exposition it is significant to point out that all Central American economic growth in recent years is taking place at the cost of a growing foreign debt and that the influence of the financiers has multiplied between 1960 and 1980.[19] National savings (public or private) now have a reduced share of the overall financing, which, added to the repatriation of foreign capital, means that foreign indebtedness is at present one of the greatest obstacles to the region's development. In the three-year period 1968–70, the average annual deficit of payments was $177 million, caused fundamentally by the remittance of profits by foreign companies: these payments totaled $120 million in 1970 alone.[20]

The internal market has expanded, relatively both because of population growth, especially in urban areas, and because of limited economic diversification deriving from two distinct processes: the modernization of agriculture, for export and for the internal market, and the creation of an industrial park producing goods for immediate consumption. But, as in the rest of Latin America, in this region economic growth follows a pattern that further concentrates income and property and maintains the relative immobility of the traditional rural sector. And the rural sector still retains a large proportion of the population.

The "marginality" characteristic of other Latin American societies—the existence of a labor force that is underemployed, unemployed, or employed in nonproductive, low-income jobs—has already appeared in some Central American capital cities. However, large populations still take refuge in the rural economy as redundant labor (because of their levels of productivity), but not as marginal population. In the cities, whose urban growth does not equal the torrential levels of other South American cities, peasant migration has only recently become an important phenomenon.

How has Central America changed in the last twenty-five years? What are the impulses and obstacles whose contradictory forces move our regional society? Today, as predictions get bleak and negative, in the midst of an international crisis insoluble by traditional means and in a local political crisis that truly constitutes a historical "rupture," where are we heading from here?

THE CURRENT "SPLENDORS" OF ECONOMIC GROWTH

Changes in the productive structure during the last two decades have had an unmistakable statistical characteristic: an average GDP growth rate above 5.4 percent, which is greater than the dizzying population increase but not great enough for the "dispersion" effect of social-wealth creation to reach the human sectors held in poverty for centuries. The relative importance of this growth rate notwithstanding, income per capita increased by only 80 percent over the 1950 level. At 1979 prices, per capita income rose from $242 (1950) to $428 (1978). To get an idea of the modesty of this growth rate, compare it to per capital income in the United States, which rose from $2,817 (1960) to $10,775 (1980), at current values.[21]

In Central America, movement within the economy obeys diverse factors generally originating in the exterior. Every time significant changes are produced in our productive system, they only reinforce our outward orientation. For example, the installation of an industrial base, requiring tremendous fiscal sacrifices on the part of the state and the low-income sectors, was not the result of endogenous historical processes. Rather, it was a literal transference of external productive factors: capital, technology, basic materials, and the like, which mobilized preexisting national resources. This also happened in other regions, but in our case this mobilization was achieved exclusively by and for the private sector, with the overt protection of the public sector.

The dynamism that characterized this industrial growth, which coincides with the establishment of the Common Market, was particularly noteworthy. The annual rate of industrial growth climbed to 8.5 percent, higher than that obtained by eighteen of the twenty-two Latin American countries. In 1979 industrial production was 3.7644 billion Central American pesos (at current prices), and the "degree of industrialization" reached 19.1 percent (1979), which, compared with the 11.5 percent average during the fifties and with the 25.6 percent for Latin America as a whole, represents a qualitative transformation impossible to ignore.[22] An important base of capital accumulation-reproduction has been formed in the urban zones, taking advantage of the fact that state power has encouraged a policy of intrazonal free trade, the common external tariff, tax incentives, and a sometimes unlimited supply for foreign resources.

These changes reflect a new international division of labor that has made possible the transfer of simple manufacturing processes to the agrarian peripheries. In the eighties, we are witnessing the relative exhaustion of this rather artificial set of impulses, which at one point seemed to favor unlimited industrial growth. In the next few years we will see a crisis of involving a new international division of labor, and a redistribution of functions within the world market.

Industrial growth was not based on internal private savings, which were replaced by international capital, foreign loans, and the consequent public and private indebtedness. The public foreign debt grew thirty-five-fold between 1960 and 1977.[23] In 1979 it rose to a total of $5.8659 billion, which the new generations will not be able to cover in the present decade. To appreciate the magnitude of this brutal imbalance, of this bottleneck in our economic growth, recall that in 1970 Central America was paying $92 million for total debt service whereas in 1979 it had to pay out $625.8 million, that is, almost seven times as much.

This tightening has increased the already recognized vulnerability of the region's national economies, even reaching dramatic levels in some of them. Moreover, all of this coincides with the "crisis" of regional integration, which obviously does not have strictly local roots. The Common Market disaster has underscored the narrow base of the industrial establishment and the inherent weaknesses in the economic growth model supporting it. The eighties pose a dilemma about integration: Is it just one experience or a rigid model as well? The integrationist processes are instruments of economic growth that require a corresponding political will. In the eighties, that will has been broken, the institutional bodies weakened, and some of their policies discredited. Will Central America in the eighties make new efforts to integrate itself as did the old Federal Republic of Central America?

In summary, industrial growth, largely the product of economic integration, produced an important differentiation in production, parallel to and superimposed upon the the traditional axis of the system, the export agriculture economy. That growth was based on the regional market, that is, the political substitute for an expanded social base for local consumption. A "nonaggression pact" between landholders and industrialists set immediate limits to industrial growth. This was feasible in the five countries because members of the same families enjoy both agrarian income and industrial or commercial profits. In addition, the integrationist project was pushed in a direction that not only ignored the market's vertical dimension, a fact that may still be remedied in this decade, but also precipitated two types of concentration, a result of the influence of those who believe in the natural wisdom of the market: socioeconomic and geographical concentration. As the fruit of the anarchy of blind market forces, which only political power can tame, foreign investments were concentrated in Guatemala and El Salvador, where entrepreneurs benefited even more from commercial traffic and spurious industrial earnings.

Even more serious is the concentration of income, which is not the effect of economic integration but of the peculiar way in which capitalism has operated in the region until now. This has involved a style of development in which social costs are always disregarded for the sake of profit, in which increases in productivity do not translate into wage increases for labor, and in which, above all, productive investment is speculative and politically protected. With an extremely short-term outlook, the Central American bourgeoisie accumulates in order to consume, and saves abroad, all of which obliges it to arrange quick cycles of return on investment at the cost of superexploiting the labor force. This is the paradise of absolute surplus value.

The distribution of income by percentage was more or less like this at the middle of the seventies (because of its confidential nature, such information is only approximate and permanently subject to challenge):

TABLE 1: *Income Distribution in Central America*
(In Central American Dollars—1970 U.S. Dollars)

Level of Annual Per Capita Income in Central American $	Income Stratum	Percentage of Population	Thousands of Inhabitants
Very high = 17,600.00	31%	5%	756
High = 5,680.00	30%	15%	2,268
Medium = 246.00	26%	30%	4,536
Low = 74.00	13%	50%	7,560

SOURCE: SIECA (Secretaria Permanente del Tratado General de Integración Económica Centroamericana), *La política de desarrollo social dentro de la integración económica* (Guatemala, 1975), 18.

There exist no plausible data to suggest that these percentages have improved for the lower-income strata in the eighties; on the contrary, the tendency toward the concentration of wealth at the monopolistic apex has not stopped. This has social and political consequences that will be analyzed below.

The descriptions of these features should not upset the characterization of Central American society in the eighties as an agrarian society. Although growth rates for agriculture and livestock production were lower in this entire period, there was nevertheless expansion in the old agro-export matrix. Over twenty-five years, coffee production has tripled and banana production doubled. Cotton, meat, sugar, shellfish, and now cardamom (in Guatemala) have appeared. The growth in agricultural-livestock production results less from increases in productivity than from the expansion of the agricultural frontier. Extensive use of land and greater exploitation of the abundant labor force were combined, along with improved technology in certain new crops to produce an increase in the value of agriculture-livestock production from $886.9 million (at 1970 prices) in 1951 to $2.3342 billion in 1979.[24] At the beginning of 1980, 79 percent of the lands best suited for agriculture and livestock raising were already being used. In the course of this decade, the agricultural frontier will be used up in two of the countries where this phenomenon has not yet occurred.

We do observe an optimistic note in the region's relative importance in Latin American agricultural-livestock exports. By the end of the seventies, we were first in exporting bananas (58 percent) and cotton (42 percent), second in meat (30 percent), and third in coffee (21 percent). It should be added that Central American sugar is not competitive in the world market, and in the eighties the regional sugar agro-industry could enter into total crisis.[25]

Clearly, the agro-livestock sector continues to be the most important factor in the formation of the regional product (28.4 percent of the GDP) and employs 60 percent of the population; moreover, 80 percent of all foreign exchange comes from the extraregional exports previously indicated. But here we find a set of paradoxes inherent in the style of growth typically found in dependent agrarian societies: (a) The average annual growth rate in the agricultural product was 4 percent (1950–78), that is, almost twice the increase in the rural population; however, in that period the rural population's share of the national income declined from 29 percent to 27 percent.[26] According to approximate calculations, the average per capita agricultural income in 1979 was projected to be 132 Central American dollars,[27] that is, less than 15 percent of the average urban income. Why should it improve in the current decade? (b) Commercial agriculture for export, increasingly modernized through incorporation of technology and chemical inputs, contrasts with the production of foods for popular consumption, which is relegated to the family plot, on the traditional *minifundio*, using backward methods. Contrary to the tendency we observe in the rest of Latin America, production for the world market grows more rapidly in Central America than does production for the internal market (4.6 percent and 3.4 percent, respectively).[28] As has already been stated many times, the agricultural economy generates foreign exchange but not food, and at the start of this decade the lack of self-sufficiency in basic grains, which has never been attained, is causing a true nutrition crisis in the population. (c) The style of growth has further emphasized the heterogeneous character of the Central American countryside; the economic and social diversification is the result of a single process, controlled by capital for its own reproduction and based on capitalist and noncapitalist economic forms, giving rise to "unequal development" of a social and economic nature.

We are beginning the eighties with one of those cyclical crises so familiar to our coffee-plantation culture. Now, however, our ties with the greater economy are no longer through coffee alone. They extend to the other export products, and the installation of the industrial park has tied the knots even tighter. Moreover, this dependency on foreign economic and political centers has given rise to structural relations that, once established, are difficult to modify. Briefly recall that the crisis of the thirties was only a contraction in foreign trade; Central American society supported the weight of that crisis on the cushion of its peasant economies, the last refuge of traditional society. Today the ties are also of a technological and financial nature. At present it would be impossible for industrial production, for example, to dispense with its raw materials, intermediate inputs, capital goods, and financing, all of which come from abroad. This iron shackle binding dependent capitalism to the world market is now tightened during periods of crisis—and not loosened, as in the past, when crisis weakened commercial dependence.

Is it possible to predict the course of the international crisis, or the forms it will take on a national level? The economic crisis, with a logic of its own, is interwoven with political crises that, although tied to economic structures in the last instance, do exhibit a relatively independent rationality. This only complicates the problem. The relative autonomy of the political sphere is acting to reinforce the economic consequences, and, almost without exception, the dominant groups have shown themselves incompetent in managing the situation. Ideologically crippled by their own neoliberal conservatism, they confront economic injustice and popular protest with manifest clumsiness.

THE FOUR-STORY SOCIETY

The old oligarchical society has been left behind. Although it was never, structurally speaking, an egalitarian society, today the inequality is even greater. Central America is more heterogeneous and more complex. While grounded in the economic mechanisms outlined above, social differentiation is superstructurally reinforced by certain factors that acquire preeminence in dependent societies, factors such as education and patterns of consumption. Income is presumably the sine qua non of social differentiation, but the actual mechanisms of this process are to be found more in cultural patterns of consumption, that is, in the ritual utilization of commodities to symbolize membership in the more privileged social groups. Imitation here assumes its full sociological value, providing those who practice it with the most important of social identifications: their own self-image.

Formed over the long course of its history, the appearance of a four-story society is nonetheless recent, and the tendencies to become increasingly pyramidal are gaining strength in this decade. In the basement "dwell" the social sectors produced by a downward social differentiation. The relative social breakdown and disappearance of the old urban crafts sector and the absolute increase of a floating population, permanently underemployed, that is improperly called the "marginal mass" swell this sector. In a semantic tour de force, this is now being called the "informal sector of the economy" in order to refer to the numerical growth of the subproletariat, a labor force that sometimes acts as a reserve but that is better defined as a "social set" without a class ascription. Many in these sectors make up the déclassés of the system, which have always existed but in a transitional way. In the European experience, the déclassé nature of some human groups represented the transition of the labor force in the process of being subsumed by capital. This is usually attributed to the breakdown of the peasant crafts sector and its subsequent productive reorganization. In dependent capitalist society, this transitional quality does not seem to exist, and the reorganization of production is permanently postponed. There is an over- or underdetermination of class that becomes very difficult to analyze.

Marginal mass or *informal sector of the economy* are terms usually applied to the process of growing urban poverty, as a consequence of the chronic sub- or unemployment inherent in this kind of industrial growth. Left unconsidered are the questions of social situation and social condition. All the more affected by social marginalization are groups of people in a situation of partial or deficient participation in the structures of the market: under twenty-four hours of work per week, below-average wages, employment in the sectors of lowest productivity, and so forth. Their condition, as a result, involves a low income, dilapidated housing, and lack of access to services or cultural benefits.

We are entering this decade with the highest unemployment rates in the last twenty-five years, but without a decrease in birthrates, except in Costa Rica. The rural subproletariat increases ceaselessly, and part of it flocks to the cities. The building's basement is filling up with more and more new and desperate inhabitants.

On the second floor are found those social sectors that have the opportunity, relatively speaking, to work and to receive an income that is not limited, temporary, or incomplete. The system rewards them by exploiting them: here we find an important nucleus of the industrial proletariat and in general the so-called working class, in the broad sense, as well as the agricultural proletariat that resulted from the modernization of commercial agriculture.

Probably the most characteristic aspect of the social change that has occurred in Central America in the last twenty-five years is the emergence of intermediate strata, which have complex origins and are even more difficult to classify; they are the direct result of the economic differentiation already alluded to and thus the beneficiaries of a *structural* upward mobility. The conditions for ascent, however, are not all economic. We refer to the belated diffusion of "middle class" culture, defined by the preeminence of certain patterns of life and social relations, consumption without solvency, and, in general, conduct that expresses one's degree of success by the degree of formality with which certain social conventions are fulfilled—for example, wearing imported clothing!

This has led more than one person to think that in this four-story building the third level is growing the most, at the expense or to the benefit of those who are above or below in this social construct. The theories of the dissolution of class barriers or of the formation of middle-class societies point to this social bourgeoisification, typified by the integration of this intermediate stratum of the society, as a factor that will supposedly balance social conflicts.

Obviously, this is not the place for a theoretical discussion of the social stratification occurring in Central America today. The phenomenon of social differentiation, familiar in other parts of Latin America, does not represent anything new. What is perhaps unique is the speed with which the mechanisms of class condition operate above and beyond those of class situation. To speak of one "middle class" is only to situate the problem on the level of appearances. In question are salaried intermediate strata, whose class affiliation is not a great problem if one agrees that in the last analysis there are no social categories external to the classes. But to speak of "middle class" is to make direct reference to "a salary group or a socio-professional category,"[29] and not to a class per se. These strata lack the income criteria and mental and psychological attitudes that define class condition.

For this reason, we are not defining the rise of a new social class, the middle class, as a new feature of Central American society. But we do want to emphasize the extraordinary importance of the gradual consolidation of these social groups. With multiple insertions into the economic structure, they are characterized less by the homogeneity of their economic activity than by their superstructural aspects: the character of the mechanisms they employ for social ascent and the styles of life they adopt. In sum, expanded education and increased employment in nonproductive (non-value-generating) jobs, above all those linked to the hypertrophy of state apparatuses, have created a complex, heterogeneous social sector in the urban centers whose presence is qualitatively important.

Certainly, its importance resides in the fact that its emergence as a social group is recent, and such changes, however relative they may be in the general societal framework, are vital and do objectively express a favorable modification of the preceding social status. However, the nature and extent of the structural mechanisms of social mobility in Central America should not be overestimated, and those that pertain to the middle groups even less so. Such mechanisms are of a nature different from the one that was typical of "classic" or endogenous capitalist development: the middle groups do not occupy this intermediate societal space as a mere transitional zone, like a petty bourgeoisie from which the middle and upper bourgeoisie would spring. Instead, it is a place of arrival, the final point in an ascent that rapidly encounters its limits (independent of the fact that the social actors in that ascent may not be conscious of those limits). This ascent is a by-product of the growth of private enterprise, and particularly of the expansion of the public bureaucracy. All this forms part of a slow process of urbanization, which is, sociologically, a mechanism for expansion of education and work opportunities.

Finally, let us speak about the inhabitants of the fourth floor, but not indicating merely what is obvious in the social stratification. Of course, there were "upper classes" in the past, and they were identified in political terms as an "oligarchy," more for their style of domination and their social privileges than for the size of their fortunes. In recent years, however, that wealth has changed in character and has become investment capital. The hoarding of treasure has been replaced by the search for surplus value. A double combination of economic and political mechanisms has facilitated processes of capitalistic concentration and centralization, in the industrial as well as in the agrarian and commercial sectors, resulting in monopolistic peaks joined together by financial capital. One is dealing with a small but powerful and multifunctional bourgeoisie.

The great landholding coffee planters exaggerated their bourgeois condition, and with that they not only did not reduce control over their production but expanded it by modernizing the processing and marketing systems. Alongside them arose cotton- and cattle-raising entrepreneurs who, strictly speaking, no longer formed what were once called the agrarian classes. This was a new bourgeoisie with urban origins, linked to other productive activities, especially in industry. There is no completed research on this process, but those on the top floor, whom we are now describing, form powerful family groups, internally diversified and with multiple insertions into the productive structure.

It is useful to point out two more features characterizing this class. Within it there are the "old" bourgeoisie, born in the period prior to 1950, and the "new," that is, the one encouraged by the Common Market. The latter is more given to climbing, having sprung up under conditions favorable to the accumulation of agrarian or commercial capital, and above all in the direct shadow of the state. Unlike the classic *bourgeoisie conquérante* of the nineteenth century, it is more adventurous and speculative in character, with a short-term outlook. This "new" group plunders the state or uses it to its advantage, through the deals that power makes possible and that, strictly speaking, have nothing to do with competition in the marketplace.

Many of these economically dominant groups have arisen because of their connection to foreign investors. The Common Market favored the internationalization of our modest internal market. A denationalized bourgeoisie? The "joint ventures" undoubtedly reduced the leading role of national capital to the advantage of internationalized management. But this conversion of the bourgeoisie into a subsidiary, contrary to patriotic opinions, only strengthens its class condition. In other words, by agreeing to be the junior partner in industrial investment, the Central American bourgeoisie does not become any the "less" bourgeois, although certainly its control over the national market may decrease. Nor has it been possible to show that it has a strictly managerial, administrative quality.

POPULATION: THE CRITICAL VARIABLES

The demographic explosion in Central America is quite dramatic on a strictly quantitative basis, for we have gone from 8 million inhabitants (1950) to more than 20 million (1980). The growth rate increased from 2.9 percent in the fifties to 3.1 percent in the following decade, and it has remained at that level in recent years. From a sociological viewpoint, we might say that Central American society has been *massified*.

This term alludes not to numbers but to changes in the quality of social relations, the presence and actions of a population of a size that permits establishing new expressions of collective life. The first of these changes is an increased tendency toward the urbanization of social life. Indicators on this point are contradictory. According to some data, more than 40 percent of the Central American population is urban; according to others, 80 percent lives in the countryside. What does it mean to be urban? It is the enjoyment, however limited it might be, of the benefits and disadvantages of industrial culture. From that point, the definition wavers empirically. What is important is not the place where one lives but the very scope of urban culture. Costa Rica and Guatemala would be, in this sense, the opposite poles of a situation that has not yet been captured statistically.

The second consequence is that massification increases the social distances between those who have nothing and those who receive a great deal. The data on employment and income, on economic activity in general, reveal, for example, the vigorous persistence of a socioeconomic structure that is difficult to modify. The impressionistic analysis of the social classes in the preceding section can be partially complemented by more reliable data, such as statistics. For example, the economically active population by category of occupation shows the following in the past two decades:

TABLE 2: *Economically Active Population by Categories in the 1960s and 1970s*

	Salaried Worker	Self-Employed	Employer	Nonsalaried Worker
1960s	1,413,525	630,142	50,114	270,197
1970s	2,453,175	1,368,311	102,611	485,250

SOURCE: Population censuses and data collected by the author.

A preliminary proportional analysis confirms that the number of salaried workers is tending to decrease (58.6 percent to 53.7 percent) and that of self-employed workers to increase (26.1 percent to 30 percent). In absolute terms, the latter group is doubling, and unremunerated family work remains proportionally stable. Such figures have to be compared with the information about unemployment and underemployment, which is contradictory in general and different according to the country considered as well.

With the help of the statistical data mentioned, and keeping in mind that such indicators have visible limitations, we want to present a comparative analysis that will enable us not so much to situate the class structure but rather to suggest tentatively the extent to which capitalist social relations coexist with other types of relations that are not fully capitalist, as well as the extent to which what we would call a process of centralization (a relation between very concentrated capital and the labor force) has been developed in those capitalist relations.

In accord with the classification by "category of occupation" and following the methodology of M. Murmis,[30] we consider in Table 3 the percentage of self-employed workers (1) an indicator of the weight of not-wholly capitalist relations; the ratio between employers (2) and salaried workers (3) suggests the degree of centralization of capital (5), that is, the point at which the large enterprise appears. Let us look at the following:

TABLE 3: *Categories of Occupation (%)*

	England (1966)	Argentina (1960)	Brazil (1960)	Central America (1970)
1. Self-employed workers	4.2	12.1	35.1	30.0
2. Employer	2.2	12.4	1.8	2.3
3. Salaried worker	90.1	69.9	48.0	53.7
4. Others	3.5	5.6	15.1	14.0
5. Worker with remuneration/ employer (3/2)	41.0	5.6	26.7	23.3

SOURCE: Miguel Murmis, *Tipos de capitalismo en América Latina* (Buenos Aires: Editorial La Rosa Blindada, 1973), 13. The figures on Central America were added by the author for comparison.

England exhibits the purest type of capitalist development, of an openly monopolistic nature, Argentina an intermediate situation, and Brazil and Central America, despite their real differences, a contradictory and uneven degree of such development, but closest to the pure type of dependent capitalism. In fact, as the percentage on line 1 becomes larger, it expresses a strong weight for noncapitalist relations, reinforced by the percentages in line 4, which hide the category of "unremunerated workers," that is, the family labor typical of agrarian societies that are still quite traditional.

Line 3 suggests the degree of wage-based social relations of production, and the larger the ratio in line 5, the more concentrated is the relation between capitalists and salaried workers. In this case, the existence of a broad layer of middle and lower bourgeoisie such as we find in Argentina distorts the relation shown by the percentages. This does not occur, for example, in the case of Central America, still a model agrarian society with a class structure in which the self-employed workers (line 1) and the "others" (line 4) total almost half the population, whereas in England they barely represent 8 percent.

There are some additional indicators, whose descriptive value complements the characterization of the social structure of the Central American population attempted in a double fashion on the preceding pages. Out of the total population, 45.2 percent are reported economically active; recent significant changes are observed in two dimensions. First, the proportion of children and adolescents who work (population between ten and fourteen years old) is tending to decrease, from 19.3 (1960) to 15.7 (1970) for the whole region, although in the rural sector it remains 21.0 percent. The second important feature appears in the changes and halts in growth of population by branches of activity. The percentage of persons working in the manufacturing industry appears practically at a standstill (11.4 percent and 11.9 percent), whereas the decrease of the agricultural EAP attains the most significant value by dropping from 63.0 percent to 53.2 percent. Services and commerce, by contrast, increased from 19.9 to 23.6 percent, which at first glance allows us to suggest what is already verified for other societies: that the subemployment, unemployment, and increasing poverty of the population is localized or concealed in these activities.[31]

Furthermore, we can consider literacy, an indicator that reveals the degree to which a society has given its population the basic tools for vocational training and, consequently, for permitting it to better understand and structure the symbolic world of culture and to relate to the collectivity in a qualitatively superior way. The data on the illiterate population generally reveal very slow changes and marked variation by nation. In general, more than half the Central American population does not know how to read and write; but comparisons between the rural and urban environments for the two decades and in the five countries prove more useful. The Central American illiterate population is unequally distributed as follows:

TABLE 4: *Distribution of Illiterate Population in Central America, by Percentage*

	1960		1970	
	Rural	*Urban*	*Rural*	*Urban*
Guatemala	81.9	18.1	81.9	18.1
El Salvador	78.1	21.9	79.2	20.8
Honduras	88.7	11.3	84.3	15.7
Nicaragua	82.3	17.7	78.3	21.7
Costa Rica	86.5	13.5	81.2	18.8

SOURCE: Population censuses from diverse years, for all Central American countries.

Obviously, the rural sector encapsulates the larger illiterate population in each country. It is worth mentioning that Costa Rica has only 3.7 percent while Guatemala has nearly half of the illiterate population for the whole region, both in the rural and in the urban sectors. The passage of time, with the styles of development corresponding to it, including the qualitative variations already mentioned in the productive sector, would seem to have no impact on this table of cultural deficiency. Two phenomena stand out, however: illiteracy is increasing in El Salvador, and it has practically disappeared in Nicaragua.

Finally, let us examine another indicator that points not only to the cultural equipment available to a population but also to the profound selectivity with which such social benefits are distributed. We are referring to higher education, determined by student enrollment in the state universities in Central America. In 1950 there were 6,535 students registered; thirty years later, in 1980, there were 156,178. This is undoubtedly an impressive figure, which reveals the magnitude of our educational effort. If the same conditions existing today continue (excluding Nicaragua, where the [National] Council on Higher Education expects the additional enrollment of 15,000 new students), then, according to a projection made for this essay, Central America will by the end of the decade have 277,000 university students in the state universities.[32]

The expansion of higher education undoubtedly continues to

favor only certain strata of the regional population. Because the data are incomplete, it was not possible to present figures on the rates of students at higher levels by social sectors, but we can conclude that in distribution by countries, Costa Rica again shows the highest rate, 15.0 percent, while Guatemala is at the opposite extreme with 3.9 percent. In between, but farther from Costa Rica, are El Salvador, 4.2 percent; Honduras, 4.4 percent; and Nicaragua, 5.3 percent.

CENTRAL AMERICA AT THE CROSSROADS

Central America in the eighties is affected not only by a significant economic crisis, which has diverse effects in the countries of the region, but also by political processes that represent, each in its own way, true historic ruptures. After the triumph of the Sandinista revolution, Central America will not be the same. The collapse of the Somoza dictatorship is less important than the total systematic crisis that its fall introduced into the core of Nicaraguan society, a result that undoubtedly obeys structural factors found in the way in which capitalism functions in the region.

The profound political crisis that is occurring in El Salvador—with all the signs of a civil war—and the politico-social breakdown that has been affecting Guatemala for years (80,000 political deaths) are circumstances that cannot in any way remain outside the analysis. We are dealing here with national processes in which what is being questioned is not, properly speaking, a matter of government, or the replacement of an arbitrary and incompetent dictator. Instead, it is the whole system that is being challenged as a system of unjust domination, incapable of resolving the elementary problems of living together in a civilized way. The political crisis being expressed in state terrorism and in revolutionary struggle represents a total confrontation that each day comes more and more to resemble that contradiction between the state, in the hands of an armed minority, and the nation, represented by millions of workers, and peasants, and other social sectors.

Whatever the perspective used, it is impossible to keep from thinking that the difficulties of economic growth and the political crisis that is violently disturbing the life of several of the region's countries are placing Central America at the most difficult crossroads in its history.

NOTES

1. The *encomiendas* involved a system of personal services and tributes that the conquered aboriginal population had to pay or give for long periods of time to conquistadores who were favored by the king of Spain. Cf. Silvio Zavala, *La encomienda indiana* (Madrid, 1935); Lesley B. Simpson, *The Encomienda in New Spain* (Berkeley: University of California Press, 1929).
2. This is what the American-born children of Spaniards were called. In the sort of ethnocultural stratification peculiar to a backward society, the Spaniards were socially superior to their American descendants, and the latter, white and literate, were far above the condition of the *castas*—the racial mixture of blacks, Indians, and *criollos*.
3. Cf. Ralph Lee Woodward, *Privilegio de clase y desarrollo económico: Guatemala, 1793–1871* (San José, Costa Rica: EDUCA, 1981).
4. The conservatives in Guatemala City wanted to join Iturbide's Mexican empire, those in San José wanted to unite with Gran Colombia, liberals in San Salvador at several points made efforts to request integration into the United States, and so on.
5. We need only recall William Walker's filibustering adventure in Nicaragua, and the English attempts to take over Roatán in Honduras, the Mosquitia in Nicaragua, and Belize in Guatemala.
6. The coffee bean must be subjected to an almost industrial process of shelling, drying, and so on, before it can be put in bags for export.
7.

Share of GDP by Agricultural Exports in Central America

1960	88%
1962	78%
1964	79%
1966	73%
1968	61%
1970	59%

Source: SIECA (Secretaria Permanente del Tratado General de Integración Económica Centroamericana), *Séries estadísticas seleccionadas de Centroamérica y Panamá* (Guatemala, July 1971), table 17, p. 28.

8. Since 1945 the volume of coffee production and exports has continued to rise uninterruptedly, to the point that by 1971 exports had almost tripled. In 1944, the last full year of World War II, Central America exported 122,120 metric tons of coffee; by 1960 that figure had grown 100 percent (to 255,494), and in 1970 it had risen to 337,331 tons. However, in the sixties the income from coffee had increased only 14 percent, using 1960 as the base year. See SIECA, *Séries estadísticas seleccionadas,* table 18, p. 29.

9.

Central American Exporting of Selected Products
New and Traditional Products
(Millions of U.S. dollars)

Year	Guatemala Cotton	Bananas	El Salvador Cotton	Bananas	Honduras Cotton	Bananas	Nicaragua Cotton	Bananas	Costa Rica Cotton	Bananas
1972	40	17.2	37.1	—	0.7	81.9	62.8	3.4	—	82.8
1974	68.3	21.4	46.5	—	3.1	51.5	135.9	5.3	—	98.4
1976	85.0	21.7	62.0	—	4.4	106.7	130.6	4.6	0.1	148.7
1978	139.2	22.2	98.4	0.2	15.7	139.2	140.9	4.8	9.5	169.9
1979	183.1	18.5	87.0	—	11.4	200.4	135.7	6.4	. . .	169.4

Year	Sugar	Meat	Sugar	Meat	Sugar	Meat	Sugar	Meat	Sugar	Meat
1972	16.1	18.0	18.0	5.1	2.0	16.0	15.2	38.7	13.1	28.3
1974	49.6	21.5	39.6	1.4	4.5	16.8	12.3	22.1	24.4	34.2
1976	106.7	14.4	40.5	9.1	2.2	25.7	52.8	40.0	24.7	40.6
1978	45.7	31.2	18.9	12.9	5.5	38.9	19.6	70.1	15.7	60.4
1979	52.9	38.3	26.8	14.0	13.3	61.2	19.6	95.1	17.0	81.6

SOURCE: SIECA, *Séries estadísticas seleccionadas de Centroamérica y Panamá* (Guatemala, 1980), 26–30.

10.

Value of Intra-Central American Trade in 1979
(Central American Pesos)

Country	Export	Import	Balance
Central America	900,066,265	879,762,408	+ 20,303,857
Guatemala	309,898,129	199,875,593	+110,022,536
El Salvador	263,615,865	256,953,270	+ 6,662,595
Honduras	59,819,041	98,514,160	− 38,695,119
Nicaragua	90,065,457	111,160,827	− 21,095,370
Costa Rica	176,667,773	213,258,558	− 36,590,785

SOURCE: SIECA, "Integración en cifras," *Anuario estadístico* nos. 4, 5, and 6 (Guatemala, 1971).

11. World Bank, *World Development Report* (New York: Oxford University Press, 1980), tables 9 and 12.
12. CEPAL (Comisión Económica para América Latina), "El Mercado Común Centroamericano y sus problemas recientes," CEPAL, E/CN. 12/CCE. 363/Rev. 1 (Santiago, Chile, March 1971), 10.
13.

Participation of Sectors I and II in the Gross Domestic Product
(In Percentages for the Year 1980)

	Guatemala	El Salvador	Honduras	Nicaragua	Costa Rica
Sector I	17.7	24.4	25.2	28.1	23.2
Sector II	22.2	15.7	16.7	17.0	24.3

SOURCE: IDB (Inter-American Development Bank), *El progreso económico y social en América Latina, 1980–81 report* (Washington, D.C., 1981), various tables, pp. 13, 28.

14. Compare the rates of industrial value added for the five-year periods 1950–55 and 1960–65, which were 6.1 percent and 8.7 percent, respectively; in the last years of the sixties—1968–69—the percentage increased to 9.3 percent. See SIECA, *Anuario estadístico* (Guatemala, 1971).
15.

U.S. Direct Investment in Central America (1974–79)
(Millions of Dollars)

	1974	1978	1979
Total Central America		793	895
Honduras	186	202	. . .
Guatemala	170	221	. . .
Costa Rica	161	143	. . .
Nicaragua	97	121	. . .
El Salvador	71	111	. . .

SOURCE: U.S. Department of Commerce.

16. Gert Rosenthal, "La inversión extranjera en el área centroamericana," *La nación,* 15 October 1971, 45.
17. *Comercio Exterior* magazine, published by the Banco Mexicano de Comercio Exterior, June 1980, 561.
18. In Guatemala the United Fruit Company became a simple banana trading company and in 1969 obliged the Méndez Montenegro government to buy the old liberal railroad for $42 million. The United Fruit Company, which in 1954 owned 20 percent of all the arable land in Guatemala, Honduras,

and Costa Rica, has sold the greater part of it; it is now involved in the production of canned food and of textiles, in meat packing, and in other areas, operating through the United Fruit Food Company, and in association with Grace and Company.

19. World Bank, quoted in CEPAL, *El carácter de la crisis económica actual, los desafíos que plantea y la cooperación internacional que demanda,* mimeographed (Mexico, 1981), 29.

20. CEPAL, *Desarrollo y política social en Centroamérica,* Doc. 76/11 (Mexico, August 1976), 56.

21. United Nations, *World Statistics in Brief* (New York, 1960 and 1980).

22. IDB, *El progreso económico y social en América Latina,* 96–112.

23. Ibid., table 111–24, p. 107.

24. Ibid., 78.

25. Calculations by the author based on data from SIECA.

26. SIECA, *La política de desarrollo social dentro de la integración económica* (Guatemala, 1975), 34.

27. Ibid.

28. CEPAL/FAO, *Veinticinco años de desarrollo agricola de América Latina, 1950–1975* (Santiago, Chile: Colección Cuadernos, 1978), table 3.

29. Nicos Poulantzas, *Las clases sociales en el capitalismo* (Mexico: Siglo Veintiuno, 1978), 67.

30. Miguel Murmis, in an essay published in *Tipos de capitalismo* in mimeograph, proposes a special methodology for using population census data. The explanation appearing in this paper corresponds to his suggestive theory.

31. Data from population censuses, various years, all Central American countries.

32. Raul Zepeda, *La población universitaria en Centroamérica,* unpublished document, Area de Educación, Confederación Universitaria Centroamericana, mimeographed (San José, Costa Rica, 1981), 17.

Reagan and Central America

STRATEGY THROUGH A FRACTURED LENS

Luis Maira

I. THE AMERICAN NATIONAL INTEREST AND INTERPRETATIONS OF CRISIS IN CENTRAL AMERICA

Central America ought to be most familiar to U.S. diplomacy, in theory. Washington's connections embraced the countries of this subregion in the first years of this century, under Theodore Roosevelt, when the international expansion of its vigorous domestic productive forces became the conscious goal of the United States. During this initial imperial expansion the great basin of the Caribbean was a privileged area. Considered to be among the foremost world-trade routes since the Panama Canal opening, the Caribbean became an "American lake," in a geopolitical position equivalent to that of the Mediterranean in European imperial disputes of centuries past.

For the tiny Central American countries, the consequences of this fact attained a brutal dimension. A mounting influx of direct North American investments began within a few years, in public utilities and agricultural enclaves. This helped generate the picturesque "banana republic" image that many analysts continue to identify with these countries even today. They also came to know the impact of an immediate presence of the U.S. armed forces, something best expressed in the regime of "protectorates" that Washington established in the Dominican Republic, Haiti, and Nicaragua. With the direct participation of its marines, the United States signaled its physical occupation of these countries for many years.[1]

The Central American peoples' perception of the immediate, sometimes asphyxiating presence of the U.S. national interest inside their own countries is nowhere better reflected than in their images of the activities of United Fruit. Partly mythical, partly realistic, these images were synthesized by Miguel Angel Asturias into the "green Pope," the core of one of the novels that brought him the Nobel Prize in literature. Things have changed. These countries are no longer a mere collection of haciendas and agrobusinesses. Yet, it is certain that ever since those early years it has been a cultural trait of broad sectors of these societies to distrust strongly anything of U.S. provenance.

But when we consider how things must look through U.S. lenses, the situation is no less singular: the behavior of the Department of State and the Washington governments can demonstrate only that despite decades of contact they have not learned the historical lessons explaining the economic and political development of the nation-states that lie along the Central American isthmus.

One should not underestimate the degree to which the current crisis in Central America relates directly to prolonged U.S. government support for authoritarian regimes in the area, despite signs of their obvious illegitimacy, exhaustion, and disintegration. The present situation was reached only after a series of endogenous democratization and modernization projects had been derailed by the regimes of force in the sixties and seventies. Washington did nothing to impede this. In Nicaragua some twenty years ago, Pedro Joaquín Chamorro and other moderate opposition figures urged the replacement of the Somoza clan's dynastic regime; for an answer they faced a series of repressions and frauds culminating in the open anomalies of the 1974 elections. In El Salvador an opposition bloc dominated by the Christian Democratic party won the presidential elections of 1972 and 1977; on both occasions obviously fraudulent government maneuverings followed by massacres of the populace blocked the opposition winners' road to power. In Guatemala the civilian government of the university professor Julio César Méndez Montenegro was smashed by the military before he even took office, in 1966; the pretext was to maintain control of public order. Since 1970 four generals on active duty have held the presidency. In the elections of 1974 and 1978, opposition groups declared illegitimate the outcome that the government had proclaimed. In recent years, as if to fix the course of history and, through force, to make the current situation irreversible, paramilitary groups of the extreme Right have assassinated the principal civilian opposition leaders, in the capital city in broad daylight.

Through various administrations the executors of U.S. policy toward Central America have refused to accept the reality of the pressure for change, preferring to maintain low-budget alliances with conservative authoritarian governments that boast of their goodwill toward the United States, their anticommunism and solidarity in the defense of Western civilization. As Edelberto Torres-Rivas has pointed out, "reasonable reformism" has been disappearing from the political ideological spectrum in the most convulsive countries at a time when the liberal democratic process has been losing all credibility in a subregion that, excepting Costa Rica, has never known stable liberal democracies.[2]

The interests at the core of the current crisis are perceived in a contradictory manner inside the United States. Such is the case even within the groups that formulate official U.S. policy, as a careful review of State Department and National Security Council reports will show. This impression is reinforced when we turn to the academic work of leading figures behind this administration's Latin America policy.

Let us examine two views regarding the origins and development of events in Central America, each implying fundamentally different policy options. These studies stand out both because they have had a large impact on those responsible for formulating hemispheric policy and because they express clearly the rationales for each point of view. One is "The Hobbes Problem: Order, Authority, and Legitimacy in Central America" (December 1980), prepared by Jeane Kirkpatrick for the American Enterprise Institute. The other is "The Deterioration and Breakdown of Reactionary Despotism in Central America" (1981), prepared for the State Department by Prof. Enrique A. Baloyra, of the University of North Carolina.

Baloyra's analysis typifies the liberal reading of the crisis. It attempts to rescue the specificity of the situations actually experienced in Central America in order to avoid theoretical contamination resulting from demands to fit conflicting forces into an East-West framework. For Baloyra, this specificity is attained by restoring a historical dimension to the political situation of each country. "We believe," he emphasizes, "that the origins of the contemporary forms of authoritarian control are the direct or indirect result of the establishment of oligarchic republics during the 1870–71 bourgeois revolutions."[3] Out of the liberal reforms arose models of oligarchic domination that suffered the tremors of the Great Depression, but ruling sectors were able to absorb opposition pressure by means of personalized dictatorial regimes (which the author calls reactionary despotism). In Guatemala and El Salvador they concentrated on restoring public order. The conservative sectors were temporarily successful with peasants, workers, and students by enforcing peace with an iron hand, thereby evading any questioning of the economic model based on raw-materials exporting.

The liberal vision stresses that the key to what is actually happening lies in the survival of worn-out political and economic models that have been upheld over the years by elites who have known how to organize themselves to protect their power. By the same token, this reading insists that the current situation cannot be understood unless one's analysis favors endogenous factors. "What is surprising is not that these regimes are deteriorating and breaking down but that they have lasted as long as they have."[4]

In a context long influenced by many elements of social malaise, existing political factors have begun to play an active role. Social and Christian Democrats began in the sixties to politicize and to mobilize the subordinate social sectors; electoral formulas failed, and irregularities constantly surrounded elections; the Catholic Church assumed a new role of social opposition and mobilization. All of this combined has strengthened the political will of opposition forces to unite in order to put an end to these regimes by any means.

This approach leads to the natural conclusion that the formulators of Central America policy in Washington should change their essential criteria with respect to what is actually happening. By attaining an understanding of the current conflicts that is both historical and structural, they might learn that what is needed is "more diplomacy and less crisis management."[5]

As if wishing to situate herself as far away as possible from this liberal point of view, Ambassador Kirkpatrick points out that centuries ago Thomas Hobbes came up with the framework essential for resolving the current crises in Central America. She begins by insisting that policymakers learn Hobbes's fundamental doctrine —that "the central problem of any society is to establish order and authority"—as if all that El Salvador needed were a stronger dose of each.

The peculiar slant of her reasoning evolves from this premise. To understand what is happening today in El Salvador (or what happened yesterday in Nicaragua), "it is first necessary to understand what kind of regimes and what kind of societies these are."[6] In countries affected by the turbulence and unrest of their recent transformations there arises, "a disagreement about the legitimate aims and means of government, growing distrust of authority, a broad internal ideological spectrum, a tendency toward privatization, limited participation in voluntary associations, preference for hierarchical entities like the church, the bureaucracy, or the Army, a long history of military participation in politics, and personalism."[7] These are factors that tend to prevent existing regimes from controlling the political process, thereby making the regimes unstable. Therefore, in El Salvador and other Central American countries, "weak governments confront strong social groups without the existence of any institution capable of establishing its authority over the whole society."[8] In such a situation, no valid procedures exist for gaining access to power, and each sector competes using the resources at hand: "the church uses ethical symbols; the workers, strikes; entrepreneurs, bribery; parties, electoral campaigns and the vote; political leaders, persuasion, organization or demagoguery; and the military, force."[9] The military usually wins out, and because of this, violence is a permanent reality, and war a constant possibility. Normally, however, "in this game, the political competitors do not destroy one another. They suffer limited defeats and they win limited victories," which accentuates further the political instability of these regimes.[10]

Into this routine and habitual (and for Kirkpatrick, acceptable) system enter guerrilla violence and the groups trained and supported by Cuba and linked to the grand schemes and alliances of the Soviet Union. These forces use terrorism to destroy order, break down the economy and daily life, demoralize the police, and mortally wound governments by proving their inability to protect personal safety and maintain public authority. Accordingly, "terrorism" constitutes "a form of revolution that replaces mass support with the employment of revolutionary military groups."

In terms of specific policy options, this framework poses some very real dilemmas, deeply disturbing to neoconservative thinking. In the first place, one has to understand that Central America is an internationalized area where other factors of power act in opposition to the North American national interest. The Socialist International, the Catholic Church, and Cuba have from distinct positions interfered in the countries of the Isthmus, contributing to their destabilization. During the Carter administration, an element of U.S. weakness was added. The government wanted to achieve its purpose by pursuing new objectives like "the internal reforms, democracy and justice that are goods difficult for any government to produce."[11]

In order to come up with a policy that works, neoconservatives advise, it is necessary to learn the simple lesson that in a case of externally supported terrorism, which they believe exists in Central America, "the status of a government depends more than usual on its ability to govern, to assure obedience, to punish those who disobey, in sum to maintain order. Only while such governments are able to guarantee an agreement with their policies can they trust in the habits of obedience; otherwise they must impose their directives by means of fear and use of force."[12]

To make more graphic for policymakers exactly what kind of solution is contemplated, Ambassador Kirkpatrick resorts to a concrete historical example to prove that "the Hero" is necessary for constructing order. In El Salvador there was one such hero: "General Maximiliano Hernández Martínez, who governed El Salvador from 1931 to 1944, was minister of war in the cabinet of President Arturo Araujo when there occurred widespread uprisings said to be the work of Communist agitators. General Hernández Martínez then staged a coup and ruthlessly suppressed the disorders —wiping out all those who participated, hunting down their leaders. It is sometimes said that 30,000 persons lost their lives in this process. To many Salvadorans the violence of this repression seems less important than that of the fact of restored order and the thirteen years of civil peace that ensued."[13]

This approach, considering the "real factors of power," encourages a policy that stresses the reconstruction of order, even if this takes force and rebuilds authoritarianism as well. After all, these conservative reflections tell us, political democracy is not a suitable model for all countries, especially not for those whose entropic tendencies are accelerated by the siege of international communism. To impede, by whatever means, the rise to power of a coalition opposed to the region remaining in loyal alliance with the United States is to serve the U.S. national interest.

The strategic optic that guides the Kirkpatrick approach has clearly come to determine Washington policy toward Central America since Ronald Reagan entered the White House. The ease with which this paradigm became dominant can be explained, in part, by the coincidence of the current government advisers' viewpoints with suppositions previously employed by the Department of State in defining its position regarding Central America.

It has been one central assumption in Foggy Bottom–style analysis that the Central American countries are increasingly less important economically and more important in terms of the security schemes of the United States.[14] None of the direct investments made by U.S. corporations in the subregion are very important. The assessment of the negative effects of another country's falling into anti-U.S. hands has again become the decisive factor for policymakers. This is complemented by the kind of analysis turned out by Reagan's teams, presenting the situations in El Salvador and in Nicaragua as the best opportunities for initiating a working policy of containment on a global scale.

With considerable influence among the experts behind the Republican foreign-policy platform, this diagnosis admits that the sharpest confrontations between the Soviet Union and the United States are occurring in areas of Africa and the Middle East but insists that the Central American countries present conditions much more favorable to a U.S. victory. Central America then, represents an opportunity for a strong "demonstration effect" for the entire Third World.

These geopolitical suppositions and concerns explain Central America's priority on the Reagan agenda as well as the tough contents of the policies that his government is applying.

II. THE REAGAN ADMINISTRATION AND CRISIS MANAGEMENT IN CENTRAL AMERICA

During the first days of the current Republican administration, Central America and El Salvador in particular seemed to be at the focus of greatest crisis confronting North American diplomacy in the Western Hemisphere. One week before the Reagan inauguration in January 1981 the FMLN-FDR (Farabundo Martí Front for National Liberation Democratic Revolutionary Front) forces had launched a general offensive against the Duarte regime, appearing to reproduce many elements of the situation just prior to Somoza's defeat in July 1979. Moreover, the Republican team had repeatedly expressed its determination to resolve developments in Central America promptly.

In a March 1980 campaign address before the Chicago Council on Foreign Relations, Reagan gave a very representative exhibition of his thinking on foreign policy.

> Totalitarian Marxists have control of the island of Grenada in the Caribbean, where Cuban advisors are currently training guerrillas for subversive action against other countries like Trinidad and Tobago, its democratic neighbor. In El Salvador totalitarian Marxist revolutionaries supported by Havana and Moscow are preventing the development of democratic government. Should we allow Grenada, Nicaragua, and El Salvador to become "new Cubas," new staging grounds for Soviet combat brigades? Shall we wait to allow Moscow and Havana to push on to the north toward Guatemala and from there to Mexico, and southward toward Costa Rica and Panama?[15]

The characteristics of the Central American subregion were such that the Reagan perspective complemented suppositions already used by the Department of State in defining its interests along the isthmus. The actual transition in policy and perspective from the original criteria of the Carter government had already occurred in the final phase of that administration. In light of the great events in Nicaragua, Iran, and Afghanistan, the Democrats revised their assessment that Central American conditions called for the application of cautious and gradual democratic measures. The door was opened to a more rigid scheme, one identifying the rising forces of the radical Left in El Salvador and Guatemala as fundamental enemies of Washington. Although these organizations moved away from identifying themselves with Moscow—even being in open conflict with pro-Soviet Communist parties in their countries —by this time various State Department analyses had begun to circulate in which they were considered elements of international communism's expansionist strategy on this continent.

These positions followed the strategic and, at root, geopolitical visions of the Republican team of experts, headed by Roger Fontaine and including various members of the Center for Strategic and International Studies, of Georgetown University; they harmonized easily with the criteria predominant within the State Department in the late seventies.[16] Let us examine the content of Reagan policies country by country.

A. Policy Toward El Salvador

El Salvador has long been the site of a potentially explosive and revolutionary situation. Being at once the smallest and most densely populated country in Latin America, it is also marked by the longevity of its military rule, by the extreme social inequality that is keeping its city and country poor in subhuman conditions, and by the closed, stony character of the oligarchic groups. These have shared power with the armed forces since they crushed the peasant rebellion of 1931, but have systematically resisted any and all proposals for change or reforms.

Many United States specialists knew this reality perfectly well. A representative example was Milton Eisenhower, who had been president of Johns Hopkins during his brother's administration and largely responsible for U.S. policy toward Latin America. In the early seventies, he characterized El Salvador in the following terms:

> . . . about 58 percent of the people are illiterate, the peasants and other workers receive wages around 50 cents per day; a handful of rich plantation owners pays minimal taxes and sends the rest of its profits abroad as investments. In the autumn of 1960, a Military Junta took over the government and attempted a land reform. A second Junta took over in 1961. It was discovered that of 2.5 million inhabitants, only nine thousand were on the list of taxpay-

ers, and the greater part of them evaded paying taxes. Landowners protested violently when the Junta proposed including as taxpayers the 50 thousand persons with highest incomes, and they threatened to bring to power a third, more conservative Junta.[17]

Eisenhower here describes what was the only attempt to open a channel for the change and modernization the country urgently needed. Occurring in the context of the launching of the Alliance for Progress, it similarly ended in failure. The military Right, organized politically around the National Conciliation party (PCN), regained control of the government after that experiment and has held it ever since. Although a group of liberal younger officers were able to unseat Gen. Carlos Humberto Romero in October 1979, they were unable to consolidate its control. The military high command quickly maneuvered the conservative officers Jaime Abdul Gutiérrez and José Guillermo García into strong positions in a regime later to be headed by the civilian José Napleón Duarte.

Despite its outcome, the overthrow of General Romero seemed to signal the exhaustion of traditional political formulas. It awoke expectations and released social energies that made the return to a traditional regime impossible. The popular organizations that had developed in the 1970s were serious actors in the political panorama.* They burst onto the stage and, seeing all the paths toward peaceful change blocked off, chose the path of arms and began the current civil war.

Without an understanding of the social dimension and the historical roots of the war, it is difficult for the Reagan Administration to find a just and stable solution. This is the principal limitation of the strategic lens that the Reagan administration applies: more like a kaleidoscope, it recasts a national conflict along an East-West axis.

The Reagan administration came to power with one clear political resolution inspired by the domino theory: as part of a new containment policy, they must prevent at any cost the rise to power of revolutionary forces in El Salvador. They defined three

---

*Contradicting Kirkpatrick's dictum about "limited participation in voluntary associations." (ED).

alternative courses of action, each with its own forms of policy designed to express the U.S. determination to intervene actively in El Salvador in defense of its national interest. First, Washington could increase aid to its internal allies (the Duarte and then Magaña governments and the Salvadoran armed forces in particular). Alternatively, the conflict could be regionalized through the formation of a military bloc of pro-U.S. forces able to engage and defeat in one or several interrelated conflicts the "anti–U.S." revolutionary potential in the area. As a third recourse, the United States could support its direct intervention with its own rapid-deployment force in order to achieve the same objectives.

The new government decided rather quickly to take the first course. The choice was based largely on Washington's evaluation early in 1981 that the FMLN's offensives in January had gotten few results. Reagan's advisers believed the opposition could be eliminated reasonably soon with greater military resources and a functional aid program to carry out reforms in a kind of social warfare. The plan included an effort to increase the legitimacy of the Salvadoran government, proposing elections of a constituent assembly for March 1982 as a project for co-opting moderate sectors away from the opposition, in order to reestablish the normal state of political affairs.

Yet another reason for choosing the first course of action, without excluding the second and third alternatives, is that Reagan's path differs only in minor details from policy already in place since the final phase of the Carter administration. North American policy toward El Salvador and Honduras was reformulated in March of 1980 as one of Carter's efforts to clarify his stand against "pro-Soviet" or "anti–North American" positions in the Third World. A request to Congress to reprogram security assistance to both countries came from Franklin D. Kramer, the principal assistant to the secretary of defense. Coherent through several previous works, his approach deserves to be called the "Kramer doctrine."

Regarding El Salvador, Kramer stressed two basic points. First, the political actor best able to find a solution to the crisis in that country was the armed forces, inspiring the most confidence, as well, for safeguarding the fundamental interests of the United States. Second, to gain the edge in the war, the government had to push through a social reform program able to place important rural and urban sectors on the side of the Duarte regime.

Washington never proposed reforms in their own right. They were part of a strategy of war, and Kramer, representing the military establishment, suggested that American advisers should supervise the projects but that their ultimate control must rest in the hands of the Salvadoran army. In the best situation to determine exactly the places and groups to be targeted, says Kramer, "the Army plays a key role in development of the agrarian reform and our military assistance will help strengthen the Army's role in the execution of the reforms."[18]

Observing the influence with which these Defense Department views oriented the Carter White House with respect to El Salvador, one should not be surprised that a team of specialists grounded in security and geopolitical considerations, like Reagan's, decided to proceed with the same strategy. One difference that must be underscored is the increase in resources pledged by the United States, as can be seen in the following table.[19]

U.S. and Multilateral Aid to El Salvador
(In Millions of Dollars)

Source	Fiscal Year 1979	Fiscal Year 1980	Fiscal Year 1981
AID	6.9	52.3	76.8
P.L. 480 (Food for Peace)	2.9	5.5	30.9
Peace Corps	1.6	0.5	—
Military Aid	—	5.9	35.4
EXIMBANK	6.4	0.7	0.7
OPIC	8.5	—	—
Export Credits (CCC)	—	4.0	30.8
Housing Inventory (HIG)	—	9.5	10.0
World Bank	23.5	—	77.0*
InterAmerican Bank	29.5	48.5	101.6*
International Monetary Fund	—	57.0	160.6**
TOTAL:	79.3	183.9	523.0

*Total cost of projects.
**Projected.
SOURCE: Center for International Policy, Washington, D.C.

To gauge the Reagan administration's commitment to the Duarte government, it is enough to cite the International Monetary Fund's estimate that, in recent years[20] the Salvadoran state's total public revenue averaged $468 million. With its own resources and through its influence over multilateral credit sources, the United States government had procured a "second extraordinary budget" for the Salvadoran government to use to fight the civil war. Taking into account the financial limits of the U.S. foreign-aid budget and the traditional reluctance in Congress to approve such allocations, it is reasonable to estimate that the 1981 figure represents a high-water mark for U.S. financial assistance to the regime in El Salvador.*

How has this aid affected the Salvadoran civil war? By any standard, the performance of the civilian-military leadership has been extremely poor. Defense Department estimates concede that the rebels effectively control one-third of all Salvadoran territory. Well-informed sources credit the Salvadoran joint chief of staff when they estimate 5,000 casualties among his soldiers in 1981 alone. International backing for the Reagan solution has grown progressively weaker.

While Washington has been raising its bets on the Salvadoran army, at home public opinion has grown noticeably colder. Various influential political forces within the United States have rejected President Reagan's projects. In the long run, this is the most decisive element acting to change views within Congress. In late February 1981 the United States Catholic Church voiced its concerns about Reagan's policy intentions toward El Salvador; echoing the Salvadoran episcopate, it called a political settlement a necessity. The same attitude now prevails in an important sector of the academic community, questioning the viability and correctness of the policies pursued by the Republicans. The position of organized labor has been just as clear. Even the AFL–CIO, which stuck to a policy of silent approval throughout the war in Vietnam, has promptly accepted nonintervention in El Salvador as part of its official platform for recent mass mobilizations.** The most

---

*In March 1983 President Reagan asked for $110 million for military assistance alone, and it seems certain that the request for economic aid will also increase (ED.).

**In January 1983 the AFL–CIO opposed presidential certification (ED)

representative organizations of the principal ethnic minorities, black and Hispanic groups in particular, have rejected the current policy explicitly.

The Reagan policy has met equally decisive resistance from the prestigious press of the eastern cities, including some of the nation's most conservative publications. When the Reagan government unveiled its "White Paper" asserting Soviet and Cuban intervention in the internal affairs of Central America, late in the winter of 1981,[21] the most effective response came the following summer, and not from the progressive sector. On 8 June the *Wall Street Journal* took the initiative, denouncing serious technical adulterations and major inconsistencies in the government document. Given this precedent, the *Washington Post* the next day ran a detailed report on the irregularities in the "White Paper" with the findings from over two months' investigations by a team of reporters. Virtually any impact from this document became a negative one after the revelations.

The sensitivity of people in Congress toward all of these facts has already changed the nature of the congressional obstacles faced by Washington's policy regarding El Salvador. By 29 April 1981 the House Foreign Affairs Committee had approved important restrictions on fiscal year 1982 military-aid procurements for the Salvadoran army. A clause added to the Foreign Assistance Act requires the president to verify that the government of El Salvador is committed to controlling the growing human-rights violations in that territory, by achieving "a substantial control over all elements of the armed forces, putting an end to the indiscriminate torture and murder of Salvadoran citizens by those forces." The amendment also expressly makes the aid conditional by obliging President Reagan to certify every six months that El Salvador is making progress in the programs of political change, including land reform, is committed to free elections, and is showing a willingness to negotiate with opposition groups in order to reach an equitable political solution to the conflict. This proposal, also approved by the Senate, basically agrees with proposals by the foreign offices of Latin American and European countries that do not partake of U.S. politics in El Salvador.

Concretely, the Washington government has committed itself

to a program of military and economic aid unprecedented for a country of El Salvador's size and population, yet the Salvadoran government is in no condition to win the war some thought would be ended quickly; rather, it can hardly prevent a worsening precarious military-political stalemate. Despite political inconveniences, the Reagan administration is committed to increasing the aid. In the budget proposal for the fiscal year 1981–82, Reagan requested $125 million for El Salvador. When the 1982–83 budget was drawn up, the request to Congress rose to $226.2 million ($194.9 million in economic aid and $61.3 in military aid).[22]

The situation has become even more unsettling since the 28 March 1982 election of the constituent assembly. On the one hand, the Christian Democrats and Napoleón Duarte were excluded from any position of power although they emerged as the greatest single political force, winning 40 percent of the votes cast in that questionable contest. On the other hand, a two-headed structure had formed in which power is shared by President Alvaro Magaña and the assembly president, the leader of ARENA, Maj. Roberto D'Aubuisson.

There was every sign of "military stalemate,"[23] as even Haig admitted by the end of 1981. The human costs of the civil war remained as high as they had been the year before, except that now the long-term aspect of the conflict had become clearer to all parties involved. This has led the Reagan administration to stand firm in its support of the civilian-military government in San Salvador, but it has also brought about new peace initiatives, such as the proposal for negotiations made by Mexico and Venezuela in September 1982.

A crucial question arises: What alternative courses are there for Washington if the failure of current tactics is confirmed? The essential political disposition of the Reagan government has not wavered, and this eliminates the option of a negotiated settlement, even though many within the State Department bureaucracy are beginning to consider such a solution inevitable, offering themselves to work on determining the settlement's contents. But for the White House, in contrast, the only alternatives to the current policy are regionalization of the conflict and open military intervention.

What kind of success do the different paths lead to?

The more drastic solution—the direct insertion of the rapid-deployment force—faces significant obstacles. These range from the process leading to the bureaucratic decision to intervene to institutional conditions for validating intervention as well as factors of political approval by the press and public opinion. One attempt to learn from the Vietnam War involved redefining the U.S. government decision-making process that could lead to direct military intervention.[24] The "Vietnam syndrome" continues to be a decisive factor in North American policy in the eighties.

In synthesis, the government of the U.S. can hardly ignore the difficulties created by its present policy. Although one might expect this policy to alter and become less bellicose, the administration will likely continue to seek to deny a military victory to the opposition. Most probably, Washington could try to regionalize the conflict, involving neighboring countries in an effort to have the conflict seen as regional and the issues interlinked. It is equally conceivable that more moderate positions within the State Department will be expressed in the elaboration of conditions for political negotiation.[25]

B. Policy Toward Nicaragua

Nicaragua ranked second on the scale of troubling situations for the United States' national interest in Central America when the current administration began. During his campaign, Reagan's experts took a deliberately ambiguous position regarding specific steps the Republican government should take. "For the moment consider Nicaragua a lost cause," said Roger Fontaine, leader of the pack of experts. He insisted, "I have no plan for the moment. . . . I can't say what we'll do with that country. I think, and this is hard for Americans to understand, that it is a matter of being patient and letting the Nicaraguan people make their own decisions."[26]

In fact, it is precisely in U.S. policy toward Nicaragua that the Reagan administration wrought the greatest changes. Carter's quest for partial agreements with the Sandinista junta was eclipsed by a conflictive approach under Reagan involving internal destabilization combined with support of Nicaraguan opponents and foreigners acting from without.

The Nicaraguan crisis was the development that buried the earlier Central America policy of the Democrats. Not having foreseen the explosive ascent of anti-Somoza forces, Carter's government planned only for the partial and gradual democratization of Nicaragua. This project was to culminate in elections in 1981, after Carter's term of office had expired.

To ignore the internal factors of change in the political processes of our countries and the increasing strength of popular political initiatives—is to handicap severely the design of U.S. bureaucratic policy. When this occurs, the projects and objectives defined in a harmonious mode in their "laboratory" exercises are contradicted brusquely by reality. A kind of paralysis is provoked in Washington's diplomacy during moments of awareness that a current policy has been exhausted without a new one to replace it.

This is exactly what happened to the Carter government after the fall of Somoza. At that moment it seemed appropriate and pragmatic to aid moderate forces and business sectors within the broad anti-Somoza forces. On this occasion, despite the Democrats' hardening line on Central America and the rebirth of a cold-war framework, Nicaragua was an exception. The Washington government took into consideration certain recommendations from Congress and especially from the major East Coast papers to support internal allies instead of repeating the siege policies that had led to the radicalization of the Cuban revolution and the confrontation between Fidel Castro and the government of the United States in the early sixties.

In a proposed aid program to countries of the "Caribbean basin," out of a total $125 million for the fiscal year 1980, the Sandinista regime was apportioned $75 million. The Department of State was handling its relations with Managua carefully, avoiding an open dispute and trying to create conditions for the free-enterprise sector to expand its influence and radius of action.

During the presidential campaign, Reagan and his team harshly criticized the Carter position, as we have seen, without disclosing the new measures to be taken. Since his inauguration, the U.S. government has seen Nicaragua as an element in the Soviet activities on this continent. Indirectly manipulated by the Cuban government, it is a kind of regional terminal for subversive and revolutionary actions Moscow hopes to promote in Central America.[27]

This kind of evaluation has resulted in a set of acts of harassment that Washington has unleashed against the Sandinista government. To begin with, the remaining $15 million from the aid approved by Congress under Carter was withheld. Later, the sale of U.S. wheat to the Managua government was prohibited in one of the first practical examples of attempts by Republican experts to use food as a weapon to pressure certain Third World countries. With the publication of the "White Paper" a short time later, Nicaragua was characterized as the principal bridge for the transfer and disposal of 800 tons of armaments destined, presumably, for Salvadoran rebels.

Since the hostile U.S. policy was set in motion, official political discourse has increasingly represented Nicaragua as an aggressor nation. In June 1981 Thomas Enders officially presented the following position:

> Cuba is trying to outfit Nicaragua as an advanced base of operations with a large army and an established intelligence apparatus, supported by 600 to 800 Cuban advisors. It is reported that armored personnel carriers, tanks and jet planes are being delivered to Nicaragua. While at a slower rate than this winter, the efforts continue to supply guerrillas in neighboring countries with armaments, operational bases and training from Nicaragua.[28]

Simultaneously, the Reagan administration expressed a lack of interest in the operation of training camps by Somocista forces openly bent on invading Nicaragua that were functioning in several parts of Florida. Secretary of State Haig in November 1981 even maintained in interviews and conferences that the United States could not discard the option of intervening militarily in Nicaragua.

The Reagan government has imposed a very significant tactical bias on policy toward Nicaragua. From an initial emphasis on weakening the political base of the Sandinistas in favor of moderate forces, the policy shifted to one that now puts more faith in actions prepared and executed by forces outside the country. This change in position is probably related to the poor performance of opposition groups inside Nicaragua. The decay of the former junta member Alfonso Robelo's leadership potential and the ineffectual state of the business sector, especially following the government action against the High Council of Free Enterprise (COSEP), were factors leading Republican experts to become skeptical about the success of a "gradual weakening" policy, such as the ones that had worked in Chile and Jamaica. But Washington policy faced a problem that went beyond mere organizational difficulty. The prolonged promiscuity of U.S. governments with the Somoza family has resulted in a kind of structural illegitimacy for any pro–U.S. force trying to operate in Nicaragua.

As part of the movement toward regionalization of conflict, Washington has accentuated its increasingly direct assault on the Managua regime. Covert action and its special $19 million budget were officially admitted to by the directors of the CIA early in 1983. Moreover, the actions of the ex-Somoza national guardsmen are more closely coordinated with those of the regular soldiers of the Honduran army. Tension along the border has reached a climax as a result of numerous incursions from Honduras into Nicaraguan territory. On his 1982 visit to San Pedro Sula, Reagan assured the Honduran president, Suazo, and General Alvarez that U.S. military aid would be intensified as need be. This prompted the Nicaraguan chancellor to redirect his diplomatic demands regarding the invasions of his country—away from Tegucigalpa and toward the Department of State in Washington.

Although the Sandinista regime is in a compromised situation, it retains important international support. Particularly significant have been its entry into the security council of the United Nations and its hosting of the ministerial meeting of the Movement of Non-Aligned Nations in January 1983, in which the Nicaraguan government received vigorous expressions of support.

The Nicaraguan government continues to be confident of its popular support. The recent military opposition of ex-comandante Edén Pastora and the resignation of Alejandro Fiallos, the former ambassador to Washington, have confirmed the Sandinistas' suspicion that the destabilization of their revolutionary process could be attempted only on the basis of a greater North American government commitment.

The Sandinista army is now the most powerful in the subregion, and the only one with recent combat experience. The 120,000 who make up the militia to support the armed forces also share this war training. The danger of deepening the Central American crisis would be greatest in Nicaragua, no matter what outside forces intervened. Experts within the U.S. military establishment view the danger of "Vietnamization" resulting from a tougher line of policy as serious indeed.

C. Policy Toward Honduras

Honduras presents no problems in and of itself, at least not for the purposes of U.S. policy toward Central America. Heavily dependent on the United States, it serves fundamentally as an operating platform for resolving more acute crises in adjacent countries. For the most part, the policy applied to it reflects and is conditioned by the U.S. objectives elsewhere in the subregion.

For various reasons Honduras has kept a low profile in Central American political history. It is the nation with the fewest political tensions and the least extremism in its political process. It has scarcely known prolonged and violent dictatorships (with the exception of Tiburcio Carías's in the thirties and forties), and although it has lived under numerous military regimes, they have been of a transitional type. Its national state was consolidated decades after this had happened in the other isthmus countries, and even today it is fair to ask whether there exists a formal Honduran state. Only in the fifties did Honduras begin to have permanent, professional military forces. Around the same time, it organized other enterprises as elemental as a survey of the national territory. Furthermore, its economy displays the smallest industrial base of any in the subregion, causing it to rely on agro-export cultigens, bananas and coffee in particular, to an extreme approaching the classic deprecatory image of the "banana republic."

In the seventies the Honduran political process was dominated by military regimes of the center right that employed a rather reformist rhetoric and at moments even tried to nudge their country closer to the Movement of Non-Aligned Nations, during the military governments of Oswaldo López Arellano and Alberto Melgar Castro, in the years 1972–78. At the end of this period, and largely as a consequence of the political crisis in Nicaragua, Melgar Castro was relieved by Gen. Policarpo Paz García, in a move to help build a rightist military bloc able to support Anastasio Somoza in his efforts to stay in power.

Paz García's taking of power represented an intention, in its first version, to build a military-political bloc out of the conservative forces along the northern flank of the isthmus. In December 1978 the Guatemalan president, Romeo Lucas García, brought his colleagues together on his retreat ranch near Guatemala City—Paz García from Honduras, Romero from El Salvador, and Somoza from Nicaragua—to discuss common strategy. The advanced state of the crisis in Nicaragua combined with the difficulty of reactivating the broken-down alliance of Central American armies, called CONDECA, kept the project from advancing further at that time. Yet this failure did not keep the Honduran high command from remaining much more closely linked to events in nearby countries. The overthrow of General Romero in October 1979 only reinforced this attitude among Honduran officers.

The Carter government maintained an ambivalent attitude toward these developments. On the one hand, it favored the projects for a return to institutional normalcy that led to the constituent-assembly elections of early 1980. On the other hand, it was toughening the role of Honduras in the broader U.S. security projects in Central America. A moment of conciliation for these two currents came when the constituent assembly decided to prolong Paz García's mandate, in order to give itself more time to complete the new constitution. The State Department liked and backed this attitude and began working toward the presidential elections for November 1981, in which the liberal candidate Roberto Suazo beat the conservative candidates.

Since February 1982 the Suazo government has been a civilian regime more in theory than in reality. It soon became apparent that the new chief of the armed forces, Gen. Gustavo Alvarez, was the real strong man in the government. Alvarez has identified closely with the Reagan government's plans, and the Suazo government has noticeably increased the ways its territory can be used by the United States. The new administration in Honduras has gotten direct aid from Washington to construct military airfields on the border with Nicaragua and to improve the training and arming of its own troops.

This attitude has heightened the role of Honduras as an honorary member of the United States and a key component in Western defense strategy. A clear sign of the ever-more-global importance of the Honduran government was seen in December 1982, when Ariel Sharon, the Israeli defense minister, paid a visit to that country. Sharon established a military-aid agreement with the Suazo government. The government appears intent on carrying through with its plans, although it has provoked discomfiting internal tensions. The reality of these tensions became perfectly clear in September 1982, when a Cinchoneros Popular Liberation Movement commando unit occupied the San Pedro Sula chamber of commerce, keeping the ministers of the economy and of the treasury, among others, hostage for several days.

The U.S. government is interested in two tasks: military support for the Salvadoran junta and collaboration in projects for harassing the government in Managua.

Honduran intervention in the political crisis of El Salvador would seem to stem naturally from the geopolitical factors linking those two countries. A good example of the Defense Department's thinking was provided by Franklin Kramer, in his presentation to Congress cited above. Toward the end of Carter's presidency, Kramer characterized the role of Honduras in the following terms:

> Situated to the north and east of El Salvador, Honduras plays a crucial role in the movement of men and materiel to the Salvadoran rebels. The Hondurans believe, and our intelligence services share this view, that their territory is being used as an access channel for men and arms into El Salvador, based on Cuban support. They are also worried that if El Salvador falls into the hands of the extreme left, Honduras will be among its first targets. . . . The Hondurans want to cut off the infiltration across their country, to prevent the creation of an insurrection against the Honduran regime as well.[29]

On the merit of these considerations, the Carter administration began providing extraordinary military assistance to the Paz García regime with an initial lump totaling $3.9 million. Priority went to the delivery of helicopters, ground-transport equipment, as well as communications and military engineering teams. The aim behind this package was to increase the capacity of Honduras for controlling its own territory, especially along the border with El Salvador. Reagan has noticeably increased these programs, requesting $10 million for the year 1981–82.

This has led to periodic coordinated actions by the Salvadoran and Honduran armies against FMLN soldiers. These joint actions have extended over the encampments of Salvadoran refugees along the Honduran side of the border. The U.S. government has favored these actions, with the same intentions that moved Washington to act as a mediator in the agreement finally ending the 1969 war between the two countries. The goal is to bring their armies closer together.

The actions carried out by the Tegucigalpa regime against Nicaragua are slightly less than official in character. Instead of using soldiers from its own armed forces, Honduras can rely on the 7,000 to 9,000 former Somoza national guardsmen who live in Honduras and attack Nicaragua from Honduran territory. Once again, Honduras is serving as a training camp, the role it has played in every major expedition aimed at overthrowing "Communist" regimes in the Caribbean basin. Out of Honduras came the forces led by Col. Carlos Castillo Armas in 1954 that overthrew President Jacobo Arbenz in Guatemala. And some of the contingents for the 1961 invasion of Cuba, defeated at the Bay of Pigs, had trained in Honduras.

To a great degree the actions by the Somocista guardsmen have consisted of attacks on Nicaraguan settlements and retreats to their bases in Honduras. That these attacks have not generalized into a sharper, public conflict is principally due to the political disposition of the Junta of National Reconstruction in Managua to avoid frontal collision with the Paz García government, out of their conviction that the attitudes for avoiding conflicts do not exist in Honduran military circles, only attitudes for aggravating them. That quality precisely coincides with Washington's strategy of expanded conflict, with the possible involvement of Honduran contingents added to their Salvadoran and Guatemalan kind, together able to confront "pro-Soviet" forces situated in governments or attempting to take them.

Whether Honduras continues in its present role or assumes a larger and more aggressive one, it will continue to be vital for the United States' plans on both the Salvadoran and the Nicaraguan fronts. Although popular organizations and parties of the left do have a certain influence in that country, especially in the peasant sectors, the conditions of political control appear adequate for the prosecution of current plans.

D. Policy Toward Guatemala

At the start of the Carter administration, Guatemala was considered part of a pilot plan for the gradual democratization of the Central American countries.

This project's failure provides various clues for an understanding of the current situation. Guatemala has been a politically unstable country ever since the actions of Secretary of State Dulles facilitated the forcible toppling of the reformist government headed by President Arbenz. For nearly thirty years, however, two political trends have been constant: on the one hand, the armed forces have become increasingly politicized, constituting a political party able to aid in the defense of the established order; on the other, the civilian political forces, large landowners in particular, have moved radically rightward. Guatemala is a nearly paradigmatic case of the Central American tendency, during the sixties, of undercutting the forces open to "reasonable reformism"[30] before they could reach power. The only civilian government recently elected in a relatively clean process, that of Julio César Méndez Montenegro in 1966, must have abdicated its prerogatives before the armed forces because of their demand for broad powers to confront the guerrilla *foco* then active in that country. Since then, power has been exercised by the army officers of Guatemala's armed forces: Gen. Carlos Arana Osorio in 1970, Gen. Kjell Laugerud in 1974, Gen. Romeo Lucas García in 1978, and, since the 23 March 1982 coup Gen. Efraín Ríos Montt.

The first two worked in frank alliance with civilian forces of the extreme Right, as seen in Laugerud's choice of a leading Central American anti-Communist leader, Mario Sandoval Alarcón, for his vice-president. The Carter government tried to break the alliance in order to foster a controlled democratic process in Guatemala based on a new alliance between the army and parties of the political center. These would include the Revolutionary party, the Christian Democrats, the Socialist Democratic party, or the United Front of the Revolution (the tendency of the last two being social democratic). But the forces of the center could neither reach an agreement with the military, with the exception of the Revolutionary party, nor muster much interest in pursuing the alliance suggested to them. As a result, when in the March 1978 elections Sandoval Alarcón's National Liberation Movement, running the ex-dictator Peralta Azurdia as its own candidate, showed too much social support to be ignored, the high command of the armed forces decided to work toward rebuilding a political bloc even to the right of the previous one.

The Lucas García government consequently applied a tougher and more repressive policy than Laugerud's, and instead of effecting the modest reforms promised during his campaign, it polarized Guatemalan society further, enhancing the rapid resurgence of guerrilla action. Failing the call to serve as a model of "viable democracy" during the Carter government, Guatemala's relations with the White House decayed to the point that traditional military-aid programs ceased. In order to prevent a reversal of this process, according to various reports presented in the U.S. Congress, paramilitary groups of the extreme Right, acting in strict coordination with the official security forces, gave themselves the task of eliminating the country's principal moderate leaders—those capable of heading a political transition. Between 1978 and 1980 the most outstanding democratic leaders in Guatemala were murdered, including Alberto Fuentes Mohr, the ex-chancellor, and Manuel Colom Argueta, the leader of the Socialist Democratic party and ex-mayor of Guatemala City.

Guatemala has been turned into a country where all forms of dissent are dangerous and any form of opposition is considered subversive. Its current political spectrum includes only parties with a clearly conservative character. In the March 1982 elections, the armed forces headed the Popular Democratic Front, running Lucas García's defense minister as their candidate, Gen. Aníbal Guevara. The Authentic Nationalist central ran Gustavo Anzueto, and Mario Sandoval Alarcón nominated himself to represent the National Liberation Movement. Alejandro Maldonado Aguirre, of the National Party of Renewal, the only candidate with a tinge of dissidence, differed from the others only in his beliefs that government repression should be placed under stricter institutional control.

The 7 March 1982 elections became a catalyst in a process of rearranging the internal situation. The conservative candidates' charges of fraud prepared the way for the 23 March coup d'état, installing Gen. Efraín Ríos Montt in power. Ironically, Ríos Montt had won the 1974 presidential elections but had been robbed of his triumph by fraud.

The ascent of Ríos Montt has allowed for political shifts that would have been harder to make in other circumstances. The new chief has reorganized the bases of the internal war, by achieving a certain calm in the urban centers and by intensifying the offensive in the rural sector. He has gone so far as to implement a program of "strategic hamlets" to eliminate communities in the areas most influenced by the insurgency, relocating the displaced population in other settlements.

The profound problems remain, unaddressed. We think they will grow only more acute once the military aid of the Reagan administration goes into effect. Aid was officially restored within weeks after Reagan met with Ríos Montt in Honduras, during his whirlwind tour of Latin America at the end of November 1982.

It is not surprising that guerrilla movements are drawing support from increasingly broad social sectors. They have recently achieved a dimension of national unity. Unions, peasant organizations, student federations, and religious base communities along with guerrilla forces constitute the political-military organizations that effect armed actions against the central government and attempt to create zones at the margin of governmental control, to begin with, and liberated zones later on. Currently, there are three major organizations of this kind: the Guerrilla Army of the Poor (EGP), the Organization of People in Arms (ORPA), and the

Rebel Armed Forces (FAR). While they all maintain their organic differences, they support each other and coordinate their action with a broad bloc of semilegal political parties making up the Democratic Front against Repression (FDCR). In the first two years of this decade, the operative capacity of these forces grew considerably, but without creating the kind of problem the FMLN posed in El Salvador. Still, the regional strengths of the three guerrilla forces complemented each other to create a national presence: the EGP on the northeastern traverse, the ORPA around El Quiché, and the FAR in the North and South.

The breadth of the insurrectional activity involves not only an organic expression of militancy but also its capacity to integrate two large sectors of the country: indigenous communities and Christian base groups. The identification of Indians and Christians with guerrilla action will determine its future advancement, given the closed course of Guatemalan process, once their legal pathways have been closed.

The United States' positions regarding the new situation in Guatemala vary considerably. As for the Reagan team, Michael Deaver is exemplary. The third man in the hierarchy of the White House executive office, he considers the firmness and anti-Communist character of the Guatemalan government to be the best guarantee of its functionality vis-à-vis the current U.S. containment policy. For many career functionaries in the State Department, however, Guatemala is almost a matter of conscience, apart from their belief that, objectively, a government of that kind is a weak point of support for any Washington project. For now, the Guatemalan military high commanders are disposed to join in any attempt at coordinated military action in the region, with or without U.S. sponsorship.

III. CENTRAL AMERICA AND THE LIMITS OF REAGAN POLICY

After examining the particular chain of events unfolding in the more convulsed countries across the isthmus, regarding specific processes of a national dimension, it is equally necessary to connect the mosaic pieces in the crisis confronting the subregion, especially if we are interested in evaluating the policy the current American government is developing.

In any policy evaluation, one underlying consideration has to be the increasingly international nature of all politics in Central America, and in Latin America as a whole. The diversification of foreign influences on the continent has resulted from two basic facts: first, the existence of well-articulated political projects elaborated by the principal political forces of Western Europe, the Socialist International and Christian Democracy; and, second, the autonomous behavior of the two "emerging powers" Mexico and Brazil in relation to the programs and objectives of Washington.

The emergence of these new international actors has a decisive impact on political developments in Central America—to the extent that it incorporates forces, programs, and material resources to strengthen the action of parties and social groups within each country seeking a progressive solution to their crises. These are the groups characterized as "anti-American" and in some cases "pro-Soviet" by President Reagan's advisers. But, in contrast to the Guatemalan experience in the fifties, when the United States had its hands free to apply a solution of force, in the eighties, U.S. force will be met with active and effective resistance.

The initiatives of European social democrats began to have an important impact on most Latin American countries in the midseventies. As part of a plan considered at length,[31] under the leadership of Willy Brandt, the principal leaders of this tendency decided to form links with a wide range of reformist and radical movements and parties having an international, *tercer mundista* (third world) line and an interest in social reform projects in Latin American countries as an alternative to military dictatorships and traditional domination.[32]

With respect to Central America in particular, this situation became clear in the aftermath of the Nicaraguan revolution. Since the beginnings of the decisive fight against Somoza, in September 1977, the Sandinista front counted on the unrestricted political, diplomatic, and even material support of the Socialist International and its parties. After the Sandinista victory, the European social-democratic parties provided the main aid and assistance to the Junta of National Reconstruction in Managua.

In the case of El Salvador, their attitude has been just as strikingly in favor of the FDR and has originated new conflicts and confrontations with the U.S. government. These discrepancies have intensified with the Reagan containment policy and increased aid levels to the Salvador regime as well as the bolder support for armed counterrevolutionary violence in Nicaragua. The electoral gains of social-democratic parties in France, Greece, and Spain should strengthen the quality of support they can lend to their Central American allies in Nicaragua, El Salvador, and Guatemala.

The disposition of Christian Democratic parties has been quite different, as they have tended to share North American apprehensions regarding the advance of leftist forces, which their Central American allied parties actively confront. This has led to an increasing concordance between Western European Christian Democracy and the U.S. State Department. After March 1979 the government of Venezuela was included, its Christian Democratic Party (COPEI) having defeated the Socialist International–linked Democratic Action Party. European Christian democrats, the West German CDU in particular, had been decisive in organizing international support behind the Napoleón Duarte government. This position has also brought them actively to oppose the government of Managua. The change to a Republican government in the United States seems only to have strengthened the Christian Democratic agreement with Washington.

But the positions of both of these international organizations, and the governments and political forces they are linked to in Latin America, have shifted especially in the aftermath of the Malvinas war. The Socialist International and the Christian Democratic Union have moved a bit closer together.

There has been increasing pressure within social democracy to draw a dividing line regarding the Sandinista regime. A major event in this process is the election of Luis Alberto Monge and the National Liberation party to power in Costa Rica. This meant that one of the parties in Central America most strongly identified with the Socialist International has turned into a staunch ally of President Reagan and into a hostile adversary of the Managua regime. Its position was seconded by the Venezuelan Democratic Action party, which even suspended an official Socialist International conference so as not to have to play host to a delegation from the Sandinista Front. These changes coincide with the also more critical positions of the Spanish PSOE and the West German SPD, which also began to revise the strategy of supporting revolutionary forces in Central America.

Meanwhile, Christian Democrats have felt the impact of the exclusion of Napoleón Duarte from the government in San Salvador. To this must be added the impact the Malvinas conflict had on the Herrera Campins government in Venezuela. At that point Venezuelan foreign policy made a real turnabout, and its chancellery became a vanguard of a Latin Americanist position that was critical of the Reagan administration's behavior toward Argentina. Reagan thus lost the principal political ally in his Central American policy.

In accordance with its new position, the Venezuelan government first coordinated actions with Mexico. At the beginning of 1983, by way of a meeting on the Panamanian island of La Contadora, it went on to form a bloc including the government of Panama and the new Betancúr administration in Colombia, as well as Mexico.

Indeed, the most important and surprising difficulties for the Reagan government's Central America strategy have come from the major Latin American countries themselves, especially Mexico and Brazil. Having normally followed State Department diplomacy and policy in the past, their attitude changed during the seventies as a result of a more general process of growth in international political stature by the most important nations of the developing world.

The strategic lens focusing current Republican foreign policy shows its limitations most clearly in this terrain. As Washington's containment approach develops, it becomes impossible to reconcile the behavior of these old allies to a conceptual model openly favoring geopolitical considerations. Nor does U.S. strategy coincide with Brazil's or Mexico's now-better-defined national interests.[33] On the contrary, both countries have expressed contradictions in their relations to the hegemonic presence of Washington in Central America, each disposed to winning a broader, more autonomous role on the international stage.

Mexico has taken steps in several directions in attempting to solve the Central American crisis. These efforts include the agreement of San José, made together with Venezuela, offering petroleum to the nations of the isthmus at better-than-market terms. Equally notably, Mexico favored the creation of the multilateral fund to aid the Caribbean basin, on the condition that the aid not be tied to military assistance and that no countries be excluded beforehand (referring to Cuba and Nicaragua specifically).

And finding the U.S. government inflexible to reasonable compromise, Mexico has broadened its accords with more compatible countries. Thus the Franco-Mexican declaration of August 1981 came about, as part of an alliance policy Mexico is disposed to deepen, even in open opposition to U.S. perceptions.

The acute economic crisis Mexico has been facing since February 1982 and the change of government—José López Portillo was replaced by Miguel de la Madrid Hurtado as of December 1982 —have no doubt reduced Mexico's international bargaining power. The de la Madrid administration's foreign policy has not yet coalesced, but it does not seem reasonable to expect great changes in Mexico's attitudes toward Central America. President de la Madrid and the new foreign minister Bernardo Sepúlveda, have always stressed their determination to carry out the policies already in place.

Since Reagan's arrival in power, Mexico and the United States have been in fundamental disagreement on how to assure a functioning political order in the convulsed countries of Central America and the Caribbean. Washington's reliance on bilateral solutions is providing progressively ineffectual, bringing that government into sharper opposition with Mexico City's. This is something the strategy of Reagan experts was unable to foresee.

Brazil shares Mexico's wish to establish an autonomous international presence. Because of its weaker economic links to the United States and because of its geographical position, however, Brazil has defined even more ambitious and global concerns for itself in the last few years. This is particularly evident because, like Mexico, Brazil's international presence was strictly subordinated to North American plans during the sixties. Following the 1964 coup, hemispheric solidarity assumed prime importance in Brazilian foreign policy.

The situation changed when Brazil began to feel the effects of the capitalist crisis of the seventies. This was accompanied by a marginal reduction of U.S. hegemony, which made it easier for Brazil to decide on its own lines of action.

The government of Brazil has sought to make Washington realize that, even though Brazil does not have direct interests in Central America, as a matter of principle, it will not accept a U.S. use of force to support its allies in El Salvador, Nicaragua, or Guatemala.

On the eve of Thomas Enders's first visit to Brazil, the foreign minister Saraiva Guerreiro declared,

> To reduce Brazil to the role of a supporting actor does not suit us. . . . We are more than that. We are not going to turn the country into a package in a system of obedient forces, as if we did not have wills and needs, as if we did not have deeply rooted traditions and options. We do not accept the formation of blocs, axes, hegemonic dispositions, arms races, tension manipulation, in sum, that entire complex of behaviors that would serve to introduce the power plays and burdens of dependency into the region.[34]

Brazil has firmly stated its position that Salvadorans should resolve the crisis in El Salvador, preferably with a representative and democratic political solution.

What conclusion can we draw from this overview of European and Latin American postures? To what extent do they define limits and restrictions on the Reagan administration's maneuverability in Central America?

There is evident a tendency for instability in the behavior of many of the actors in the conflict. A kind of zero-sum game appears to be at work, in which individual countries might change sides but in which the balance between blocs remains roughly equal. Political events during 1982 in Costa Rica, Panama, Guatemala, Peru, and Ecuador have been favorable for Washington. But changes occurring in Venezuela, Argentina, Bolivia, and Colombia are beginning to deprive U.S. diplomacy of some of its early allies.

Reagan administration policy regarding Central America might yet find encouragement among the bloc of authoritarian governments in the stable of U.S. supporters. Apart from some countries already considered, this bloc would include Chile, Uruguay, Paraguay, Haiti, and Jamaica.

In the long run, however, the crisis in Central America as well as the solutions Washington has tried to apply, and the supporting alignment of conservative forces behind them, are an important part of a broader process leading, perhaps, to the stable division of the capitalist camp into two sub-blocs—one more conservative and the other more open to change in the international system.

Through its disposition to unilaterally dictate the solutions for resolving world tensions, the Reagan government has functioned like a catalyst to accelerate the transformation of the international power structure. If these are in fact the circumstances, then the dangers of forcing the struggles of Central American people onto an East-West axis become patent, and the weakness in the Reagan foreign policy will become disastrously clear.[35]

NOTES

1. U.S. intervention in the Dominican Republic began in 1905, when that country was required to accept a revenue director (designated by President Theodore Roosevelt and backed up by the U.S. Navy) who took over the customs service, collected taxes, and issued bonds to guarantee payments of the debts to foreign creditors. The situation grew even worse between 1916 and 1924, when some 2,000 marines occupied the country, withdrawing only when the local government accepted the treaty that institutionalized the protectorate system.

   In Haiti, the presence of U.S. Navy forces helped to impose the 1915 treaty that established a U.S. high commission to supervise Haiti's economy and politics. Starting in 1924 a U.S. official took over the recently created Office of Internal Taxes, which further emphasized Washington's control over Haiti.

   Finally, in Nicaragua, after the imposition of such agreements as the 1910 Dawson pact or the Knox-Castrillo agreement of 1911, military intervention occurred in 1912, with 3,000 men and nine warships. Fifteen years later, in 1927, and up until 1932, U.S. troops occupied Nicaraguan territory. It was against this intervention that César Augusto Sandino, the principal national hero in Nicaragua's history, struggled and eventually won. The proclamation of the "good neighbor policy" by President Franklin Delano Roosevelt led, starting in 1933, to the withdrawal of the overt U.S. military presence in Central America and the Caribbean, but the impact of that stage has left a deep impression in Central American history, which one must keep in mind when evaluating the course of the current crisis.

2. The viewpoints of Edelberto Torres-Rivas have been presented principally in his book *Crisis del poder en Centroamérica* (San José, Costa Rica: EDUCA, 1981); and in his articles "Síntesis historical del proceso político centroamericano," included in *Centroamerica hoy* (Mexico City: Siglo Veintiuno, 1975), and "Poder nacional y sociedad dependiente," included in *La inversión extranjera in Centroamérica* (San José, Costa Rica: EDUCA, 1974); and in the essay "Elementos para comprender la crisis centroamericana," mimeographed (Mexico: CECADE, 1981).

3. Enrique Baloyra, "The Deterioration and Breakdown of Reactionary Despotism in Central America" (Paper submitted to U.S. Department of State, 1981, mimeographed).

4. Ibid., 45.

5. Ibid., 64.

6. Jeane Kirkpatrick, "The Hobbes Problem: Order, Authority, and Legitimacy in Central America" (Paper presented at the American Enterprise Institute for Public Policy Research, December 1980, mimeographed), 4.

7. Ibid., 6.

8. Ibid., 7.

9. Ibid., 8.

10. Ibid., 9.

11. Ibid., 12.

12. Ibid., 18.

13. Ibid., 17.

14. In 1977 Sally Shelton, a key aide in the State Department, made the following representative appraisal:

> Contrary to what the majority of Latin Americans think, United States economic interests in Central America are rather limited. Our total annual trade with the region is around 1.8 billion U.S. dollars, that is, less than 1 percent of U.S. foreign trade. U.S. investment in the area is about 700 million dollars, or 0.5 percent of direct U.S. foreign investment. The region does not possess any strategic raw materials.

Sally Shelton, "Estados Unidos y Centroamerica," *Cuadernos semestrales de Estados Unidos* 6 (Mexico, 1979), 17.

15. Ronald Reagan, "Peace and Security in the 1980's" (Speech to the Council on Foreign Relations, Chicago, 17 March 1981).

16. With regard to the organization and activities of the task force that prepared

the proposal on Latin American policy for the current Republican administration, one can consult the analysis and documents contained in volume 9
of *Cuadernos semestrales de Estados Unidos* (1981), which is devoted to the
topic of the Reagan administration and the crisis of U.S. hegemony.

17. Milton Eisenhower, *Vino amargo: Estados Unidos y América Latina* (Bogota:
Ediciones Tercer Mundo, 1964), 43. There is an English version: *The Wine
Is Bitter* (Garden City, N.Y.: Doubleday, 1963).

18. Statement of Franklin D. Kramer, principal assistant of the secretary of
defense for international security affairs, before the Foreign Appropriations
Subcommittee of the House Appropriations Committee of the U.S. Congress (Washington: U.S. Government Printing Office), 25 March 1980, 6.

19. "The Aid Package for El Salvador," International Policy Report, Center for
International Policy, Washington, D.C., April 1981.

20. Because of the drop in productive activity in 1980 as a result of the civil
war, the IMF uses the last year of normal activity, 1979, as the reference point
in its recent studies. See IMF, "International Financial Statistics," Washington, D.C., March 1981, 142ff.

21. The so-called White Paper on El Salvador, officially entitled "Communist
Interference in El Salvador," was distributed by the State Department on
23 February 1981; it marked the beginning of a strong diplomatic offensive
by the Reagan administration in support of José Napoleón Duarte and the
Salvadoran armed forces.

22. In the original request for the aid program for fiscal 1982–83, the Reagan
administration sought $125 million in total direct assistance for the Duarte
regime.

23. A good demonstration of the internal effect of the state of the war on the
armed forces was the rebellion of Col. Sigifrido Ochoa in early January
1983. He accused the minister of defense, Gen. Guillermo García, of mis-
managing the political situation and of forgetting the political aspects of the
conflict. It is significant that the heads of the U.S.-trained special forces—
the Atonal and Ramon Belloso Brigades—as well as the air force command,
gave initial support to Ochoa's demands.

24. In this regard, see Graham Allison, Ernest May, and Adam Yarmolinsky,
"Limits to Intervention," in *After Vietnam,* ed. Robert Gregg and Charles
Kegley (Garden City, N.Y.: Doubleday Anchor, 1971).

25. The existence of dissident views in the State Department has for some time
been the subject of intense commentary in Washington. In November 1980
an extensive, articulate "dissent paper" on El Salvador circulated in Congress
and in the academic world. In this unsigned text a policy of political
negotiation was proposed, following the pattern used by the British foreign
office in the case of Zimbabwe. Officials of the State Department denied the
authenticity of the document and refused to consider its content. But along
the same line, and this time without the need for speculation, one can
consider the official conversations held in Washington between representa-

tives of the Reagan administration with a delegation from the politico-diplomatic commission of the El Salvador's FDR, headed by Rubén Zamora, a distinguished leader of the Social Christian Revolutionary Movement, a group that broke off from the Christian Democrats. Setting aside the fact that specific agreements between the parties were not reached in that meeting, which took place in the third week in December of 1981, the mere fact that it was held represented a great triumph for the Mexican and French foreign ministries. Perhaps through this meeting the Reagan government was recognizing the Salvadoran opposition's status as a "representative political force ready to assume its political obligations," precisely the recognition that the United States had categorically denied it five months before.

26. Roger Fontaine, statement to *Miami Herald,* 24 August 1980.
27. Thus, according to the characterization by Constantine Menges,

> In Nicaragua two very different political groups united to defeat Somoza in July 1979: the Communist guerrilla force and the activists who had been receiving Cuban aid since 1972 and a variety of genuinely democratic parties and business and labor groups. . . . President Carter failed to aid the democratic forces effectively, notwithstanding that he knew of the massive Cuban supplying of arms for the final offensive of June and July 1979 and that Cuban secret agents were providing extraordinary resources that would be able to assure control by Marxist-Leninist groups with total disregard for the hopes of the Nicaraguan people.
>
> Nicaragua has received more than $600 million in economic aid from the democracies and international credit institutions. But none of this has been translated into effective incentives for democracy. Elections were postponed until 1985, and those "would serve to reinforce and enhance the revolution." The communications media are virtually under complete control, with the exception of *La Prensa.* The revolution constantly puts pressure on all non-Sandinista parties and unions, and in November 1980 an unarmed leader of the Businessmen's Federation was murdered by the police, probably as a warning. At the end of August 1980, four democratic parties issued a call to the O.A.S. and to democratic governments to require the FSLN to fulfill its strict promise of free elections; however, not a word of this dramatic call was published by any of the prestige papers in the United States. In foreign policy, Nicaragua has given clandestine support to the revolutionary terrorists in El Salvador, signed friendship agreements with the Soviet Union, and taken pro-Soviet, pro-Cuban positions on almost all issues in the United Nations.

Constantine Menges, "United States and Latin America in the 1980's," in *National Interests of the United States in Foreign Policy,* ed. Prosser Gifford (Lanham, Md.: University Press of America, 1981), 73ff. It is possible that Menges's opinions are even more important now that President Reagan has appointed him to a high position in the Latin American section of the Central Intelligence Agency (CIA).

28. Thomas Enders, speech on relations between the United States and Latin America, Council of the Americas, Washington, June 1981.

29. Kramer, statement, 4.

30. Torres–Rivas, "Elementos."

31. See *The Social-Democratic Alternative* (Barcelona: Blume, 1977), dialogues between Willy Brandt, Bruno Kreisky, and Olof Palme. There is a German edition: *Briefe und Gespräche: 1972–1975* (Frankfurt: Europäische Verlagsanstalt, 1975).

32. This disposition materialized in a 1977 international conference in Caracas, Venezuela, where the principal leaders of European social-democratic parties (Brandt, Felipe González, Mario Soares, François Mitterrand, and Bettino Craxi, among others), established contact with various leaders from Caribbean and Central and South American countries. From the beginning, it was clear that this new relation between European and Latin American reformist parties could run up against the policies and criteria upheld by the United States government.

33. A systematic presentation of Mexican positions and attitudes toward the United States can be found in Olga Pellicer, "La política de Ronald Reagan hacia México: La difícil recuperacíon de la buena vecindad," *Cuadernos semestrales de Estados Unidos* 9 (1981): 255ff.

   The attitudes that inspire the new Brazilian foreign policy are lucidly expressed in Rolando Sardenberg Mota, "A Politica externa do Brasil e a America Latina" (Instituto de Relacoes Internacionais, Universidade Católica do Rio de Janeiro, 1980, mimeographed). Sardenberg is currently one of the principal intellectual figures in the Brazilian ministry of foreign relations and has been one of the authors of the new foreign policy vision of Itamarati.

34. See *Jornal do Brasil,* 15 August 1981, 12.

35. The replacement of Secretary of State Alexander Haig by George Shultz, in mid-1982, has had no important impact on U.S. policy toward Central America. It is true that Haig's departure marked a change from an outlook closely tied to strategic analysis and that the coming of Shultz represented the return to the pragmatism characteristic of traditional Republican administrations. This pragmatism has caused the new secretary of state to concentrate on areas of greater priority for Washington, especially in the affairs of the Middle East and Africa. Control over Central American policy has remained in the hands of the assistant secretary of state for inter-American affairs, Thomas O. Enders, who has proceeded without change.* Within this framework, we can only point out a few modifications brought on by the Malvinas war. They can be summed up in the observation that

---

*Both Enders and Deane Hinton, the ambassador in El Salvador, have now been replaced. It is still early to assess the significance of these changes (ED.).

the United States has chosen one of the variants of the "Central-Americani-zation" of the war: restricted regionalization. Since the White House and the Department of State can no longer count on political support from Venezuela and on military support from Argentina, they have sought a series of changes and adjustments within the Central American countries them-selves. For constitutional reasons, or by force of circumstances by the end of 1982, all the heads of government of Central American countries, with the exception of Nicaragua, were different from those who had governed at the end of 1981. But within this context, the criteria of the Reagan administration remain the same. An East-West perspective on the situation continues to be favored. Military victory is still the goal. And negotiations with radical governments or political forces continue to be rejected.

Liberation and Revolution

CHRISTIANITY AS A SUBVERSIVE ACTIVITY IN CENTRAL AMERICA

Tommie Sue Montgomery

*T*he political and economic oppression that has plagued all but one of the Central American nations has long provided conditions for revolt.[1] Other factors have helped produce the political turmoil currently sweeping through the isthmus; they include the influence of the Roman Catholic Church and, in Nicaragua, of many Protestant churches. Since the late 1960s, a new message—liberation theology—and a new medium—Christian Base Communities—have contributed to the transformation of both church and society in Central America. Although that process of transformation is far from complete and is characterized, in part, by conflict, the churches have played and are playing important roles in the process of social change currently under way.

This essay examines the changes in theology and church social doctrine that undergird the churches' changing role; discusses the experiences of churches in Nicaragua, El Salvador, and Guatemala that illustrate how they have sought to implement that theology and doctrine; and concludes with a summary and prognosis for future intrachurch and church-state relations in the region.

THE THEOLOGY OF LIBERATION—AND THE LIBERATION OF THEOLOGY

When organized religion takes political positions supportive of the status quo, it is generally praised by the temporal powers that be, or is at least ignored. When it dares, however, to challenge the status quo, then it is condemned, harassed, and persecuted. Since the late 1960s, liberation theology has been challenging the status quo in Central America, frequently with dramatic results. It challenges military dictatorships, human-rights violations, economic oppression—in its own words, "structural injustice" and "institutionalized sin." Liberation theology rejects capitalism as a viable means to the development of Latin American society and accepts Marxism as one tool of socioeconomic analysis. At the same time, it rejects atheistic communism, which it finds as dehumanizing as capitalism because it denies that there is a spiritual dimension to life.

Liberation theology flourishes in the social and economic context of the abject poverty characteristic of the vast majority of Central Americans. Its parishioners live in shacks made of sticks and mud, with thatched roofs and dirt floors. They rarely receive medical attention during pregnancy, or for any illnesses. Entire families, including children, work when they can, which means perhaps three months a year picking coffee beans. When there is work, the head of the household earns perhaps $3.00 a day maximum. During the rest of the year work is often not available, even though men and women leave home for days or weeks at a time, seeking any kind of a job. The consequences of this kind of poverty are immediately apparent in the low levels of nutrition, the high rates of infant mortality, and the generally poor physical condition of the population. Schooling is almost never available, and even religious participation is sporadic, because for a long time clergy have served these rural people only occasionally. The message in the priest's homilies is always the same: accept your lot here on earth and wait for your reward in the hereafter; poverty is a blessing; the poor shall inherit the Kingdom of God.

Then, one day, a priest comes to town, this time to stay. At his first mass in the village, he reads from the third chapter of Exodus:

> Then the Lord said, "I have seen how cruelly my people are being treated in Egypt; I have heard them cry out to be rescued from their slave drivers. I know all about their sufferings, and so I have come down to rescue them from the Egyptians and to bring them out of Egypt to a fertile and spacious land. . . .
>
> Go and gather the leaders of Israel together and tell them that I, the Lord, the God of their ancestors, the God of Abraham, Isaac, and Jacob, appeared to you. Tell them that I have come to them and have seen what the Egyptians are doing to them. I have decided that I will bring them out of Egypt. . . .[2]

In his homily the priest explains that the Exodus story shows that God is a god of justice, who has acted throughout history on behalf of the poor and oppressed, and that people, just like the Israelites, can act together to throw off their oppression. People leave mass shaking their heads, wondering what kind of crazy man their bishop has sent to their parish.

The story is a composite, but portions of it occur thousands of times throughout Central America. This kind of reaction of the faithful to their new priest's homily was precisely what happened in the parish of San Antonio Abad, in San Salvador, when a young Salvadoran priest, Alfonso Navarro, arrived in the early 1970s. Navarro had also told his people that, before God, they were the equals of the large landowners for whom many of them worked on occasion.

The story does not end here, however. In the following days, the priest visits all the other families in the neighborhood. He says he would like to organize Bible study groups in the parish. Will they come? The group, comprising perhaps twenty or thirty people, begins to come together first in a two-week-long course that meets every evening. Each session is similarly structured: it starts with the celebration of the Word, a worship service less formal than the mass. Then the priest gives a short talk based on a biblical passage; he discusses not only its theological meaning but also the church's social doctrine. [He invites the people to relate the scripture and his words to their temporal condition, to say what the scripture means to them. He breaks the group up and asks each subgroup to select a discussion leader and a recorder who will also report highlights of the subgroup's discussion to the whole community at the end of the evening.]

The contemporary social doctrine of the Roman Catholic Church comes out of the Second Vatican Council (Vatican II), which met in Rome between 1962 and 1965, and the Second Latin American Bishops Conference, held in Medellín, Colombia, in 1968. Penny Lernoux, in *Cry of the People,* wrote that Medellín was "one of the major political events of the century: it shattered the centuries-old alliance of church, military and the rich elites."[3] Vatican II brought the laity into the daily life of the church by changing the language of the mass from Latin to the vernacular, by calling for lay participation in the mass, and by declaring that the laity are equal, as a result of baptism, to the priests and bishops. No longer were people to be merely passive objects; now they have to be active participants in church life.

It was at Medellín, however, that the church changed sides. Sin ceased to be simply a personal failure between oneself and God. Sin, the bishops wrote, may also be institutional: where there are social, economic, or political structures that violate one's personhood, reduce one's humanity, or prevent one from living a less than fully human life, the church has an obligation to condemn those structures, people have the right to work to change them, and the church must accompany them in that process.

Now, what "accompany" means in practice has become one of the major sources of conflict within the Central American church. The issue, simply put, is this: how does a priest, nun, or bishop support parishioners' right to organize politically but remain apart from that organizing activity? And what happens when one's parishioners begin to suffer the consequences of their actions—consequences that might include arrest, disappearance, and death?

Liberation theology tackles this situation first with its bold assumption that there must be a continuing dialectic between reflection and action. Theology must move out of the cloister and seminary and into the everyday world, both in the way texts are interpreted and in who is doing the interpreting. The Bible itself talks clearly about fundamental social and political questions, in terms that lay people can easily grasp. Everyone can "do" theology —that is the basic premise of the Bible study courses—and the messages the verses deliver are clear and consistent: (1) God is a god of justice who acts in history; (2) oppression and injustice are condemned throughout the Old and New Testaments; and (3) there is not only condemnation but also the promise of a better life here on earth. The injustices to be condemned include fraudulent commercial practices and exploitation, hoarding land, dishonest courts, ruling-class violence, slavery, unjust taxes, unjust bureaucrats, and oppression by the rich.[4]

Isaiah, Jeremiah, Amos, and Micah, among other Old Testament prophets, consistently condemn all forms of social and economic injustice, and their words are read in study groups. Isaiah, in the tenth chapter, condemns the Assyrians: "You are doomed! You make unjust laws that oppress my people. That is how you keep the poor from having their rights and from getting justice. That is how you take the property that belongs to widows and orphans." He goes on to warn of the Lord's inescapable wrath. Similarly, Jeremiah, in the twenty-second chapter, warns Jehoiakim, the son of the king of Judah, "Doomed is the man who builds his house by injustice and enlarges it by dishonesty; who makes his countrymen work for nothing and does not pay their wages." Amos warns the piggish Samarians, "As the Sovereign Lord is holy, he has promised, 'The days will come when they will drag you away with hooks; every one of you will be like a fish on a hook. You will be dragged to the nearest break in the wall and thrown out'" (Amos 4:2–3).

By the time of Micah, near the end of the Old Testament, God has directed his wrath at the Israelites:

> You mountains, you everlasting foundations of the earth, listen to the Lord's case! The Lord has a case against his people. He is going to bring an accusation against Israel. The Lord says, "My people, what have I done to you? How have I been a burden to you? Answer me. I brought you out of Egypt; I rescued you from slavery; I sent Moses, Aaron, and Miriam to lead you. . . . The Lord has told us what is good. What he requires of us is this: to do what is just, to show constant love, and to live in humble fellowship with our God. It is wise to fear the Lord. He calls to the city, "Listen, you people who assemble in the city! In the houses of evil men are treasures which they got dishonestly. They use false measures, a thing that I hate. How can I forgive men who use false scales and weights? Your rich men exploit the poor, and all of you are liars. So I have already begun your ruin and destruction because of your sins. You will eat, but not be satisfied—in fact you will still be hungry. You will carry things off, but you will not be able to save them; anything you do save I will destroy in war. You will sow grain, but not harvest the crop. You will press oil from olives, but never get to use it. You will make wine, but never drink it." (Micah 6:2–4, 8–15)

But the condemnation of social, political, and economic injustice is only a part of the Old Testament message and only the beginning of liberation theology. The Old Testament also offers the promise of something better,—the new Jerusalem:

> There will be no weeping there, no calling for help. Babies will no longer die in infancy, and all people will live out their life span. Those who live to be a hundred will be considered young. To die before that would be a sign that I had punished them. People will build houses and get to live in them—they will not be used by someone else. They will plant vineyards and enjoy the wine—it will not be drunk by others. Like trees, my people will live long lives. They will fully enjoy the things that they have worked for. The work they do will be successful, and their children will not meet with disaster. I will bless them and their descendants for all time to come. (Isaiah 65:19–23)

Here in Isaiah, then, liberation theology finds the message that it is God's will not that his people wait for their reward in the hereafter but that they enjoy a fully human life *here on earth*.

For Christians, this message is carried forward in the New Testament. When Mary learns that she is pregnant by the Holy Spirit, she sings a "Song of Praise," which includes the words "He has brought down mighty kings from their thrones, and lifted up the lowly. He has filled the hungry with good things, and sent the rich away with empty hands" (Luke 1:52–53). The fact that these words come from the mouth of a poor peasant woman is not lost on poor Central American *campesinos*.

If the Exodus story is the central passage for liberation theology in the Old Testament, Jesus' proclamation of the "good news" is the key passage in the New Testament. At the beginning of his ministry, Jesus returns to Nazareth, his hometown, and on the Sabbath visits the synagogue. When handed the Scripture, he reads from the sixty-first chapter of Isaiah:

> The Spirit of the Lord is upon me, because he has chosen me to bring good news to the poor. He has sent me to proclaim liberty to the captives and recovery of sight to the blind, to set free the oppressed and announce that the time has come when the Lord will save his people. (Luke 4:18–19)

He then announces to those present, "This passage of scripture has come true today, as you heard it being read" (Luke 4:21).

Again, liberation theology interprets this not as a promise of the condition of life after death but as an obtainable objective of life on earth.

The Old Testament not only denounces poverty and makes general promises of a better life. It also speaks of concrete measures to prevent poverty from developing among God's people. In Leviticus and Deuteronomy there is detailed legislation designed to prevent the accumulation of wealth and resulting exploitation. For example, what remains in the fields after harvest should be left for the widow, orphan, and alien. Fields should not be harvested to the edge, so that something remains for the poor and alien (Lev. 19:9–10, 23:22; Deut. 24:19–21). The Sabbath has social as well as religious significance, for it is a day of rest for the slave and alien (Exod. 23:12; Deut. 5:14). Interest on loans is forbidden (Exod. 22:25; Lev. 25:35–37; Deut. 23:20). Slaves are to be granted freedom after seven years (Exod. 21:2–6) and debts pardoned (Deut. 15:1–18).

Why is the Bible—or God—so explicit? Because poverty represents a sundering both of solidarity among people and of communion with God. Poverty makes it impossible to achieve a spiritual relation with God. Poverty is an expression of a sin: a negation of love.[5]

THE SUBVERSIVE ACTIVITY OF CHRISTIAN BASE COMMUNITIES

The theology of liberation does not suggest that these biblical laws be adopted; rather, it argues that people must draw upon them and creatively develop means appropriate to their contemporary situation. At Medellín, the primary means recommended for conveying the church's message on justice and peace were Christian Base Communities.

Christian Base Communities (CEBs) (Comunidades Eclesiales de Base) are, perhaps, the most subversive institution the Latin American church has developed. Their impact has differed from country to country, but in general they have changed the lives of participants in four ways. First, CEBs provide a forum for bringing people together—an organization. In many areas of Central

America, this was a unique opportunity. In El Salvador, for example, peasants have been impeded from organizing since the 1932 peasant uprising. Second, grass-roots leadership emerges in the form of catechists (lay teachers) and delegates of the Word (lay preachers). These lay leaders are chosen by the people, not by the priests, and once selected, receive additional training from the priest or in centers set up for this purpose. In El Salvador during the 1970s seven such centers were established, and over 15,000 catechists and delegates were trained there.

Third, the CEBs provide experience in participatory democracy; all decisions in the life of the CEBs are made by the participants, not imposed by the priest. Dr. Charles Clements, a U.S. doctor who provided medical care to civilians and guerrillas in a "controlled zone" of El Salvador[6] beginning in 1981, tells of peasants who said that when Father José Alas came to Suchitoto in December 1968 and began developing CEBs, "it was the first time anyone ever asked me what I thought." Doña Olivia Guevara, a native of Solentiname, Nicaragua, related how the arrival of Father Ernesto Cardenal in 1965 and the development of a Christian community in those islands changed the lives of the people forever.

Finally, the CEBs are the medium by which the message of liberation theology is delivered. Through Bible study courses, homilies, and priest-parishoner dialogues during the Mass, people begin "doing theology"—interpreting the biblical message in the context of their own life and experience. Nowhere is this process more clearly captured than in the four-volume *Gospel in Solentiname,* a collection of dialogues on the scriptures read during the Mass.[7]

Solentiname, Nicaragua

The experience of the Christian community in Solentiname began in 1965 when Father Ernesto Cardenal, a Nicaraguan priest who had studied for several years with Thomas Merton in the Trappist seminary at Gethsemane, Kentucky, returned to his homeland at Merton's urging to found a contemplative lay community. Cardenal chose the islands of Solentiname, in the southern part of Lake Nicaragua, near the Costa Rican border, because of their isolation and their poverty. The people survived on subsistence farming and fishing. In his masses, which were described above, Cardenal invited the people to comment on the scriptures in the light of their own experiences. Over several years, the discussions grew more radical, as the political and economic conditions in Nicaragua deteriorated and as the repression of the Somoza regime grew.

Solentiname had by the mid-1970s become world famous, primarily because of its religious life but also because of what the community was accomplishing in the arts. From the beginning Cardenal, himself a poet, encouraged the people to express themselves through painting, sculpture, and poetry. These activities brought recognition as well as some additional income for the people. The people also established an agricultural cooperative that enabled them to improve their diet.

By the mid-1970s many young people in Solentiname were convinced that the Nicaraguan political and economic system would not change until Somoza was gone. They also believed, as Christians, that both Scripture and church social doctrine justified their decision to join the Sandinista National Liberation Front (FSLN). The community paid for that decision in October 1977 when a group of young Sandinistas from Solentiname, all of whom were members of the Christian community, decided to attack the National Guard barracks in San Carlos, a town on the southeastern coast of the lake. The object was to persuade the guardsmen to desert, but when the Sandinistas surrounded the barracks and invited surrender, the response was gunfire. At the end all was quiet inside the barracks, and Alejandro Guevara, one of Doña Olivia's sons, was assigned to burn the barracks. On entering, however, he found wounded guardsmen and was unable to burn them alive. The Sandinistas withdrew, but on the next day a National Guard contingent arrived in Solentiname and burned the community to the ground. The people went into exile in Costa Rica or fled to the mountains.

After the revolutionary triumph in 1979, Ernesto Cardenal became minister of culture. Alejandro Guevara had by 1981 become director of reconstruction in Solentiname.

Suchitoto, El Salvador

In December 1968 a young Salvadoran priest, José Inocencio Alas, was sent by Archbishop Luís Chávez y González to Suchitoto, thirty miles north of El Salvador's capital, San Salvador. Alas had studied in an Ecuadoran center for pastoral development founded by the progressive bishop Eduardo Proaño. Immediately on arriving in Suchitoto, Alas began developing Christian Base Communities and within a few months had created over thirty of them. In February 1969 Alas began a two-month course in which the CEBs discussed biblical themes and the direction the CEBs would take. The objective of the course, Alas has said, was "to prepare the people, following Medellín, to succeed in constructing their own destiny."[8] When the course ended, the participants elected nineteen of their peers as delegates of the Word. The delegates then received additional training, including a course in public speaking.

As the years passed, Alas continued to hold courses, primarily on biblical themes. By 1973, however, they had begun systematically to study socialist and capitalist ideology. Meanwhile, three events intruded on the life of the parish. In 1969 two wealthy landowners purchased a local farm, announced that it would be a private-enterprise effort to redistribute the land, and then put the parcels on the market for a sum that represented a 300 to 700 percent increase over the purchase price. This enraged the peasants, who had been led to believe they would be able to buy the land at a reasonable price. They mounted a demonstration, 3,000 strong, in front of the farm. The landowners were unmoved, whereupon 400 peasants went to San Salvador and demonstrated in front of the National Assembly. At the time, the progressive opposition was just two votes shy of controlling the assembly. The demonstration moved the assembly to pass a law obliging the landowners to sell the land for no more than a 100 percent profit on the original investment. The peasants were elated, the landowners outraged.

A few months later, in January 1970, the National Assembly convened an agrarian-reform congress, in which governmental, nongovernmental, labor, and business groups were invited to par-

ticipate. The Roman Catholic Church was among the nongovernmental groups that accepted, and Father José Alas was asked to
deliver the church's position, a ringing endorsement of agrarian
reform. Hours after he delivered the speech, he was abducted by
men in civilian clothes in front of the National Palace in down-
town San Salvador. Monseñor Arturo Rivera y Damas, at the time
the auxiliary bishop of San Salvador, staged a sit-in the office of
the minister of defense, Fidel Torres, and announced he would not
leave until Alas was produced—alive. Several hours later Torres
persuaded Rivera that Alas would be released unharmed, and
Rivera left. Alas was beaten, drugged, and left naked on the edge
of a cliff in the mountains south of San Salvador.[9]

The third event was the government's decision to build a hy-
droelectric dam, the Cerrón Grande, on the Lempa River near
Suchitoto. When completed the dam inundated thousands of hectares of peasants' land, for which they received little or no compensation. On the one hand, these events convinced the people that
they faced formidable opponents whose interests were fundamentally different from their own; on the other hand, they gave them
a sense that, organized, they could accomplish many things. By
early 1974 they had also decided that they needed a more formal,
explicitly political organization. After two meetings in Suchitoto,
the peasants, accompanied by José Alas and joined by representatives of several labor unions, student and teacher organizations, and
political parties, gathered in the Basilica of the Sacred Heart in San
Salvador and organized the first of the mass popular organizations,
the United Popular Action Front (FAPU). This was the first time
in Latin American history that an explicitly mass, revolutionary
organization had come out of the pastoral work of the church
through Christian Base Communities.

In the mid-1970s Father Alas was increasingly denounced as a
"subversive" and a "Communist." Finally, after Alfonso Navarro
and another priest were assassinated in March and April 1977, the
new archbishop of San Salvador, Monseñor Oscar Romero, persuaded José Alas to go into exile. By 1983 much of the parish lay
within the FMLN-controlled zone of Guazapa and many of
the peasants joyfully told visitors about the years with Father
Alas.[10]

El Quiché, Guatemala

During the 1950s, Catholic Action, a pastoral organization known throughout much of Latin America for being extremely conservative, moved into the Guatemalan highlands and began to develop study groups that were forerunners of the Christian Base Communities. For reasons that are not clear, Catholic Action took a more progressive stand in Guatemala than elsewhere, with the result that many catechists were trained even before the Medellín era. After Medellín, encouraged by El Quiché's bishop, Monseñor Juan Gerardi Candedera, the development of CEBs and catechists began in earnest. By the late 1970s the Quiché diocese alone had several thousand catechists, and the CEBs were closely integrated with the traditional Indian community institutions. After 1976 government repression led a slowly increasing number of Indians to join the Guerrilla Army of the Poor (EGP). In the spring of 1980, after the army murdered six women as well as five men in Nebaj, the main Ixil community, a number of Ixil communities collectively decided to go over to the EGP. The following August Bishop Gerardi, who had himself been the object of a kidnapping attempt in June, met with all the priests, nuns, and representatives of the diocese's catechists. They decided to close the diocese officially, concluding that only such a dramatic step could attract worldwide attention to the growing repression, which had taken on genocidal proportions.[11] This decision was widely interpreted, especially in the international press, as abandonment. Such was not the case. Some of the priests and nuns and most of the catechists remained in the diocese clandestinely to maintain an official presence. Others moved to Guatemala City and set up clandestine clinics and safe houses. Every three months the catechists come down from the mountains to receive liturgical training for the next quarter and to carry back the Host (consecrated bread) for the Eucharist. The remainder, including the bishop, left Guatemala and created the Guatemalan Church in Exile.

THE BISHOPS RESPOND

Although these events might imply a certain unity within the church, nothing could be further from the truth. In fact, the development of liberation theology and of CEBs has created divisions within the Catholic Church unmatched since the Reformation. However, only the most pessimistic and those unfamiliar with the sense of unity that pervades the Roman Catholic Church in Latin America (and elsewhere) suggest the possibility of schism. As we will see, those who expend the most energy demanding church unity are those who are uncomfortable with liberation theology and the legacy of Medellín.

Thus far we have focused on the church at the base, for that is where most of the evangelizing or pastoral efforts of the church in Central America have been directed since 1968. But the most profound divisions in the church are between the hierarchy—the bishops—on the one hand, and the priests and religious (nuns and brothers) and parishioners, on the other. This division is particularly sharp where the majority of priests and religious have chosen to follow the Medellín path but where a majority of the bishops continue to be more concerned with their hierarchical prerogatives and authority than with what the Latin American church was by 1979 calling a "preferential option for the poor."[12]

The conflicting ways of thinking within the church are of three kinds. The first is, in the words of the Argentine Jesuit Juan Carlos Scannone, "a conservative preconciliar theology" that emphasizes "the values of tradition, the institutional and sacral aspect of the church, and hierarchical authority."

The second and third categories both reflect, again in Scannone's words, a "liberation theology predominantly concerned with being a theology of popular pastoral activity," which "underlines the values of popular culture, the 'already' existing unity of the church as the People of God, the Christian sense of our people and their religiosity, and historical roots of the current liberation process, and openness of this process to a qualitatively new society. . . ." (Both stress "social criticism of injustice, ethico-prophetical denunciation, and identification with the poor and oppressed.")

The difference between the last two categories lies in their receptivity to Marxism. The second emphasizes "a liberation theology predominantly influenced by Marxist categories and methodology in its concern to analyze and transform reality." Those who fall into this category range from people who find Marxist tools of analysis useful in examining and understanding Latin American reality to those who consider themselves both Christians and Marxists and who see no inherent contradiction between the two. The third category hopes that the liberation process will lead "to a qualitatively new society that would be neither capitalist nor [Communist]."[13]

These divisions are present in every national church in Central America. In the respective hierarchies, however, the bishops tend to fall into either the first (traditional) or third (progressive) category. There are no bishops in Central America who, like Sergio Méndez Arceo, the retired bishop of Cuernavaca, Mexico, openly embrace Marxism.

In El Salvador four of the five members of the Salvadoran hierarchy and a minority of priests generally adhere to the first, or traditional, category. Included in this group is the bishop of San Miguel, José Eduardo Alvarez, who is commonly known as "the colonel from San Miguel," a reference to the fact that he is a colonel and a chaplain in the Salvadoran army. Also in this group are the bishop of Santa Ana, Marco René Revelo, who acquired a certain fame in 1981 for going to the air force base at Ilopango, near San Salvador, to bless some U.S.–supplied war planes, and the bishop of San Vicente, Pedro Aparicio. The latter, owner of a large hacienda that had been a gift from the then-president of El Salvador, Col. Arturo Molina, was generally inclined to share the views of his fellow landowners. In May 1982 an active lay member of the church inside El Salvador said, "Here everyone knows Aparicio as 'the strong arm of the right.' "[14] Although the new auxiliary bishop of San Salvador, Gregorio Rosa Chávez, is not as conservative as those just described, he is known for his close ties to the Christian Democratic party (PDC), which by mid–1980 had lost much of its base of popular support with the exodus of progressive members, who soon formed the Popular Movement of Social Christians (MPSC) and who helped create the Democratic Revolutionary Front (FDR) in April of that year.

The remaining prelate, Archbishop Arturo Rivera y Damas, of San Salvador, fits into the third category, as did his predecessors, Oscar Arnulfo Romero and Luís Chávez y González. Chávez was a personally conservative man who took seriously Vatican II and

Medellín and immediately began encouraging priests to implement the new social doctrine. It fell to his auxiliary, Rivera y Damas, to confront the oligarchy and the army periodically, as he did at the time of José Alas's abduction. As a result, Rivera was the choice of everyone to become archbishop when Chávez retired in 1977 —everyone, that is, except the army, the oligarchy, and the papal nuncio. Thus, Oscar Romero was chosen because they did not want someone who would "oppose the government."[15] In fact, Romero had his first run-in with the government on the day after his installation as archbishop.[16]

Approximately one-quarter of the priests still in El Salvador in mid-1983 shared the most conservative of these positions, while about one-half shared the perspective of Rivera y Damas. The remainder, in the words of Father Benito Tobar, use "the analysis of Marx because it is objective and scientific. But we are not Marxists. We cannot understand Marx as a religion, because we are Christians."[17] By 1983, the priests and nuns in this category themselves fell into three groups: those who were in exile, most of whom were working with Salvadoran refugees in other countries and/or with the FDR and the Farabundo Martí Front for National Liberation (FMLN); the eight to ten priests who were carrying on their pastoral work in one of the FMLN's controlled zones; and those whose sympathies were with the revolutionary organizations but who had chosen to try and continue their pastoral work openly inside the country.

In Nicaragua, as in El Salvador, only one bishop, Rubén López, of Estelí, was most open in sharing the perspective of Romero and Rivera. Other bishops, such as Salvador Schlefer, of Bluefields (department of Zelaya), permitted, if not openly encouraged, their priests to implement the new social doctrine of the church—which meant the widespread development of CEBs in Zelaya. Two bishops, López Fitoria and Pablo Antonio Vega, were pro-Somoza but were not inclined to speak out, as bishops have done in El Salvador. Other bishops, notably Carlos Santí, of Matagalpa, and Julián Barní, of León, both of whom were named to their posts in 1982, made clear their willingness to try and work with Nicaragua's revolutionary government. Santí, in his first homily after his installation in June 1982 stated flatly, "Anyone who says there is repression of religion in Nicaragua is a liar." Archbishop Miguel Obando y Bravo, of Managua, was the best-known of the Nicaraguan bishops because of his increasingly outspoken opposition to Somoza during the 1970s. But Obando was anti-Somoza, although never prorevolution, as his positions after the triumph clearly revealed.

In Guatemala, once again we find only one bishop, Gerardi of El Quiché, who openly embraced the teachings of Vatican II and Medellín. What finally moved the bishops to begin expressing concern over the political situation in the country was not government repression but the taking of power by a born-again Christian, the retired. general Efraín Ríos Montt, in a coup d'état on 23 March, 1982. Ríos Montt immediately began encouraging conservative Protestant sects from the United States to come in. He also surrounded himself with advisers from his own church, the Church of the Word (El Verbo), which is itself affiliated with the California-based Gospel Outreach. Medical missionaries and preachers began to appear in outlying villages, having been ferried in by military helicopter. Reports that thousands were being "converted" to Protestantism sent tremors through the Guatemalan Catholic Church. It began to appear that the bishops had something to fear even more than revolution. Meanwhile, Gen. Efraín Ríos Montt's brother, progressive Bishop Ríos Montt, left the country for an indefinite period.[18]

Whether the bishops in Central America fell into the "traditional" or "progressive" camp determined to what extent they supported or encouraged the development of Christian Base Communities in their respective dioceses. In Nicaragua CEBs were formed, but not in any systematic manner. Outside Zelaya, there existed no strong encouragement of CEBs. In Zelaya the Capuchins responsible for the diocese trained 900 delegates of the Word, and CEBs were established in Estelí, Carazo, Matagalpa, Jinotega, and Yalí and in several barrios of Managua.

In El Salvador, Archbishop Chávez began immediately after Medellín to encourage the development of Christian Base Communities, and many priests followed his lead not only in the archdiocese but in the other dioceses as well. The archdiocese, then, was a center of ferment in the Salvadoran church, and its influence was felt in every corner of the country.

In Guatemala, as in Nicaragua, the development of CEBs was sporadic—outside Quiché diocese—and was very much a result of the local priest's effort. In all three countries the development of CEBs was positively related to the political development of the population that was organized in the CEBs. In other words, there emerged a clear correlation among the development of the CEBs, the political radicalization of the people, and the presence of political organizations. The FSLN in Nicaragua organized in many areas, but people became most radical where CEBs were present. In El Salvador many of the 15,000 catechists and delegates along with innumerable CEB members entered the ranks of the revolutionary organizations as combatants, militia, or political organizers or did political work outside the country. Dozens of the revolutionary leaders have been catechists or delegates. Of these, perhaps the best-known was Juan Chacón, a catechist who was secretary general of the Popular Revolutionary Bloc (BPR), the largest of the popular organizations, and who, like his catechist father, was assassinated by state security forces.

Only in Guatemala has another factor been critical: many of the parishes in which CEBs were established were largely Indian. The cohesiveness of the Indian communities and the traditional practice of collective decision making within those communities meant that the involvement of large numbers of indigenous people in the revolutionary organizations did not come until the entire community made the decision to go over to these organizations. The clearest example of this occurred in El Quiché in 1980 when the Ixil and the Quiché Indians made the collective decision to join the Guerrilla Army of the Poor.

THE PROTESTANT CHURCHES

Central America is over 90 percent Catholic. It is thus easy to ignore the Protestant churches. To do so, however, is a mistake because, in different ways, they have had a significant impact on the process of social change in each country.

In Nicaragua between 10 and 12 percent of the population is

Protestant, an unusually high proportion in Latin America. In El Salvador, Protestants make up less than 5 percent of the population. In Guatemala accurate figures are difficult to come by because of the claims by various sects of the numbers being converted to Protestantism.

In Nicaragua the December 1972 earthquake proved to be the turning point for the Protestant churches.[19] Four days after the earthquake, a Protestant doctor, Gustavo Parajón, issued a radio appeal for a meeting of Protestant pastors. Within three weeks twenty denominations were participating in five different aid programs for those who had been left destitute. All these programs were organized under the recently created Protestant Committee for Assistance to the Dispossessed, or CEPAD.

Three months after the earthquake CEPAD changed the last word of its name to "development," as it began to think in a more long-term context and to focus on the spiritual bases of social action. Between 1974 and 1980, CEPAD sponsored sixty pastoral retreats throughout the country. By 1977 these Protestants were moving in a direction that culminated less than two years later in strong support for the revolution. During and after the September 1978 offensive, the Protestant churches, through CEPAD, provided broad support to the FSLN both by turning their churches into refugee centers and by secretly providing food and medicines to the combatants. This work was coordinated with that of the Evangelical Committee for Agrarian Progress (CEPA), an organization created by Jesuits in 1969 to train *campesino* leaders, and other Catholic relief agencies around the country.

In El Salvador, until the early 1980s, there was only one Protestant Church, a Baptist church in San Salvador that created its own CEBs and that became committed to the revolution. Because of its work, its membership of 150 almost doubled between 1980 and 1982, and by 1981 the great majority of them were participating, in some capacity, in the revolutionary process. In the early 1980s other churches of the same denomination came to share the commitment of their fellow church. In addition, other Protestant churches found a new role in providing assistance to refugees (mostly peasants) from the countryside. The remainder of the Protestant churches in El Salvador are either apolitical, or they support the present government. In fact, the government, like that of Guatemala, has approved the development of churches by certain fundamentalist Protestant sects like the Central American Mission. Salvadoran refugees in Nicaragua have told me in interviews that the National Guard tells people in their villages that "the true Christians" go to the Protestant churches because "those who go to the Catholic Church are communists."[20]

The situation in Guatemala resembles that in El Salvador, but on a much larger scale, as we have already seen. In Guatemala, as in El Salvador, a handful of mainstream Protestant churches are attempting to make a "preferential option for the poor" but are finding it extremely difficult because of the repression.[21]

JOHN PAUL II'S "JOURNEY FOR PEACE"

The visit of Pope John Paul II to Central America during the first ten days of March 1983 was preceded by elaborate preparations. There was much hope that his "journey for peace" would somehow be a catalyst in resolving the conflict that plagues the region. In retrospect, however, it seems that the visit had a lasting impact in only two countries. In El Salvador the pontiff named Arturo Rivera y Damas archbishop of San Salvador, after Rivera had served as apostolic administrator for almost three years—an almost-unheard-of tenure. (In contrast, Poland had a new archbishop within three weeks after the death of Cardinal Wyszynski in 1981.) On his arrival in El Salvador, John Paul's first act after leaving the airport was to visit the tomb of El Salvador's slain archbishop Oscar Romero. Then, during the mass, he pointedly praised Archbishop Rivera, recalled in positive terms the pastoral positions of Romero, and delivered a homily whose major theme was a call for "dialogue"—that is, negotiations between the contending sides in the war.

Through these and other acts the pope's visit to El Salvador strengthened both Rivera y Damas within the Salvadoran hierarchy and the church as a potential mediator between the revolutionary organizations and the government. By visiting Romero's tomb and speaking of him during the mass, he lifted the curtain of silence that had surrounded Romero's name in El Salvador. To mention

Romero was to invite death; but three weeks after the pontiff's visit, 3,000 people jammed the cathedral for a requiem mass on the third anniversary of his death—a number that would have been unthinkable one or two years earlier.

John Paul's visit to Nicaragua, in sharp contrast, was a disaster both for the church and the government. In general the Pope accepted the position of the archbishop in each country. The archbishop's description of the situation thus becomes decisive. In Nicaragua, Archbishop Obando has chosen to define those parishes with strong CEBs and members committed to the revolution as the "popular church," further labeled "parallel church," that is, outside the official church. This was the position presented to the Vatican and the pope over a three-year period—with the implication that the "popular church" rejects the authority of the bishops and is potentially schismatic. John Paul accepted this definition and came to Nicaragua preaching unity. His homily during the mass in Managua was the most hierarchical and authoritarian he has ever delivered as pope. It contained not one word of compassion, of reconciliation, of love. It is not surprising, therefore, that the same Sandinistas who at the beginning of the mass were chanting "Long live John Paul II!" by the end were screaming "People's power!"

The irony—and tragedy—is that people who are members of the CEBs defined as the "popular church" *never* use that term to describe themselves. They do not see themselves as being outside mainstream Catholicism in any sense. They do not question the authority of their bishops. They *do* ask for dialogue, something that Archbishop Obando is clearly unwilling to engage in,[22] and something that Vatican II and Medellín clearly mandate.

Another irony is that in El Salvador there exists an organization called the National Conference of the Popular Church (CONIP), one that, while it does not challenge the bishops' authority, openly identifies with the revolutionary process and recognizes both the FDR and the FMLN as the "vanguard" of the revolution. But Archbishop Rivera y Damas has chosen to ignore CONIP rather than to confront it. He maintains a dialogue with members of CONIP, but he has refused to define member priests, nuns, and CEBs as being outside the church. As a result, no confrontation has developed. In El Salvador there was no mention of the need for unity, although it can be argued that the divisions in the church are much more profound than those in Nicaragua. In El Salvador, however, the conservative bishops were effectively silenced by the pope's call for dialogue, something several of them have openly opposed.

In Guatemala, John Paul's visit had the effect of making General Ríos Montt defiantly order the execution of six people days before the pope arrived. He announced a few days after the visit that he had "sinned"—but Guatemala's military policy of destroying indigenous communities in order to eliminate the social base of the guerrillas has not changed. The bishops there continue to be more concerned with the inroads made by conservative Protestantism than with human-rights violations.

FUTURE ROLES FOR LIBERATION THEOLOGY

The church in Central America, as throughout Latin America, is at the beginning of a new reformation. Historically, the church worldwide has adapted to changing socioeconomic realities. Its last major upheaval—the Reformation—accompanied Europe's transition from feudalism to capitalism. The new reformation is occurring at a time when various forms of socialism are replacing capitalism, especially in the Third World.

These upheavals in the political and economic arena are likely to be long-lived, as those with power struggle to hold on to it while those without power struggle to obtain it. The tensions within the church are thus likely to continue for several decades, though how exacerbated they become will be determined, to a large extent, by how the bishops choose to define the situation.

These tensions do not necessarily mean schism. We may be witnessing a new reformation *within* the Roman Catholic Church and within various Protestant denominations. Because the lessons of the sixteenth century have been learned, history will not necessarily repeat itself.

Nonetheless, *liberation* shows no evidence of becoming a less dominant theme; liberation theology and Christian Base Communities are now an integral part of the institutional structure of the churches in Central America and cannot be easily eliminated as one would extract a bad tooth. In addition, wise heads in the churches are likely in growing numbers to recognize their two practical choices: make their peace with the revolution or be completely marginalized, as the church in Cuba was in the early 1960s. As a result, the church will probably be an important actor in revolutionary societies in Central America—and may indeed keep its revolutions humane.

Making a "preferential option for the poor" has meant, for the churches in Central America, internal tensions and divisions, persecution, and life. That the churches have come to play this role, and that they have been condemned by many for doing so, is not surprising. As Archbishop Oscar Romero said shortly after two of his priests were murdered by right-wing death squads in the spring of 1977, "The moment the defense of the poor is raised in this society you call the whole thing into question. That is why they have no other recourse than to call us 'subversive.' That is what we are."

NOTES

1. The exception is Costa Rica, which has enjoyed a progressive democratic government since 1948. For general studies that discuss this oppression and repression, see, e.g., John A. Booth, *The End and the Beginning: The Nicaraguan Revolution* (Boulder: Westview Press, 1982); Tommie Sue Montgomery, *Revolution in El Salvador* (Boulder: Westview Press, 1982); Stephen Schlesinger and Stephen Kinzer, *Bitter Fruit: The Untold Story of the American Coup in Guatemala* (Garden City, N.Y.: Doubleday, 1981).

   This essay is based on research carried out over a four-year period in Nicaragua, El Salvador, Mexico, and the United States. Portions of this article previously appeared in "Cross and Rifle: Revolution and the Church in El Salvador and Nicaragua," *Journal of International Affairs* 36 (Fall–Winter 1982–83): 209–21. I am grateful to the Centro de Investigación y Asesoría Socio-Económico, in Managua, for providing support during the essay's first incarnation, and to Hernán Guerrero, Dennis Gilbert, and Martin Diskin for their comments.

2. Exod. 3:7–8, 16–17. The translation is from the *Good News Bible*.

3. Penny Lernoux, *Cry of the People* (Garden City, N.Y.: Doubleday, 1980), 37.

4. See, e.g., Exod. 23:11; Lev. 25:2–7; Exod. 21:2–6; and other citations in the text, below.

5. This discussion is drawn from José Míguez Bonino, *Doing Theology in A Revolutionary Situation* (Philadelphia: Fortress Press, 1976), chap. 1.

6. A "controlled zone" is an area of several hundred square kilometers where the revolutionary forces have established a presence sufficient to guarantee that government troops cannot enter except in massive numbers during a military offensive. Life in the controlled zones is fairly normal. There are schools, clinics, hospitals, agricultural production, a rudimentary judicial system, and "town meetings," called "popular assemblies," where the civilians living in the villages of the zone make decisions that affect their daily lives. The Guazapa zone lies twenty miles north of San Salvador and covers an area of 400 square kilometers.

7. Ernesto Cardenal, *The Gospel in Solentiname,* 4 vols. (Maryknoll, N.Y.: Orbis Books, 1976–82).

8. Interview with José Alas, April 1980.

9. Interviews with Monseñor Rivera y Damas, Ricardo Urioste, and José Alas.

10. Interview with Charles Clements, May 1983.

11. The deaths in Nebaj were significant because previously virtually all the victims had been men. Indian elders rationalized these murders by thinking that the men must have been doing something wrong. After Nebaj, the elders began to say, "They're killing our people." To the Indians, women were the source of life and therefore were key to the survival of the community. Information in this section comes from interviews with Father Sean McKenna, an Irish priest who remained in El Quiché after August 1980, and Father Javier Guerriarán, who left and helped form the Guatemalan Church in Exile.

    Systematic repression in El Quiché had begun in July 1975 when thirty-seven members of a cooperative were seized by government troops. A year later sixty-eight of its leaders, who were also catechists, disappeared. One hundred other community leaders were killed during 1976. Father Guerriarán reports steadily increasing repression against the CEBs between 1976 and 1978. Between 1976 and 1980, four priests were killed in El Quiché and eleven in other parts of Guatemala; in May 1980 a convent was attacked with bombs and grenades. *Witness to Political Violence in Guatemala: The Suppression of a Rural Development Movement,* by Shelton H. Davis and Julie Hodson (Boston: Oxfam-America, 1982), contains a chronology of the political violence from 1976 to February 1982 on pages 47–52.

12. A "preferential option for the poor" was a term coined at the Third Latin American Bishops Conference, held in Puebla, Mexico, in January 1979.

13. Juan Carlos Scannone, "Theology, Popular Culture, and Discernment," in *Frontiers of Theology in Latin America,* ed. Rosino Gibellini (Maryknoll, N.Y.: Orbis Books, 1979), 221–22. Scannone uses the term *Marxist* in place of *Communist.* But many who fall into the third category could accept a socialist regime with Marxist leaders if freedom of religion were guaranteed and honored. As a Peronist, Scannone is profoundly anti-Communist. He

denies to Marxist-oriented liberation theology any *pastoral* concern. But research in both Nicaragua and El Salvador reveals that priests and religious who fall into the second category have a profound concern for genuine pastoral work—that is, visiting the sick, saying mass, holding Bible study groups, and in general sharing parishioners' joys and sorrows on a daily basis. I have thus adapted Scannone's categories to reflect more accurately the empirical evidence.

I am grateful to Javier Igviñiz Echevarría, of the Catholic University in Lima, Peru, for providing pertinent information on Scannone's background.

14. Interview, San Salvador, May 1982.

15. So Rivera y Damas was told in Rome by a cardinal with some responsibility in the selection process. Information from a privileged interview.

16. One of his priests had been captured by the National Guard, and Romero went to President Molina and successfully demanded his release. See Montgomery, *Revolution in El Salvador,* 109.

17. Interview, San Salvador, January 1980.

18. Speculations on why Bishop Ríos Montt left Guatemala ranged from too much pressure to threats on his life by right-wing Protestant fanatics.

19. Information about the Nicaraguan Protestant churches is taken from Dodson and Montgomery, "Churches in the Nicaraguan Revolution." This article originally appeared in Spanish in *Nicaráhuac,* no. 5 (April–June 1981): 137–59; also in *Nicaragua in Revolution,* ed. Thomas W. Walker (New York: Praeger, 1982), 161–180 with the same title.

20. Privileged interviews, Nicaragua, 1981–82.

21. Guatemala cannot be discussed in more detail, because naming churches or individuals would jeopardize many lives.

22. These generalizations are based on research carried out over three years in Nicaragua, including interviews with Archbishop Miguel Obando y Bravo and with members of several CEBs and priests.

Reactionary Despotism in El Salvador

AN IMPEDIMENT TO DEMOCRATIC TRANSITION

Enrique A. Baloyra

THE MODEL OF REACTIONARY DESPOTISM IN CENTRAL AMERICA

As a way of describing the basic features of the authoritarian regimes of Central America, a model proposed for the countries of Mediterranean Europe by the Spanish sociologist Salvador Giner seems relevant. Giner identifies a form of political domination, *reactionary despotism,* in which (1) a reactionary coalition of landowners, and industrialists and financiers closely related to them, (2) imposes an exclusionary political regime, (3) to try to legitimize their control of the economy and the limited pluralism that the regime can accommodate, (4) in which the power of the state is implemented through service classes from the middle strata who are dependent on the expansion of government for employment and job security, (5) in which potential and actual opponents of the regime are denied citizenship, and (6) in which co-optation and passive obedience replace the active consent of the population.[1]

Despite the obvious differences in levels of development between Central America and Mediterranean Europe, Giner's model seems applicable since it draws upon a comparable sociohistorical experience. His discussion of the rise of capitalism in backward societies and of the developmental path of reactionary despotism is grounded in the model offered by Barrington Moore. According to Moore, the emergence of a system of labor-repressive agriculture as in El Salvador creates conditions in which able leaders can drag along the less perceptive reactionary elements concentrated in the landed upper classes and establish a powerful bureaucratic apparatus and an efficient machine of law and order, consolidating the "conservative route to modernization."[2]

According to Moore, weak commercial and industrial classes

lose any possibility of becoming the more dynamic element in the society once they accept the hegemony of a landowning class. The consequence of this is a conservative trend and the consolidation of semiparliamentary forms of authoritarian domination.[3] In Giner's elaboration of this model, the Mediterranean Europe of the nineteenth and early twentieth centuries conforms to the conservative blueprint described by Moore: weak bourgeoisies unable to dominate the precapitalist element, a bloated bureaucracy serving a noninterventionist state, and oligarchic rule.[4] In addition, some features borrowed from the "world systems" perspective appear in the model of reactionary despotism: the subordinate and secondary role of these capitalist economies, the penetration of foreign investment, and economic enclaves.[5]

The prevalence of the export model and the oligarchic nature of the Central American republics between the mid-nineteenth century and the Great Depression are well established. There is little need to dwell on the details of how each country was affected by the transition to export agriculture—they are made abundantly clear elsewhere.[6] What remains to be clarified is which combination of factors in a particular sociohistorical sequence of development is responsible for the differences observable today.

This essay utilizes El Salvador to illustrate how the model of reactionary despotism could help us understand the development and deterioration of authoritarian regimes in Central America.

II. REACTIONARY DESPOTISM IN EL SALVADOR

In the case of El Salvador, it can be argued that a preindustrial capitalist state[7] has existed since the late nineteenth century. That state represented a fusion of the liberal economic ideology of the 1870s and the political hegemony of the planters. The result was an oligarchic republic—formalized by the constitution of 1886—which evolved into a political regime that could be termed a "dictatorship of notables," or simply an authoritarian regime,[8] but not a functioning democracy. The government[9] was under the control of planters, and the control and the execution of public policy were by and for them.[10] State power was very much privatized, and it remained so until the crisis of 1931.

The absence of foreign economic enclaves, or at least of any significant elite group that could dispute their power, enabled the planters to remain politically hegemonic and socially dominant during most of this time. The Asociación Cafetalera (Coffee Growers' Association) emerged as a state within the state, as the coffee growers were able to dictate economic policy to suit their narrow interests.

The changes brought about by the bourgeois revolution of 1870 included a redefinition of relations inside the power bloc. Creole *latifundistas* (large landowners), urban merchants, and the church lost power to the new coffee entrepreneurs. The latter were primarily the officers of the liberal armies—claiming the spoils of their victory over the conservatives—liberal politicians, merchants connected to these two groups, the *ladino* (non-Indian) upper middle class, and some immigrants. Tensions remained among producers, financiers, and intermediaries, as well as between producers and exporters, but there was a tendency toward the fusion of these interests. During boom periods producers were able to move laterally into the finance sector, and during busts the financiers had the upper hand and were able to acquire property through foreclosures. In essence, planters wanted to become bankers to preserve their properties, whereas merchants wanted to become planters in order to increase their social prestige.

Planters and merchants remained at odds over monetary and fiscal policy, but there was little doubt as to who was dominant. For example, the planters were able to keep El Salvador within the silver standard, even though some reform governments like those of Carlos Ezeta in the 1890s and of Manuel Enrique Araujo in 1911–13 tried to impose the gold standard and to fix the exchange rate, respectively.[11] The bimetallic-currency situation enabled them to utilize the monetary system to keep everyone else in the Salvadoran economy at a disadvantage. Their control of the banks that issued currency—including the Internacional, the Particular, the Occidental, and the Agrícola Commercial—gave them an additional advantage, as did the control of credit, which enabled them to have much say about the diversification of the economy.

Incidentally, Ezeta was overthrown by the planters and Araujo was assassinated, and although four men were blamed and punished it never became clear who was behind his death.

The crisis of the Depression was the first of a series of opportunities in which El Salvador could have embarked on a process of transition to democracy. In 1931 the incumbent president Pío Romero Bosque allowed a truly competitive election to take place; it was won by Arturo Araujo. Araujo's government was soon overwhelmed by the deepening economic crisis, by his inability to meet popular demands and to rely on his supporters to organize viable political organizations, by the hostility of the oligarchy, and by the increasing restlessness of the military.

Araujo's overthrow on 2 December 1931, the peasant uprising and the *matanza* of 1932, and the personal dictatorship of Gen. Maximiliano Hernández Martínez have been described in considerable detail.[12] For our purposes, the importance of this crisis is that it marks a watershed in the evolution of reactionary despotism in El Salvador. General Martínez and the oligarchy reached an accommodation: Martínez thought that El Salvador had to live within its means; the oligarchy believed that only the army could maintain control in the countryside, at least for the foreseeable future.

In other capitalist countries, including Mexico, the crisis of the Depression brought about a reform of the capitalist state. The government became more involved in economic matters, and a compromise between laissez-faire and welfare economics was worked out. In El Salvador, following the Depression, the government finally assumed control of the monetary system and imposed some order in the banking community. That these measures came so late in the development of the Salvadoran state testifies to the power of the oligarchy and its ability to privatize the use of the powers of the state for economic policymaking. In other words, it took a personal dictatorship to rein in the oligarchy in these matters, but the measures were not redistributive. The economic-reform package enacted by Martínez, in collaboration with Miguel Tomás Molina and Napoleón Viera Altamirano, left the state unreformed in the sense that the supremacy of the private sector was not compromised and that no basic mechanism of redistribution was put in place. The measures had to overcome the opposition of the oligarchy, which managed to retain control of credit mechanisms, but their intent was to protect proprietors at all levels, to promote the capitalist system, and to reconcile the contradictory interests of individual capitalists.[13] In essence, therefore, Martínez curbed the oligarchy's predatory capacity and diminished its ability to engage in reckless monetary speculation.

At no time was the laissez-faire orientation prevalent in the country displaced as the dominant ideology, and although the crisis of the Depression put an end to the oligarchic republic, the regime became *explicitly* authoritarian. The reactionary coalition was displaced from power to the extent that it no longer monopolized control of the government. However, it retained sufficient economic power, social prestige, and political influence to prevent the rise of an alternative coalition and to thwart any attempt to reform the traditional system of export agriculture.

It is possible to describe the period of military rule begun in 1932 in El Salvador by means of a number of variants that a capitalist state may assume. The term *Bonapartism* could perhaps be applied to the personalist dictatorship of Martínez (1932–44) and his successors (1944–48). The epithet *military dictatorship* would certainly do no injustice to the basic configuration of the Salvadoran government since 1948. The last year of the Molina administration has been described as a "regency."[14] This writer has referred to the Romero administration (1977–79) as "militarized capitalism" and as an attempt to restore the reactionary coalition to the government.[15] The possibilities, in short, are vast and the space available insufficient for a detailed examination of each.

However, we should not overlook a continuous theme that is perhaps the most important contradiction of Salvadoran politics during the last fifty years. As a working hypothesis, I would like to propose that the alliance between the military and the oligarchy, begun in 1932 and formalized by the constitution of 1950, became increasingly contradictory, rendered more acute by the inability to maintain the formula of reactionary despotism without an increasing amount of repression. Under the pact of 1950, the armed force assumed—"was given," some would say—control of the state institutions while the private sector retained sole custody of the economy and its operation. The pact was increasingly difficult to maintain because the overall process of social change and the political activation of more dynamic actors periodically presented the system with the alternatives of change or repression.

Elsewhere I have suggested that the military failed to undermine the bases of oligarchic power.[16] The military did not create a party or a coalition sufficiently broad to challenge the oligarchy if this became necessary. Instead, the crises of 1948 and 1960 were handled in a manner suggesting that the military did not want to share power with reform factions that could imperil its monopoly of the government. The result was that the processes of transition initiated then were nipped in the bud by the oligarchy. Neither the Partido Revolucionario de Unificación Democrática (PRUD) nor the Partido de Conciliación Nacional (PCN), the "official" parties of the Salvadoran military experiment initiated in 1948, resembled Mexico's Partido Revolucionario Institucional (PRI) in any real sense. More important, the basic features of Salvadoran political economy were not altered by the creation of this experiment, since it was predicated on a division of labor between the two actors that the official party came to replace in the Mexican case— namely, the military and the oligarchy.

The pact had two parts. First, the military would maintain an exclusionary political regime by preventing the participation of government critics and would refrain from tampering with the economy. The private sector in turn, would manage exports and provide the fiscal revenue and the foreign exchange necessary to maintain El Salvador's role in the international division of labor. Beyond the normal frictions one could anticipate in an alliance like this, the scheme from the very beginning showed a number of additional flaws. First of all, neither the oligarchy nor the military was totally cohesive or homogeneous (more on this below). Second, the linchpin of the system, namely, the availability of redundant labor, could be maintained only by a stifling of the political activity of the peasantry and the agricultural workers. The lack of substance of the Salvadoran elections usually guaranteed this, but the emergence in the late sixties of the petite bourgeoisie as a political force to be reckoned with forced the regime to obstruct the electoral process completely during the seventies. With the neutralization of the moderate forces represented by the Christian Democratic (PDC) and Social Democratic (MNR) parties, the political process became radicalized. This forced the military to reevaluate its relation with the oligarchy, and after the embarrassing defeat suffered during the agrarian-transformation crisis of 1976 (see below) and after Romero's attempt to stop the deterioration of the model, the reformist faction prevailed and the military redefined its role in October 1979.

In essence, then, the first aspect of our working hypothesis is that the present Salvadoran crisis has its organic roots in the oligarchy crisis of 1931–32 and in a flawed attempt to save the export model through exceptional forms of the capitalist state. The crisis that began in 1932 dragged on, as the military was unable to break with the oligarchy or to attack the real bases of its power. Thus, any talk about a "catastrophic balance"[17] in El Salvador must refer to the deadlock between the military and the oligarchy. The deterioration of the reactionary despotism, brought about by the inability to deal with this contradiction, forms the historical background to the present crisis.

Given the ambiguous and multifaceted role of the armed force in the Salvadoran process of transition begun in October 1979, and given its unwillingness to submit to the rule of law and its indiscriminate use of force, other observers will challenge this interpretation. However, the interpretation of the present behavior of the Salvadoran military as a staunch defender of oligarchic interests in El Salvador is very flawed.

III. CONFLICT AND CONSENSUS IN REACTIONARY DESPOTISM

Students of the Salvadoran oligarchy have uncovered at least two different groups within this social formation. In the mid-1960s Robert Aubey found three: agriculturalists, merchants, and a mixed group.[18] Rafael Guidos Véjar saw a *frente agrario* (an agrarian front) and *grupos industrializantes* (industrializing groups), more or less resembling a growing differentiation between a traditional landed oligarchy and a small industrial bourgeoisie.[19] Italo López Vallecillos also perceived two factions: one agro-financial, the other agro-industro-financial.[20] In essence, these and other scholars described a situation of "shared economic power" in the context of very fluid relations, in which the interests of the traditional agrarian faction usually prevailed.

Which of the different economic family groups of the oligarchy constituted the core of the reactionary coalition? Luis de Sebastián suggested that the economic basis of oligarchic power in El Salvador was a concentration of land ownership, finance, production, and export activities, which amounted to a "magic square" of economic domination.[21] The degree of concentration increased as one moved from ownership and production to credit and export activities. Therefore, the ability to profit from this "magic square" situated a group or an individual at the very core of the coalition.

The data presented by Aubey and by Colindres suggest which of the economic groups benefited the most from the "magic square."[22] Leaving the question of surnames aside, one can determine that the core of the reactionary coalition of El Salvador was composed of the 240 or so largest agricultural planters, the twenty-six major groups engaged in export agriculture and specializing in coffee exports, cattle ranchers with interests in the banking sector, large merchants dedicated to the supply of agricultural machinery and other agricultural inputs, financiers and bankers associated with export agriculturalists, the major speculators in real estate, and some entrepreneurs of the food-processing and textile industries. Linked very closely to these were former military officers who had retired at the top of the ranks and who had played key roles in pacifying the country during one or more of the periodic political crises; former high government officials who because of their legal or technocratic skills could fill managerial functions in the private sector; and, on a lesser scale, local commanders of the National Guard who offered protection to the largest farms, and individuals connected to the repression of opposition elements. As a whole, this group had the most to lose from the installation of a democratic regime in the country and from any successful attempt to change the nature of the Salvadoran state. It could be argued that until October 1979 that state existed primarily to permit the reproduction of the "magic square."

Some qualifications must be made. First, this core element of the reactionary coalition was not necessarily the most anti-Communist, conservative, and violent element but the one that had the most to lose from any process of change. Individuals included in this core may or may not have shared all these characteristics. What they did all share was a direct and very major interest in the preservation of a regime, reactionary despotism, that sheltered their usufruct of the "magic square." But it does not follow that they manned the barricades at all times in their defense of privilege. As a matter of fact, a large number of them began to export their capital in 1979 and took up residence in Guatemala and in the United States following the coup of 15 October 1979. There is evidence to suggest that they subsidized violent activities against the popular organizations in the 1970s and against the Junta Revolucionaria de Gobierno during the period 1979–82.[23] It is also apparent that many of the smaller fry, meaning entrepreneurs of more modest means who used to follow the guidance of the core sector, were the ones who stayed behind, unable to change their location, and who confronted the situation created by the economic policies of the JRG with vociferous criticism.

Second, in times of crises, precisely when it would be most useful to make finer distinctions between the oligarchic and the bourgeois factions, these have showed a tendency to act as one. In other words, the agricultural and the industrial factions, whatever the frictions and contradictions between them, have stood together. Therefore, the distinction between the core and the peripheral elements of the reactionary coalition—the latter including the more recent bourgeois groups in certain sectors of industry, transportation, and even in some subsectors of agriculture—becomes blurred just when it would matter the most.

This resulted not only from the control of the leading associations of the private sector by the agricultural faction but also from the ideological pressure they could exercise thanks to their advantageous economic position. According to Rubén Zamora, the Salvadoran bourgeoisie has been consistent in its opposition to any restriction or limitation on property.[24] The predominance of a laissez-faire conception of economic activity and class solidarity have overcome any desire for change and any hegemonic aspirations on the part of the bourgeois faction. That is why it has tagged along every time the agricultural faction has gone on the warpath against a government initiative. This happened in 1976, when President Molina tried to enact a modest program of agrarian reform but had to shelve it because of private-sector opposition. It also happened during the tenure of the Christian Democratic juntas of 1980–82.

It is very interesting to note the strong continuity of the dominant economic ideology within the Salvadoran private sector and its ability to resist change. The denunciations of the 1976 agrarian-transformation project by the Asociación Nacional de la Empresa Privada (ANEP) are strikingly similar in tone and tenor to the criticisms of the economic policies of the Christian Democrats in 1980–82, whether those criticisms came from the Alianza Productiva or from the Federación Nacional de la Pequeña Empresa de El Salvador (FENAPES). Even more remarkable is the continuity between these arguments and those utilized by the *cafetaleros* (coffee growers) against Ezeta in the 1890s and against the Araujos in 1911–13 and 1931. Whatever the changes in the modalities of the regime, in the identity of the cast of characters, or in the names of the sectoral associations, the paradigm remained the same.

The only occasions on which the agricultural and industrial factions parted company after 1932 were those involving the organization of political parties and the recruitment of presidential candidates to challenge the military. The agriculturalists were content to support the official candidate; when necessary, if aroused by the "reformist demagoguery" of a military president, they chose to support individuals and groups more attuned to the needs of the agrarian front—for example, Gen. José Alberto "Chele" Medrano's FUDI in 1972 and the former major Roberto D'Aubuisson's Alianza Republicana Nacionalista (ARENA) in 1982. The industrialists, by contrast, tried to organize parties and movements that could attract some petit-bourgeois and working-class support, but the latter found their own avenues of expression. Therefore, the Partido Acción Renovadora (PAR) in the late forties and fifties; the Partido Acción Nacional (PAN) in the fifties; the Partido Popular Salvadoreño (PPS) in the sixties; and, most recently, the Acción Democrática party (AD) remained interesting possibilities but were unable to attract much popular support or to form an alternative and more progressive coalition with anyone.

In essence, then, the core element of the reactionary coalition remained very stable during the period 1870–1979, even though it was displaced from its monopoly of the government in 1932. The coalition itself was reactionary because it was first and foremost, bent on the preservation not of economic freedom but of privilege. Since 1932 the coalition has been unwilling to check arbitrary rule or to replace it with a just and rational system, and it has opposed letting the general population participate in the conduct of government.[25]

The coalition is also reactionary because it has shown a willingness and ability to support and promote exceptional forms of the capitalist state in order to protect its economic privilege. This is not merely a question of whether the government should not bend too much in the direction of union demands, spend too much on welfare, link public policymaking to the electoral process, or try to push taxes beyond reasonable limits. The leaders of the reactionary coalition of El Salvador *do not believe in unions or in welfare economics or in suffrage.* Their basic premise is that government exists to protect the entrepreneur from undesirable and improper interference by other social actors, so that the reproduction and accumulation of capital can proceed without any restraints. They demand total deference to their vision of the capitalist system, and to promote this they have been willing to espouse a disloyal and antidemocratic conservatism for more than a century.

IV. THE ATTEMPT TO RESTORE REACTIONARY DESPOTISM IN EL SALVADOR

The agrarian crisis of 1976 reveals the degree to which the relation between the military and the oligarchy deteriorated during the seventies. On the one hand, the administration of President Arturo Molina was in power as a result of a blatant electoral fraud perpetrated against an opposition coalition of Christian and Social Democrats and Communists in 1972. The military needed some kind of program or accomplishment that they could wield in trying to gain some badly needed legitimacy. More specifically, they wanted to offer some benefits to the basic constituency of the

Partido de Conciliación Nacional (Party of National Conciliation, PCN) among the more traditional segments of the peasantry. On the other hand, the increasing mobilization and radicalism of some sectors of the popular classes were a source of mounting concern to the military, some of whose members felt that repression alone could not keep the situation under control.

In 1975 Molina created the Instituto Salvadoreño de Transformación Agraria (ISTA). The U.S. Agency for International Development (AID) pledged a substantial sum of money to compensate landowners affected by a pilot program of agrarian reform. A new peasant union, the Unión Comunal Salvadoreña (UCS) was organized with the assistance of the American Institute for Free Labor Development (AIFLD). On 29 June 1976, Law Decree No. 31 created the First Project of Agrarian Transformation. Shortly thereafter, between 70,000 and 100,000 peasants were trucked into San Salvador to participate in a government-sponsored rally supporting the project. Details of the project were explained to public employees and military officers during July. In short, it is obvious that the government prepared the ground and that it anticipated strong opposition from the oligarchy.

Despite all this careful planning on the part of the Molina administration, the oligarchy was able to rally the support of the most important organizations of the private sector, mounting a vociferous campaign and defeating the measure. By October 1976 the government had lost the initiative and the will to continue the fight, and the project was shelved. This was a defeat for the military institution and not merely a personal setback for Molina. To be sure, Molina became the scapegoat and was unable to govern during the rest of his term. He could not even select his own successor.

If Molina had been acting alone, his neutralization would have sufficed and the matter would have ended there. However, this was not true, because the agrarian front not only created its own separate organizations, beginning shortly before the onset of the crisis, but also managed to create closer links with conservative military officers and to attempt an outright restoration of the reactionary coalition in office. The ISTA crisis and the march of the Salvadoran political process at the time suggested to the elements of the reactionary coalition that the pact of 1950 could no longer be maintained and that anything short of a *direct* control of the government would be insufficient to protect thier interests.

The coming to office of Carlos Humberto Romero, the most conservative military president since 1944, indicates that the oligarchy did indeed manage to restore itself to power in 1977.

Two interpretations are possible here, and they follow from the two extant views of the relation between the oligarchy and the military. Those who perceive the military as the errand boys of the oligarchy interpreted the ISTA episode and the imposition of Romero as one more instance in which the masters had to discipline the servants. Those who believe that the relation was more symmetrical saw the episode in a different light.

On the surface it would appear that the first interpretation is the more adequate. After all, despite the careful planning, the AID and AIFLD support, the fact that the lands involved were for the most part in the public domain, and the government's mobilization of the peasantry, the oligarchy was easily able to prevail. However, this interpretation would fall short in explaining how and why the oligarchy was able to beat back the very modest challenge posed by ISTA, and unable to prevent measures aimed directly at the core of the reactionary coalition three years later in 1979.

It is possible to argue that, after the Nicaraguan revolution, the United States was more adamant about the need for reform in El Salvador—that, therefore, U.S. insistence made the difference in 1979–80.

Elsewhere, in analyzing the degree to which the Salvadoran military experiment inaugurated in 1948 produced a workable copy of the Mexican model of one-party domination, this writer concluded that the Salvadoran copy had fallen short because it failed (1) to create a true political party controlled by a *civilian* bureaucracy, (2) to impose civilian supremacy on the military, (3) to break up the alliance between the oligarchy and the bourgeoisie and to create the historical project that would make the latter hegemonic, and (4) to displace laissez faire as the dominant ideology.[26]

In 1976 the reformist wing of the Salvadoran military stood helplessly alone. To be sure, some progressive mavericks like Enrique Alvarez and a group of technocrats were on the side of the government, but Molina had burned his bridges to the petite bourgeoisie and labor. The country was in the middle of an increasing campaign of civil unrest and terrorism, which hardliners exploited to argue that counterinsurgency, and not reform, was the first priority. Moreover, despite the AID support, the Ford administration was not every concerned about El Salvador.

In essence, therefore, the agrarian initiative failed because of the *structural* difficulties of the model of repressive reformism that the military had tried to use to constrain reactionary despotism in El Salvador. The reformers were isolated from society, they lacked a truly hegemonic party, and, though they could play around with reformist rhetoric, they could not challenge the dominant ideological paradigm. However, this failed attempt lit a fuse and provoked a reaction of the opposite kind.

Unlike any of the governments inaugurated since 1948, the Romero government dropped any pretense of reformism and simply set up a very thorough repression. The conflict with the church and with the popular organizations escalated, and the right-wing paramilitary organizations were given a free hand. In November 1977 Romero enacted a draconian public-order law, which aimed to legalize the repressive policies of the government. The law had the support of the majority of the private-sector organizations that had been clamoring for a clampdown. Under Romero the number of political assassinations, of disappeared persons, and of prosecutions for political offenses increased dramatically, compared with similar data for the Molina period. Although these increases pale by comparison with post-1980 levels they seemed alarming at the time and brought the Romero administration the dubious distinction of being considered "one of the world's worst violators of human rights."

There can be little doubt that, in fact and form, the Romero period brought, if not the actual presence, at least the program of the reactionary coalition to the policies of the government during the years 1977–79. That presence was still detectable in the very contradictory government organized following the coup of 15 October 1979, which deposed Romero. Many have argued that after this government fell apart, primarily because of the continued onslaught against the popular organizations and because of the military's unwillingness to accept a complete subordination to the government, the situation reverted to "business as usual," but this assessment ignores a very important aspect of the policies of the Gobierno Provisional Revolucionario.

During the first junta, in the fall of 1979, Decree No. 75 nationalized the export trade, and all land titles were frozen. Following the exit of the Social Democrats from the government, and the covenant between the Christian Democrats and the military, the Junta Revolucionaria de Gobierno enacted Decree No. 153, affecting the largest agricultural enterprises, and Decree No. 158, nationalizing the banking industry. In other words, during late 1979 and early 1980, the highly unstable coalition of military reformers and moderate democratic parties was able to enact policies aimed directly at the "magic square of oligarchic domination." When this is put side by side with 35,000 deaths, the uprooting of one-tenth of the population from their homes, and a devastating civil war, the tendency is to belittle the significance of that fact. After all, how could anyone pretend that these new heights of "repressive reformism" were to be commended? However, despite these "mixed results," the fact remains that the economic bases of the "magic square" were broken by these policies. The problem was that this significant development was not accompanied by a dissolution of the authoritarian regime. And this was the case not because the military continued to serve the oligarchy, most of which had left the country, but because its use of violence was based on anti-Communism—on the need, to put it in the words of the defense minister José Guillermo García, to manage what the military interpreted as a "black conflict."

There is little need to recount the efforts and activities of the "disloyal Right" to derail the Salvadoran process of transition.[27] The question is, If nothing of real substance had taken place, why would the disloyal Right and the Salvadoran private sector have conducted a determined and bitter campaign against the policies of the PRG? Why would the more reactionary element of the private sector—which in 1980–81 stood behind the Frente Amplio Nacional and the subversive efforts of Roberto D'Aubuisson— have made strenuous efforts to unseat the Christian Democrats?

Why would the ANEP, the Alianza Productiva (organized in 1980), the industrialists' association (ASI), and the rest of the organizations of the private sector have remained on the warpath since January 1980? Why would the attempts by the United States to reconcile the private sector and the Christian Democrats have failed so thoroughly despite American prepotence?

But let us not confuse the actions of a dependent bourgeoisie and of reactionary conservatives against the reforms with the actions of those who had been hit more severely by such reforms. Most of the leaders of the reactionary coalition were not in El Salvador during 1980 and 1981, and the fact that others picked up where they left off attests to the resilience of a dominant ideology, not to the everlasting presence of those who have the most to benefit from it. The reality that it was the "small fry" and those sectors not yet affected by any reform who mounted what was essentially a defense of privilege is grounded on historical experience. In addition, reactionary elements who had not been in the core of the coalition before could now entertain hegemonic aspirations of their own. Finally, as was true in the ISTA crisis of 1976, those in the private sector who criticized the reforms were careful not to make direct allusions to the military institution, which they now praised for its heroic battle against communism.

These dynamics are not what one would find if this had been a continued defense of oligarchic privilege by the military; they are the ultimate result of the many contradictions expressing themselves simultaneously in the context of an ongoing civil war. This situation poses a classical *coyuntura*. However, the rupture of the historical pact between the oligarchy and the military has not been accompanied by a rupture of the authoritarian regime, nor has it produced a realignment of the bourgeoisie.

In its most recent attempt to regain control of the government, made possible by the outcome of the election of 1982, the reactionary coalition has launched a concerted drive, on the one hand, to reorganize its core element and, on the other, to undo the measures that struck the pillars of the system of economic privilege. These concerns figure very prominently in the campaign of the ARENA and were put on the table the minute the constituent assembly and the new provisional government got down to business. Decree No.

207 (Land to the Tiller) was suspended. The next targets are the nationalized banks and the foreign trade. This is another test of strength in a process that has failed to resolve the most important issue that must be dealt with to bring about a democratic outcome, namely, the restoration of the rule of law. Incidentally, this seemed to be the most generalized and intense motive expressed by Salvadorans at the time of the elections of 28 March 1982. This means not that they are against the reforms but simply that their first priority is to be secure in their persons.

V. PROSPECTS

According to Giner, reactionary despotism gave way to pluralism in southern Europe because of the exhaustion of traditional patterns of legitimation and because of the economic transformation that altered the nature of the society.[28] In El Salvador the traditional ideological schemes are represented by the laissez-faire liberalism of the economic elite and by the values of deference, religiosity, and hard work preached constantly to the popular sectors. In an ideological sense, the core actors of the reactionary coalition still have a tight grip, but there are "aspirants to the throne." Their ideological dominance has been eroded by a new social stance on the part of the Catholic Church, by the PRG's use of a different set of symbols and values to legitimize the reform measures, and by the realities of the civil war. To be sure, values are among the most resilient and difficult elements to change, but the dike has burst and the underlying normative structure has changed.

The most relevant of the economic changes experienced since 1979 have to do with the massive flight of capital, the lack of investment, and the depressed situation of export prices. These have done more to change the economy than have the economic sabotage of the guerrillas, the destruction brought about by the war, and the short-term impact of the economic reforms. The absence of oligarchic capital poses a dilemma because it creates a vacuum that must be filled by the government, by a new set of (oligarchic) actors, by the bourgeoisie, or by the military. Given the uncertainty in the Salvadoran process, it is not very likely that the capital that left the country will reappear anytime soon, at least not as massively and as suddenly as it left. With industry and agricultural functioning at about half of their capacity and with the structure of profits in dire straits, it is difficult to see where the investment capital will come from, especially given the credit squeeze of the early eighties. Ironically, the behavior of the oligarchs now living in exile may undermine the attempt to restore reactionary despotism. These exiles may demand a set of conditions that even Roberto D'Aubuisson may be unable to deliver. Anything short of a complete routing of the "Left," which in their view includes the Christian Democrats, and anything short of a complete reversal of all the reforms, which will incur the wrath of the U.S. Congress, will make them keep their money abroad. In addition, what has become a wartime economy gives individual military officers generous opportunities for personal enrichment, and the ongoing rift with their former associates may induce them to engage in the direct appropriation of public resources to increase their own financial independence.

It is always problematic to try to be specific and to identify major social actors in a fluid situation, not to mention a civil war. In addition, the Salvadoran private sector continues to behave as one actor. The major private-sector associations—including ANEP, AP, ASI, the chamber of commerce, and the sectoral associations representing growers and cattlemen—were hard at work in 1982 trying to restore reactionary despotism. They perceive the ARENA and the figure of Roberto D'Aubuisson as the ideal vehicles for that restoration. Analytical efforts to determine whether and how the core sector of the reactionary coalition is being remade will have to focus on the ARENA and its relations with the PPS and the PCN. The PPS is dominated by figures associated with the Romero administration, who were always perceived as the more conservative among the industrialists. By contrast, the former official party, the PCN, continues to get its clues from the military and may be a less reliable ally to the ARENA. The AD does not seem to travel in the same undemocratic orbit as these and could drift closer to the PDC.

This is hardly the place for a psychobiographical analysis of Roberto D'Aubuisson, who shares with the military and with

Salvadoran conservatives a visceral and, in his case, fanatical anti-communism. D'Aubuisson's authoritarian populist tendencies could be instrumental in forging a new type of conservative or even reactionary coalition but one in which the role of the state would be redefined to replace the loss of the traditional core actors. He would have to battle the Christian Democrats and confront them head on, because although their constituencies are poles apart ideologically, they are very similar in social composition. Both seem to be battling for the support of the petite bourgeoisie and of sectors of the peasantry opposed to the guerrillas. The PDC has a more ample base, however, for it includes a segment of labor and of the marginal classes of the larger urban areas. If D'Aubuisson prevails, the result could be a regime very similar to fascism; if the PDC overcomes the very adverse present situation, a more tolerable outcome could ensue. However, in either case, a new pact with or redefinition of the role of the military would have to accompany this.

Two final observations seem particularly appropriate. First, the election of 1982 left intact a situation in which a number of actors have the ability to curtail the actions of others but lack the power to become hegemonic. The Christian Democrats won the election but lost control of the government. The United States and the military got the safe and genuine election they wanted, but they also got a government dominated by a group set on a collision course with the U.S. Congress and American public opinion. The reactionary conservatives who financed ARENA put their man in office, but his initiatives are being kept under scrutiny by the military and by the United States for fear that he may upset a very delicate balance. Finally, the guerrillas and the FDR could neither stop nor discredit the election, but its outcome kept them afloat.

Second, despite this multiple-player game, the process of transition in El Salvador has returned to the fore the old questions about the military and the oligarchy or, better, the issues of civilian supremacy and the reform of the economic model. The long-term, sociohistorical view that opened this discussion suggests that reactionary despotism is a consequence of a social situation in which a weak bourgeoisie, unable to become hegemonic and forced to be the junior partner of a traditional oligarchy, cannot create the historical project that has characterized the development of democratic capitalism. Although the transition process has thus far failed to sever these links in the Salvadoran case, the behavior of this one actor (the bourgeoisie) may determine the future course of that country to a far greater extent than the behavior of any other single actor. If precedent prevails, the bourgeoisie will continue to parrot the old lines of the oligarchy and to make common cause with it to find security through the restoration of privilege. The traditional core of the reactionary coalition may not be reconstituted, and the bourgeoisie may find itself in a new alliance with the state bureaucracy. It is also possible that it will split and that at least a substantial segment will gravitate toward collaboration with the democratic actors. The question, therefore, is not whether the Salvadoran state will change but what the direction of the change will be.

NOTES

1. Salvador Giner, "Political Economy and Cultural Legitimation in the Origins of Parliamentary Democracy: The Southern European Case" (Paper presented at the roundtable The Transition from Authoritarianism to Democracy in Southern Europe and in Latin America, Madrid, 19–22 December 1979), 19, 22, 24, 25.

2. Barrington Moore, *Social Origins of Dictatorship and Democracy* (Boston: Beacon Press, 1968), 434, 441.

3. Ibid., 424, 437–38.

4. Giner, "Political Economy," 8–12.

5. Ibid., 10–12.

6. Thomas L. Karnes, *The Failure of Union: Central America, 1824–1960* (Chapel Hill: University of North Carolina Press, 1961); Ch. D. Kepner, Jr., and J.H. Soothill, *El imperio del banano* (Buenos Aires: Triángulo, 1957); William Krehm, *Democracia y tiranías en el Caribe* (Buenos Aires: Parnaso, 1957); Franklin D. Parker, *The Central American Republics* (London: Royal Institute of International Affairs, 1964); Mario Rodríguez, *Central America* (Englewood Cliffs, N.J.: Prentice-Hall, 1965); Edelberto Torres-Rivas, *Interpretación del desarrollo social centroamericano* (San José, Costa Rica: EDUCA, 1971); and Ralph Lee Woodward, Jr., *Central America: A Nation Divided* (New York: Oxford University Press, 1976).

7. By *state* I mean the formula of political domination utilized to invest an incumbent government with public power and to legitimize the utilization of that power to regulate social and economic relations.

8. By *regime* I mean the mode of government—that is, the manner in which public officials relate to the citizenry, including how they gain incumbency, formulate and implement public policy, and deal with political opponents.

9. By *government* I mean the network of public officials who are identified with the chief executive, who participate in the policymaking process as members of that network, and whose tenure in office depends on the tenure of that chief executive and/or on his ability to govern effectively.

10. For more details, see Knut Walter, "Trade and Development in an Export Economy: The Case of El Salvador, 1870–1914" (M.A. thesis, University of North Carolina at Chapel Hill, 1977).

11. John C. Chasteen, "President of a Coffee Kingdom: El Salvador's Manuel Enrique Araujo, 1911–1913" (Unpublished MS, Chapel Hill, 1981), 31–36.

12. Thomas P. Anderson, *Matanza: El Salvador's Communist Revolt of 1932* (Lincoln: University of Nebraska Press, 1971); and Alejandro Marroquín, "Estudio sobre la crisis de los años treinta en El Salvador," *Anuario de Estudios Centro Americanos* 3 (1977): 115–60.

13. Stephen Webre, *José Napoleón Duarte and the Christian Democratic Party in Salvadoran Politics, 1960–1972* (Baton Rouge: Louisiana State University Press, 1979), 10.

14. Rafael Guidos Véjar, "La crisis política en El Salvador, 1976–1979," *Estudios Centro Americanos* 34 (1979): 514–16.

15. Enrique A. Baloyra, *El Salvador in Transition* (Chapel Hill: University of North Carolina Press, 1982), chap. 4.

16. Ibid., chap. 3.

17. "Catastrophic balance" refers to a situation in which no one actor is hegemonic and in which two or more actors have sufficient influence to veto or neutralize the initiatives of the rest, but lack enough power to impose themselves or their political projects on the rest.

18. Robert T. Aubey, "Entrepreneurial Formation in El Salvador," *Explorations in Entrepreneurial History*, 2d ser., 6 (1968–69): 270–71, 275–76.

19. Guidos Véjar, "Crisis política," 512–13.

20. Italo López Vallecillos, "Fuerzas sociales y cambio social en El Salvador," *Estudios Centro Americanos* 34 (1979): 558.

21. Luis de Sebastián, "El camino económico hacia la democracia," *Estudios Centro Americanos* 34 (1979): 950–51.

22. Aubey, "Entrepreneurial Formation," 272–76; and Eduardo Colindres, "La tenencia de la tierra en El Salvador," *Estudios Centro Americanos* 31 (1976): 471.

23. Evidence introduced by the former U.S. ambassador to El Salvador, Mr. Robert White, during a hearing of the Senate Foreign Relations Committee, established the support that wealthy Salvadorans living in Miami and in Guatemala City gave to the conspiratorial activities of Roberto D'Aubuisson in the spring of 1980. Senate Committee on Foreign Relations, *The Situation in El Salvador: Hearings*, 97th Cong., 1st sess., 1981, 116–59.

24. Rubén Zamora, "¿Seguro de vida o despojo? Análisis político de la transformación agraria," *Estudios Centro Americanos* 31 (1976): 512.
25. Moore, *Social Origins,* 414.
26. Baloyra, *El Salvador,* chap. 2.
27. Ibid., chaps. 6 and 7, for more details.
28. Giner, "Political Economy," 31.

Revolution and Crisis in Nicaragua

Richard Fagen

POWER AND HEGEMONY

Who rules Nicaragua? A legalist would say that executive power resides in the Junta de Gobierno, operating through a standard array of ministries; legislative power resides in the Consejo de Estado, or Council of State, inaugurated on 4 May 1980, after a long-drawn-out controversy over its composition; and judicial power is lodged in the Supreme Court and lesser magistrates—except for special tribunals established to try ex-members of the National Guard.

This formalistic overview of the structure of government in Nicaragua would not include a separate box for or perhaps even mention the Sandinista National Liberation Front. Yet the answer to the question "Who rules Nicaragua?" is the FSLN. The FSLN named the Junta de Gobierno, FSLN commanders hold several of the most important ministerial positions, and all other ministers and high officials were selected by the FSLN. The Frente decided on the composition of the Council of State (in which it has a clear majority); the armed forces (Ejército Popular Sandinista), the police, and state security are all down-the-line Sandinist organizations; and no major decision—either domestic or international—would be taken without prior approval by the national directorate of the FSLN.

The hegemonic role exercised by the FSLN does not mean, however, that what the Frente wants the Frente gets. To the contrary, a great deal of political bargaining takes place in Nicaragua. Policy options are constrained, both by domestic and by international factors. Hegemony is not the same as control; if economic realities and social forces were not so complex, for example, it certainly would not have taken the Frente months of pulling and hauling to constitute the Council of State. Nor does hegemony imply that the FSLN is actually able to govern in a direct, day-to-day manner. Not only is the new state necessarily staffed by many persons who by no means fully agree with official policies, but even with the best of will the multitude of projects under way outruns the technical and fiscal capacity of the state to respond. There is thus a sharp, double constraint on making Frente-designed policies come to life.

Moreover, the policies themselves contain substantial tensions and even contradictions. In a coffee-growing area north of Managua, I witnessed sharp confrontations between peasants and landowners in the streets of the provincial capital. Peasants (not paid during much of the insurrection) were demanding back wages and better working and living conditions. They were counseled by organizers from the ATC, the Sandinista-led association of peasants and rural workers. The confrontations were being adjudicated by employees of the Ministry of Labor.

I asked a young Sandinista cadre how the Frente felt such disputes should be settled. He answered that the most important overall goal was to maintain agricultural production, that the situation on each *finca* (farm) was different, that the Frente did not have nearly enough cadres to investigate individual cases, that the ATC would do a good job of representing the workers' interests, and that the final word would have to rest with the Ministry of Labor—many of whose provincial employees had served under Somoza as well. Such are some of the problems of turning hegemony into coherently implemented policies at the grass roots.

Throughout the period prior to the August 1978 assault on the National Palace, the FSLN was still not a mass organization. Although it had acquired sympathizers among high school and university youth and more radicalized sectors of the middle class, it did not command the loyalty of most of the huge number of Nicaraguans who opposed Somoza.

With the mass uprisings of September 1978, this situation changed. The uprisings, sparked by the FSLN, were truly insurrectional in the sense that thousands of citizens grabbed whatever weapon was at hand, built barricades, and launched themselves against the guard. In many instances the major role of the thinly stretched regular FSLN combatants was simply to try to instill some order and coherence in what was a spontaneous overflowing of hostility toward Somoza and the guard.

Somewhat chastened by this experience, the FSLN worked diligently during the fall and winter of 1978–79 to prepare the citizenry for the next round of insurrectional activity. The response to the Frente's call was so massive, so *popular,* that the thousands of *milicianos* with their red and black kerchiefs and assorted pistols, shotguns, rifles, Molotov cocktails, and contact bombs were never fully organized by Frente cadres or always led by known Sandinistas. In fact, in the hour of victory, anyone who had built a barricade, thrown a bomb, fired a gun, carried a message, or cared for the wounded had earned the right—at least temporarily—to call himself or herself a Sandinista.

In July 1979 the leadership of the Frente was faced with several problems deriving from this multifold expansion of the rank and file. Most urgent was the task of putting order into the armed forces. Common criminals released by Somoza just before he fled had grabbed weapons and uniforms and were posing as combatants. Honest but untutored *muchachos* who had actually earned the right to bear arms began to give the FSLN a bad name, seizing houses and automobiles, getting drunk, firing weapons indiscriminately.

Of more lasting importance was the task of deciding how to organize the FSLN for the purpose of governing Nicaragua rather than overthrowing the dynasty. The organizational issue embodies a prior question: What should be the role of the FSLN in post-Somoza Nicaragua? The Frente has a one-line answer: *El FSLN es la organización de vanguardia del pueblo nicaragüense.* The definition of the Frente as a vanguard in turn implies a double imperative. First, it implies a continuing dominant place for the FSLN in Nicaraguan politics. It is a claim that FSLN hegemony, in the sense previously mentioned, ought to be a structural, not just a temporary, feature of the political economy of the nation. Second, it implies that membership in the FSLN must be strictly controlled. Not everyone can belong, no matter how heroic he or she might have been during the final insurrection.

Although not at present formally constituted as a political party, the FSLN is moving in that direction. A membership structure with three levels is envisaged: militant, premilitant, and affiliated member. Local committees (Comités de Base Sandinistas) will link the party with the masses, and existing mass organizations like the CDS (Sandinista Defense Committees) and the Central Sandinista de Trabajadores (labor confederations) will then be oriented more directly by the party as well.

IDEOLOGY AND LEGITIMACY

The objective reality of Nicaragua substantiates and reinforces the claims of the FSLN to vanguard status and thus to a special place in the political life of the nation. On the other hand, the dominant ideological umbrella under which much of the struggle against Somoza was waged locates the operational definition of legitimacy in an electoral process in which all come equally to contend in the "free" political marketplace. Both visions can agree on the importance of basic human rights and certain developmental goals. Both could also agree that in a transitional period after Somoza an extraordinary role would have to be taken by the group that spearheaded the dictator's downfall—the FSLN. But their longer-term understandings of the proper nature and organization of the state are in fundamental conflict.

This conflict reflects economic interests, long-standing political divisions, and international actors and forces. At least during 1979 and until late 1980, however, it was being played out largely at the ideological level. This in no way diminishes its seriousness. To the contrary, since what is at stake is nothing less than the future format of the Nicaraguan political economy, the battle is deadly serious. The ideological conflict is a sometimes murky cover through which the social forces bubbling just below the surface can be viewed. The pot has boiled over in the past, and it will undoubtedly do so again.

Interestingly, among the major open clashes of 1979 and early 1980 was a series of confrontations with the "left" opposition to the FSLN, groups which felt that the Frente was not fulfilling its class *compromiso* with the popular sectors—in wages, worker control, and the like. Because the challenge to Frente hegemony was serious, the possible economic costs important, and *mano dura* easier to use against the ultra-Left than against the private sector, the crackdown was swift and evidently effective. Dozens of persons were jailed, and a sharp ideological campaign against the "ultras" was launched.

That voices such as the MDN (Nicaraguan Democratic Movement, headed by the industrialist Alfonso Robelo) and the PSC (Social Christian party) could speak unhindered in Nicaragua in 1980 indicates the high degree of political freedom that existed. Equally impressive and perhaps more revealing of the "tone" of politics in Nicaragua in the first year and half of the revolution was the manner in which ordinary citizens were voicing complaints and participating in the pull and haul of reconstruction. In union halls, workplaces, and neighborhoods and on street corners, Nicaraguans were for the first time in their history speaking out in large numbers. As one very highly placed but non-Sandinista member of the government said to me, "There is more freedom in Nicaragua today than at any time in the last forty-six years."

ECONOMICS IN COMMAND

The politics of austerity that characterizes the Sandinista economic recovery program takes different forms. For example, in a situation characterized by severe shortages of basic goods, high unemployment, and 60 percent inflation, the official goal in 1980 was to limit salary increases to rises in the cost of living, thus keeping real wages constant. In some cases, the actual increases granted did not even meet this goal. Yet there seems to be a widespread understanding and acceptance of the Sandinista slogan "La revolución no es piñata" ("The revolution isn't a bag of goodies").

No one but a *Comandante de la Revolución* could tell the workers that "pressures to raise wages [above the rate of inflation] are pressures directly against the *Plan*," and then continue by saying, "Brother workers and peasants, it will be necessary for you to make adequate use of what salary you have this year, meeting your family responsibilities and not spending your money on unnecessary things. Begging your pardon, but you will have to get drunk less and dedicate more of your salary to your family."

In mid-1979 there were stories to the effect that Somoza's

confiscated properties would amount to as much as 50 percent of all the productive facilities of the nation. Although the holdings of the dynasty were impressive—and thus the newly formed Area of People's Property very significant—when an interim inventory became available, it was disclosed that the majority of productive facilities were still in private hands, particularly in certain key sectors of the economy. In the critical agrarian sector (the main earner of foreign exchange), 80 percent of the production remains in private hands. In manufacturing, the corresponding figure is 75 percent. Only in mining and construction does the balance tip in favor of the state, with 95 percent of the productive facilities of the former and 55 percent of the latter in public hands. Overall, it is estimated that 59 percent of the nation's total gross domestic product will be produced by the private sector and 41 percent by the state in 1980. That the state achieves even this level of participation in production is due to the large and predominantly state-run service sector.

The implications of this superficial sketch of the pattern of ownership of productive facilities in post-Somoza Nicaragua are obvious: without the cooperation of the private sector, even the modest targets of the plan of economic reactivation cannot be met. Take a crucial crop like cotton, for example. The 1980 plan set a planting target of approximately 170,000 *manzanas* (a *manzana* is about one-half acre). Of this total, only about 21,000 *manzanas,* or 12 percent, were to be the responsibility of the INRA, the national agrarian-reform agency. The rest remained in the hands of more than 5,000 private producers, most of them owning fewer than 50 *manzanas* each. The INRA made emergency plans for moving onto the majority of these farms to plant cotton if the owners refused to do so. But the agency also offered a package of incentives to get these farmers to plant. They did. The package of state-delivered credit, agricultural inputs, and price guarantees motivated the farmers to produce. With appropriate modifications, similar incentive packages have been given to other sectors of private enterprise.

A special kind of mixed economy has thus developed in Nicaragua in the aftermath of Somoza's overthrow. The state controls the financial system, has important participation in other key sectors, and uses its significant instruments of pricing and credit to structure the operation of various markets. But the rules of the game are still capitalist rules—as the FSLN acknowledges—and when hard choices have to be made between production and other goals, those choices are almost always made in favor of production.

If local capitalists decide not to participate in productive activities in Nicaragua today, they are making a political decision. The government has not made it difficult for them to operate profitably. To the contrary, official policies are designed to keep the margin of profitability large enough that decisions not to participate will be clearly seen to be class-based, politically motivated attempts to weaken the Sandinista state.

The FSLN has charged the Government of National Reconstruction to accomplish the fundamental national task: economic recovery. Thus "making the economy work"—with all the compromises implied therein—takes precedence over political and social goals that are closer to the hearts and central to the longer-run program of the men and women who fought so long in the name of Sandino and *el pueblo* to overthrow the dictatorship. This contradiction produces tension and often ambiguous situations in which the intent of public policies is not always clear.

THE CLASS QUESTION

Within weeks after the victory, it was clear that the particular constellation of groups and organizations that came together in the anti-Somoza coalition and that were thus to "share legislative functions with the Junta" did not reflect the realities of revolutionary Nicaragua. Most glaring was the omission of any mention of or representation for mass organizations—of women, youth, workers, peasants, indigenous peoples, and neighborhood committees (Sandinista Defense Committees or CDSs). But to include mass organizations, essentially created and organized by the FSLN, was to pose a double threat to those who opposed the hegemonic role of the Frente: first, it tipped the balance of the council in favor of the FSLN and gave additional institutional legitimation to the notion of the FSLN as vanguard; second, it added a host of new voices speaking for the *clases populares* in a forum that might otherwise have overrepresented the bourgeois opposition to Somoza.

The composition of the Council of State became an issue which embraced the key question: In whose interest should Nicaragua be ruled? The FSLN provided for ample representation of the mass organizations on the forty-seven-seat council. The FSLN's class position was made clear. Robelo's Nicaraguan Democratic Movement, the Social Christian party, and the Conservative Democratic party all initially responded by refusing to take the seats allotted to them. COSEP, the Higher Council of Private Enterprise, allotted five seats, debated for a week, and then finally decided to participate.

For six months the uneasy truce remained in force. Then, early in November 1980, after the government had banned a political meeting of Robelo's MDN and some Sandinista youths had stoned the MDN's headquarters in Managua, eleven members of the council walked out. Among them were all the representatives of COSEP as well as the representatives of the MDN, other opposition political parties, and non-Sandinista trade unions.

The position taken by COSEP vis-à-vis the council does not mean, however, that there is an implacable and unrelenting tension between private enterprise in general, on the one hand, and the Sandinista state representing the *clases populares,* on the other. To the contrary, the class question in Nicaragua today involves the struggle for the hearts, minds, and energies of those tens of thousands of small and medium-sized capitalists, both urban and rural, who are essential to the politics and economics of reactivation and national unity. This is well understood by both those who oppose and those who support the programs of the FSLN and the junta. Thus, under the banner of the "sacred" defense of private property, some seek to band together persons as disparate as the owners of huge agrarian estates and neighborhood shoe-repair stalls. Meanwhile, Sandinista state policies take cognizance of the importance of both the economic necessities and the values of small and not-so-small capitalists and the diffuse "middle class" to which some belong and with which many others identify.

An example illustrates the detail to which such policies go. Prior to Mother's Day, 1980, a discussion was held in the Ministry of Planning with regard to the norms that should govern the importation of the traditional (middle-class) Mother's Day gifts of candy and other luxuries. In foreign-exchange-poor Nicaragua, all such discussions imply important trade-offs: Candy for middle-class mothers or rice for peasant children? Because of the political sensitivity of the issue, it was decided to allow for the import of modest amounts of Mother's Day luxuries. Thus does the class question percolate into multiple layers of society and bureaucracy.

The other key aspect of the class question is located in the relationship of the *clases populares* to the Sandinist state. The FSLN says that the new Nicaragua will be ruled in favor of the *clases populares.* But the contradictions that arise from the dual needs of austerity and benefits for the masses also complicate the relation between long-run goals and short-run exigencies. The pressure to redistribute is very strong; worker grievances are real and poignant. "We haven't had a vacation in three hundred years," said one leader of the Association of Rural Workers. The temptation to take that vacation is great.

Furthermore, the *clases populares,* like the capitalists, are not a homogeneous and unified group. While organized workers are doing relatively well, the unemployed are not. The government's public-works programs have not been able to employ more than a minority of those without jobs. The more marginal urban youth who fought so heroically during the insurrection have also caused special problems. Ironically, these urban *muchachos* formed the backbone of the FSLN-led militias. Thousands were killed and wounded. But they were marginal to the Nicaraguan economy before the insurrection, and they are not central to the reactivation process either. Those who have found a place in the new Sandinista Popular Army or the police are among the most fortunate. Others have found pick-and-shovel work, usually temporary, in the physical reconstruction of the country. But many more remain on the streets. Their incorporation into a new Nicaragua will have to await future structural transformations of the society and the economy.

TOWARD SOCIALISM

Nicaragua is not socialist. The 1980 plan was designed to revitalize capitalism and to set up an important sector of state ownership and state production. But many Nicaraguans understand that they have been given a historic opportunity to construct a socialist system that is not a Central American imitation of what has been attempted in Cuba, Eastern Europe, or elsewhere. What happens in Nicaragua will, of course, depend not only on decisions taken there but on events and decisions in a host of other countries and institutions as well. But at a minimum there are four broad tensions that will have to be dealt with in the course of socialist construction in Nicaragua.

Centralization and Decentralization

A planned economy requires a significant degree of centralization. To combine this centralization with institutions that allow for local initiative, decisional autonomy, and participation has been the most difficult task facing those who believe in socialism with a human rather than a bureaucratic face. In war-damaged Nicaragua, there exists a powerful pull toward the centralization of decision making. The arguments are familiar—and compelling —"a firm hand at the helm as we sail through stormy seas"; a necessary period of tutelage while the masses learn the skills and discipline needed to participate more fully in the management of their lives and labors. But even were Nicaragua not war-damaged, the pull toward centralized decision making would be very strong. With its population of 2.5 million, relatively homogeneous culture (with the exception of the extensive but thinly populated Atlantic coast), and uncomplicated economy, Nicaragua does not seem to offer insurmountable problems to those who advocate strong centralized control.

There are, however, tendencies that pull in the opposite direction. The massive, only partially coordinated participatory experience of the insurrection strengthens the pressures toward decentralization. In addition, the shortage of trained cadres and bureaucrats—and the presence of holdovers from Somoza's time in the public sector—suggest that not all decisions should be taken nor all activities administered at the center.

However, basic tensions still exist: mass organizations are charged both with implementing state policies and with representing the interests of their constituents to the state. Thinly staffed national ministries attempt to administer programs that are beyond their human and material resources; yet devolving some of these responsibilities to the citizenry is certainly not a solution that springs automatically to the bureaucratic mind. Leaders schooled for years in military discipline turn easily to command models to solve obdurate developmental problems, while at the same time appreciating the importance of mass action without necessarily knowing how or to what degree it should be encouraged in the new Nicaragua.

Consensus and Dissent

No complex system ever has worked or ever can work on the basis of full consensus. In modern societies conflicts of interest and differences of opinion are inevitable; even in a well-functioning socialist system, conflicts would have to be adjudicated, some voices given priority over others, and hard decisions on the allocation of scarce resources made. There will be dissent, openly expressed if the costs to the dissenters are not too high, or expressed in other ways if mechanisms of social control operate "effectively." The key question is not how much dissent will be "allowed" but what forms and channels of dissent are most compatible with the construction of a working consensus supportive of a new political-economic order.

The international discussion (which does have ramifications within Nicaragua) pivots institutionally, but not in class terms, on the legitimacy of classic liberal and bourgeois notions of elections and the freedom of the press. The fascinating thing about that ideological battle is that elections and a rich political discussion in the mass media are not antagonistic to the Sandinista revolution. But the Sandinistas are constantly backed against the wall and sometimes made to appear antidemocratic by the opposition's use of particular abstract symbols, "democracy" and "freedom," which have very little historical reality in Nicaragua. Objectively and concretely, there is very clearly more political freedom, more political discussion, more personal liberty in Nicaragua today than at any other time in the last half century. Enemies of the revolution count on people's having short historical memories.

It is precisely in this tangled area of consensus and dissent that liberal and religious fears and critiques gain their most sympathetic audiences inside and outside of Nicaragua. Socialist practice to date has emphasized national unity as a prerequisite for development. This has meant the silencing of those voices that fall outside a centrally determined view of how society should be run. Many fear that when even tougher times come, when bedrock contradictions in the construction of socialism are reached, and when and if external and internal pressures of a clearly counterrevolutionary nature increase, the space for criticism that now exists will be among the first casualties.

An acute class struggle goes on, and it is very difficult to predict its direction. When I was in Nicaragua in February 1981 and talking to someone from the FSLN, he said, with a great deal of passion, "If the Reagan administration forces us to the wall, either directly or through their class surrogates who surround us, we will have no choice except to go on a war footing. And if we do, it's questionable whether we will be able to create the political and pluralist space which many of us hope this revolution will have."

Public and Private Property

While the incorporation of private enterprise into the process of reactivation of the economy does not mean that the private sector "commands," it does imply serious contradictions for the future. The more deeply entrenched and even legitimate a "patriotic" private enterprise becomes, the more difficult it will eventually be to gain control of its productive facilities without serious conflict. This is particularly true for the large enterprises whose owners have very substantial political and economic resources (both domestic and international) with which to oppose the socialization of the economy. Yet it is precisely these large enterprises that eventually must pass into collective ownership if the socialist promise is to be fulfilled. Many people inside Nicaragua, including people in the FSLN, hope that such is the case, but it is too early to tell. While there is a kind of conjunctural expediency on the part of many different groups, many persons within the FSLN genuinely believe it is necessary to construct new institutional frameworks for the practice of socialism. These will be both political and economic frameworks that will have a decentralized character and provide some kind of counterbalance to bureaucratic tendencies and allow substantial scope for autonomous bases of criticism. But that innovative socialist vision remains abstract and in the future.

None of this is news to Nicaraguans. To the contrary, as one official noted, the game being played in Nicaragua is chess, not poker. Everybody can see everyone else's hand. This means that the fragility of the alliance between the state and the private sector is evident. At the moment, neither the state nor the private sector is motivated to fracture the alliance permanently—although their reasons for restraint are different. But the game is dynamic, and certainly both the tactics and even some of the players will change (despite the chess metaphor, there are many players, not just two). It can be predicted with some certainty that the particular mix of public and private property that characterized Nicaragua at the beginning of the 1980s will not hold through much of the rest of the decade.

The Present and the Future

As I emphasized at the outset, each of the tensions that we have mentioned must be understood historically. The past conditions the present, and the present in turn shapes—but does not determine—the future. In addition, however, there is a basic present-future tension that is not captured by this historical perspective alone. Socialism, particularly developmental socialism, elevates the dialectic of present-future to the center of its political economy. If all works well, the 1980 plan will create the initial conditions for a surplus in 1981.* This surplus, in turn, will increasingly be

---

*A serious interruption in this sequence was caused by the disastrous floods of spring 1982. Furthermore, the diversion of national resources to militia activity, and other costs of defending against the U.S.-financed threat on the Honduran border, have been very harmful (ED.).

captured by the state and will be used quite otherwise than if it were to remain in private hands. Each successive cycle, it is hoped, will thus transfer more real control over production and distribution away from the private sector and into the public domain.

This long-run political-economic dynamic involves not only the relation of the state to private capital (particularly large capital) but also the relation of the state to the *clases populares.* Productivity increases in both industry and agriculture are essential if significant surpluses are to be generated. And this in turn means that hard work, discipline, and sacrifice are necessarily part and parcel of the development model. Economics-in-command and a policy of austerity are required, however, not just in conventional terms (the pie is not now big enough for everyone to have a larger piece) but also in terms of collective investment in the future. The construction of socialism requires that the postponement of current gratifications—and in some cases the postponement of necessities of life—be undertaken *consciously and collectively.* This shared understanding is at the core of the cultural transformation without which the promises of structural transformations dissolve into bureaucratic and inegalitarian forms. It also implies a promise to the *clases populares* that the surplus generated by the sweat of their brows will, in fact, be used in their interests.

But to emphasize this domain of socialist construction is not to define what constitutes "proper" decisions regarding the allocation of scarce resources between what in shorthand we can call consumption and investment. All of the other tensions interact with this. The dialectic of present and future will be resolved differently if strong, decentralized participatory institutions have been constructed. Patterns and channels of consensus and dissent are also obviously relevant, as is the particular mix and stratification of public and private property. The prospect of socialist construction in Nicaragua is so exciting at the moment because none of these issues has been definitively decided. One hopes, in fact, that within certain broad boundaries they will be the subject of just as much discussion years from now as they are today, for only a dogmatist would believe that in a well-functioning socialist society these issues can or should be settled once and for all.

The Developing Crisis

In Nicaragua 1982 was officially, the "Year of Unity against Aggression." Unofficially, it was the year of difficulties, contradictions, and — in many ways — the radicalization of the Sandinista revolution.

There is more than ample justification for the official characterization. Beginning with the electoral rhetoric of Reagan and his advisers, the current U.S. administration has waged an unremitting campaign to make life difficult and costly, if not impossible, for the Nicaraguan revolution. Although the accusations have varied in tone and detail, more recently the claims that Nicaragua is "totalitarian," or rapidly moving in that direction, and that it is a "platform of terror and war in the region" have been used to justify a program of diplomatic and economic pressures and covert action against Nicaragua.

Washington's ultimate goal is not entirely clear. Undoubtedly, some U.S. officials dream of the day when Edén Pastora, the ex-Sandinista commander, will march triumphantly into Managua at the head of a "liberating army." Others may harbor no such illusions but nevertheless feel that with the right mix of finely tuned pressures it will be possible to tame and deradicalize the revolution. Yet others may quite pointedly calculate that a more radicalized and Soviet-oriented Nicaragua is a much-to-be-desired outcome: only then, using Nicaragua as "proof" that the Soviets and Cubans are the real masterminds and beneficiaries of discontent in the region, will it be possible to mobilize the public opinion, dollars, and firepower needed to destroy other revolutionary movements in Central America.

Whatever Washington's hopes, however, Nicaraguan realities are at once more complex and less easily manipulated from the outside than its enemies would like to believe. Not surprisingly, the complexities are rooted in the extremely serious economic difficulties facing the revolution—difficulties that at first glance seem almost insurmountable. But the revolution also has significant strengths, stemming from its capacity to organize and reorganize the economy and society in response to challenges and threats.

This capacity is at the heart of the revolutionary paradox. On the one hand, a fundamental social transformation of the sort under way in Nicaragua creates a range of problems over and above those encountered by other poor societies. On the other hand, this process of transformation also unleashes energies and resources not available to elites in nonrevolutionary situations. The revolution is simultaneously a problem maker and a problem solver. The men and women who with much courage and tenacity defeated Somoza and his allies understand this. They will not easily abandon what was so dearly won on the battlefield—the right to make their own mistakes, to determine their own future, and ultimately to make the basic transformations sorely needed in Nicaraguan society.

AFTER THE DELUGE

In May of 1982 western Nicaragua was hit with the heaviest rains in decades. The floods that followed swept away highways, bridges, houses, crops, and people, causing damages estimated by the United Nations at more than $350 million, equal to 70 percent of the value of all Nicaraguan exports for 1981. Little wonder that religious members of the opposition to the Sandinistas claimed that the same God who had sent the 1972 earthquake to punish Somoza had now sent the floods to punish the revolutionary government.

Even before the floods, however, the economic situation of Nicaragua had been very serious. The balance sheet of its open, agro-exporting and energy-importing economy was already disquieting. Despite the fact that the gross domestic product grew at better than 8 percent in 1981, total exports barely topped $500 million while imports edged up toward $1 billion (an underestimation of their true costs, since official import figures do not include almost $200 million in freight, licenses, insurance, and other associated expenses). The year-end negative balance on the current account was over $500 million, inflation was officially calculated at 24 percent, and unemployment was beginning to rise.*

---

*For a detailed and careful analysis of flood damage, implications for the Nicaraguan economy, and other relevant data, see United Nations, *Nicaragua: The Floods of May, 1982, and Their Implications for the Economic and Social Development of the Country* (Economic Commission for Latin America, July 1982).

For 1982, the picture is much darker. Post-flood estimates of expected growth for the year vary between zero and 1 percent. Inflation will surely be higher than in 1981, exports will be lower, and imports will drop as foreign-exchange shortages become even more acute. As imported inputs for manufacturing and agriculture become scarcer and economic activity slows down, unemployment —particularly in urban areas—will increase. Salaries and purchasing power in general will not keep up with inflation, so levels of consumption will decline. The shortage of foreign exchange will intensify already serious problems of transport and the maintenance of existing services in everything from health to education. In sum, Nicaragua's still largely capitalist economy is subject to and is being assaulted by the same cyclonic winds now buffeting other small dependent nations. All are in a struggle to survive in a world of increasing indebtedness, high interest rates, worsening terms of trade, rising energy prices, regional strife, and global recession.* As one high official remarked, "Even without the floods and imperialism, we would have plenty of problems."

If we add to this scenario some basic structural characteristics of the Nicaraguan economy, the situation appears even more complex and potentially difficult. Although about 40 percent of the gross domestic product is generated in the state-owned sector of the economy, about 73 percent of all productive activity is still in private hands. In agriculture, which accounts for over 70 percent of all exports, an even higher percentage of productive assets is in private hands—almost 86 percent. Nicaraguan development, particularly export performance, is thus highly dependent on the behavior of capitalists, large producers as well as small.

In this context, the Sandinista state must necessarily play a double game. On the one hand, it must give sufficient incentives, opportunities, and security to these producers. It must treat them like the capitalists they are. In fact, it must actually "overincentivize" them, because to the normal uncertainties of the market are added uncertainties generated by the revolutionary process itself.

*A comparison with neighboring Costa Rica is instructive. With a slightly smaller population, Costa Rica in 1981 had twice the inflation, a higher total foreign debt, and a slightly higher negative balance on its current account than Nicaragua. Costa Rica also registered negative growth (−1.5 percent) in its GNP for 1981.

On the other hand, the state must also ensure sufficient benefits and dignity both to urban and to rural workers. It must honor its vow that this is a revolution of workers and peasants, a revolution for the majority.

Under the best of circumstances, it would not be easy to run a mixed economy of the sort being attempted in Nicaragua. In a country not yet fully recovered from the war of 1978–79, still very underdeveloped technologically and managerially, under assault by its huge neighbor to the north and by counterrevolutionaries much closer to home, it seems a herculean task.*

THE WORLD TO THE RESCUE?

The Sandinista leadership has no illusions about the possibilities of eradicating in a few years the unequal relations and developmental weaknesses that were centuries in the making. Thus, Nicaraguans speak not of the possibility of ending dependency but rather of the necessity of "diversifying dependency." This means new markets for exports and new sources of imports. It means receiving technology (including weapons) from Western as well as Eastern countries. It means vigorous attempts to break away from the political and economic hegemony of the United States, so long the dominant actor in Nicaragua's international—and often domestic—relations. Perhaps most important, in this period of economic crisis, diversifying dependency means searching for as much foreign aid, from as many different sources, as possible.

In search of this aid—and of international solidarity in general —representatives of the government of Nicaragua must by now have broken the small-country record for hours spent in airplanes flying from one capital to another. In April and May of 1982, for example, Sergio Ramírez of the governing junta and other high officials visited twelve countries in Western Europe. During the

---

*The United Nations estimated that in the period 1977–79 direct war damage to infrastructure, plant, and inventories was $480 million. Approximately 50,000 Nicaraguans were killed, and another 100,000 wounded (out of a total population of about 2.5 million). Hundreds of millions of dollars more were lost in crops not planted or destroyed. Capital flight of at least $1.5 billion further damaged the economy during this period. So serious was the disruption that by the end of 1981 real per capita income was still 25 percent below what it had been at the end of 1976, the last "normal" year.

same period, Commander Daniel Ortega of the junta and Commander Henry Ruiz, the minister of planning, were in the Soviet Union. Days later Commander Bayardo Arce of the national directorate of the Sandinista National Liberation Front (FSLN) was in Finland to attend a meeting of the Socialist International. Meanwhile, Commander Victor Tirado, also a member of the national directorate, was visiting North Vietnam and Poland. During these same two months, other officials traveled to the United States, Germany, Bulgaria, Brazil, and Argentina.

By 19 July 1982, the date of the third anniversary of the triumph of the revolution, the leadership would look back on this vigorous effort with substantial satisfaction. In three years, almost $1.5 billion of new loans, credits, and donations had been secured. Much of the old debt contracted during the Somoza period had been renegotiated on favorable terms, and the new debt was quite well distributed across various countries and institutions: about 39 percent had been contracted with multilateral organizations, 18 percent with the United States and Western Europe, another 18 percent with Latin America, 17 percent with the socialist countries, and 8 percent with Libya. The announced policy of "walking on four legs"—Latin America, Western Europe, the socialist bloc, and Arab oil exporters—seemed to be working.

But the big question had by then become, will it continue to work? Much more aid was needed if Nicaragua's crisis of short- and medium-term foreign exchange was to be met. The country's total public foreign debt had climbed to almost $2.5 billion, one of the highest per capita in Latin America, helping to make Nicaragua substantially less attractive as a credit risk than it had been less than a year earlier. Furthermore, the vigorous campaign being waged by enemies of the revolution, by Nicaraguans as well as foreigners, was straining relations with at least some previous supporters in Latin America and Western Europe.

Thus, in the near future, "walking on four legs" may well become "limping on two." Some pessimists were suggesting that a self-reinforcing spiral might be beginning. To the extent that support from Latin America and Western Europe becomes problematic, the necessity of turning to the socialist bloc becomes more urgent. But the closer Nicaragua's relations with the socialist bloc are, the more problematic further support from Western Europe and Latin America becomes.

The more conventional response to a foreign-exchange crisis of the sort that Nicaragua is now suffering would be, of course, to turn to the IMF. Removal of restrictions on the operation of market forces both internationally and domestically, reduction of public expenditures, and devaluation are typical components of an IMF-imposed program of "recovery." It is difficult to imagine, however, that the government of Nicaragua would accept such conditions—with their clear implications of subordination and distortion of revolutionary priorities—in exchange for a loan. As one planner said to me, "We are not about to sell our revolutionary birthright for a mess of IMF pottage."

If an IMF-imposed solution is not probable and if walking on four legs—much less, limping on two—cannot fully address the profundity of the crisis, what then is the answer? Nicaragua seems headed for a period of austerity deeper and longer than anything yet experienced in more than three years of revolution. The key questions thus become how this austerity will be distributed and experienced in Nicaraguan society and what its political consequences will be.

THE PRICE OF SQUASH

A visitor to Nicaragua soon grows aware of opposition to the revolutionary government, for among the Reagan administration's many falsehoods about Central America, none is more gratuitous than the characterization of Nicaragua as "totalitarian." A vast array of political, social, and cultural forces are at work in the country. Professional and business associations in deep disagreement with government policy meet openly and protest loudly. Opposition political parties, although not able to mobilize wide popular support, are nevertheless active and vocal. The opposition trade-union movement is small but vigorous. The Catholic Church, some of whose members are supportive of the Sandinista revolution and some of whom are in opposition, continues as a major cultural and political force. A multitude of Protestant sects flourish. Private schools, both religious and secular, remain open. Even in the state of emergency decreed in March 1982, as a result of multiple threats from the Reagan administration and the constant incursions of former national guardsmen across the border from Honduras, the opposition newspaper *La Prensa* continues to publish—albeit under the censorship that is also applied to other publications. And certainly in the streets, markets, churches, bars, and buses of the country one hears plenty of openly voiced complaints and criticisms—hardly what one would expect in a "totalitarian" society.

In this context of debate, criticism, and economic difficulties, the first half of the revolutionary paradox mentioned earlier operates with a vengeance: not only do people look to their government for improvements in living and working conditions—thus creating expectations that are very difficult to fulfill in a situation of scarcity—but the relatively permissive political climate presents ample opportunities to those who wish to embarrass or discredit a revolution whose accomplishments inevitably fall short of popular expectations in many areas.

Thus, in an inflationary economy, in which real purchasing power is declining, every trip to the market is an opportunity to hear and perhaps to internalize messages that assault the prestige of the revolution. That things are much worse in Costa Rica is not important or even known to the Nicaraguan shopper buying vegetables. The point of comparison is much closer to home: last month a squash cost one *córdoba,* and this month it costs one and a half. Who is to blame?

At this point, however, the second half of the revolutionary paradox comes into play. Just as the revolutionary process creates certain problems (unfulfilled expectations, disruptions in production and distribution), it also creates special opportunities and new resources. Ideally, at least, the FSLN should be in a position to fight back, not only ideologically, but also in the distribution of real benefits.

As a successful example of the latter, the massive literacy crusade of 1980 is outstanding. In only five months, illiteracy was reduced from almost 50 percent to about 13 percent. Moreover, during this period hundreds of thousands of Nicaraguans working as temporary literacy instructors received their first real taste of what life in the most backward sectors of their own nation was really like. Unfortunately, both individuals and whole segments of society tend to forget the long-term material and moral benefits of such revolutionary undertakings when confronted with expensive squash.

In the long run, victories for the revolution in the ideological struggle depend on the effective functioning of the Sandinista National Liberation Front. Here the Reaganite view of the iron hand with which the FSLN rules Nicaragua is totally misleading. It is true that at the level of macropolitical decisions the Frente is in command. But at the level of day-to-day, grass-roots organization needed to educate and mobilize the population to confront problems in the revolutionary process, the FSLN is actually quite weak. This is equally true in the affiliated mass organizations of women, youth, urban and rural workers, and even in the Sandinista political party-in-the-making.

In part the organizational thinness of the FSLN and affiliated mass organizations is to be expected, given the relatively short time since the victory over Somoza and the fact that the FSLN was initially organized to do battle against the tyranny, not to govern. But the current grass-roots organizational weakness of the FSLN also reflects the legacy of forty-six years of despotic rule. At the time of Somoza's defeat, Nicaragua basically had only a political culture of opposition, and a very narrow and undemocratic political culture at that. Thus, the revolution must quite literally create a citizenry with the skills, attitudes, and experiences appropriate to participatory politics. It must do battle against apathy, against suspicion, against the subculture of corruption that characterized the Somoza years, and against dogmatic tendencies and errors committed by the Frente itself. In this situation, it should come as no surprise that the revolutionary government is not always well prepared to explain the price of squash—or, for that matter, to counter the criticisms and often the outright lies that emanate from certain sectors of the Catholic hierarchy, the private sector, the opposition press, and Washington, D.C.

COUNTRYSIDE AND CITY

I talked to Sandino
And he told me
That you don't have to be big
To fight against the enemy.

If it weren't for Sandino
And the revolution
I wouldn't be singing
My humble little song.
    —VERSES WRITTEN BY A NICARAGUAN PEASANT

To travel in the Nicaraguan countryside is to enter a world very different from the cities, particularly from the capital city of Managua. The peasants, rural workers, and even many of the private producers stand more solidly with the revolutionary process than do most urban dwellers. In part this reflects an agrarian reform that is both sophisticated in design and administered with honesty and substantial efficiency. Combining direct land grants to peasants, the establishment of cooperatives, state ownership of certain large production units (primarily those confiscated from Somoza and his followers), and incentives to private producers, the reform has been one of the most successful revolutionary programs.

Rural support for the revolution also draws strength from the comparisons that most peasants and rural workers make with the wretched conditions under which they previously lived. Not to be insulted and kicked around by the foreman and not to be cheated on payday (or in the boss's store) represent a vast improvement over what prevailed just a few years earlier. A peasant may not be making much more money or living in better housing, but he or she is probably now at least marginally literate and is for the first time being treated like a human being.

In addition, almost everywhere in the countryside the multiple irritations that perturb urban dwellers, from food prices to crowded buses, are less immediately felt. When food is grown locally, and when most simple folk have always walked or ridden horses, high prices and shortages have a different meaning. "We can get by" is a rural, not an urban, response.

Substantial rural support for the revolution is also, somewhat surprisingly, to be found among the thousands of small and medium-sized landowners who produce most of the cotton, coffee, and other agricultural commodities that constitute the bulk of Nicaragua's exports. Many such producers are, of course, deeply distrustful of the revolution. Many hold investment to a minimum, producing only what is necessary to keep their farm or ranch from deteriorating or being nationalized under the "idle lands" provisions of the agrarian reform law. But others, realizing that they have no place to go, respond to the credit and marketing incentives provided by the government. If they encounter a consistent set of problems in trying to produce in the Nicaraguan mixed economy, those problems are more likely to derive from the acute shortage of foreign exchange that affects all sectors than from their political differences with the revolutionary government.

In his Worker's Day speech on 1, May 1982, Commander Tomás Borge, the only surviving member of the group that founded the FSLN, in 1961, emphasized that workers were "correct to continue demanding their economic rights." He also added, however, that their first responsibility was to consolidate revolutionary power—implying that in these difficult times salaries were going to have to take a backseat to other national priorities. At this massive May Day rally in Managua, Borge was literally and figuratively speaking to the urban population, for it is in the city-based activities of manufacturing, services, and government that Nicaragua's economic difficulties are and will continue to be felt most acutely. It is also in the cities that unemployment translates most immediately into hardship and discontent.

How the balance between countryside and city, between support and opposition to the revolution, will play itself out over the next months and years is impossible to predict with any accuracy. As noted earlier, much will depend on the organizational capacity and the political skills of the FSLN. But it *can* be predicted with a high degree of certainty that Managua will continue to provide more than its fair share of problems as well as the lens through which most outside observers will view the Nicaraguan revolution.

It is in Managua that the major opposition leaders who are still in the country hold forth. It is there that visiting journalists make their contacts and assess "public opinion." It is in the capital that a political confrontation or a police action is immediately known and given meaning—or many meanings. Thus, the city plays its many roles: stronghold of the old and often antirevolutionary culture and values; generator of problems that are both different from and often more intractable than those of the countryside; amplifier and broadcaster of these problems to the rest of the nation and to other nations as well. No wonder one frustrated municipal official said, only half in jest, "What we really need around here is another earthquake to get rid of what the quake of 1972 left standing."

THE STRUGGLE CONTINUES

In Nicaragua today, class struggle is not simply some dusty Marxist concept; it is an everyday reality. Political power has passed from the Somocistas and what allies they had among the middle and upper classes to the FSLN and other revolutionary organizations speaking in the name of *las clases populares*—the majority of Nicaraguans who never before had a voice in how or for whom their country was run. This process is neither easy nor complete. The interests of the wealthy and comfortable are inevitably hurt, or at least deeply threatened; social tensions not allowed expression under the old order now surface and are given voice in streets and workplaces. It cannot be pleasant for middle-class families to hear the common folk marching through their neighborhoods chanting revolutionary slogans that promise the end of the old class-based system of power and privileges.

In revolutionary Nicaragua, as one would expect, class struggle reflects very directly the way in which economic power is related to political power. This relation is very different from what one would find either in a fully developed capitalist economy or in its socialist counterpart. In either case, one would expect a high degree of congruence between economic and political power. But in

Nicaragua, such is not the situation. While the mixed economy depends on very substantial participation by the private sector, this sector has only minority participation in the political system.*

Two related sources of tension are embedded in this state of affairs. First, the social classes represented by or affiliated with the private sector resent the fact that they neither have nor are going to get the political clout to which they feel their economic role entitles them. Second, since most of the private sector still remaining in Nicaragua was either neutral during the insurrectionary period or openly anti-Somoza, many of its members feel that, in addition to their economic claims on power, they also have claims based on their opposition to the dictator. But all of this argumentation matters little, for a self-proclaimed government of the *clases populares* is not about to shape its new institutions to suit the desires of classes that are numerically in the minority and whose overall average income is perhaps twenty to thirty times higher than that of the impoverished majority.

This understandable intransigence on the part of the FSLN has important implications for the way in which the current economic crisis has been and will be handled. Every effort will be made to soften the blows that fall on the mass of the citizenry. If petroleum products have to be rationed, it is the owners of private automobiles (a small but vocal fraction of the total population) who will feel the pinch most acutely. As food becomes scarcer and more expensive, it is the supply and distribution of rice and beans that will receive first priority. As complaints and dissent mount, it is the voices of the poor that will be listened to most attentively.

The economic crisis thus implies a reaffirmation and deepening of the class character of the Nicaraguan revolution. Almost by definition it also implies a radicalization of the revolution—understood as a quickening of the pace at which the economy is moved away from the market orientation that still guides most of its operations. The management of scarcity in favor of the *clases populares* cannot be left to the vagaries of the market or to capital-

---

*The expression *private sector* refers to medium-size and large capitalists who find their most organized expression in COSEP, the Higher Council of Private Enterprise. Technically, private enterprise includes everyone from the smallest peasant producer to the owner of the largest factory. COSEP, however, represents only the upper reaches of this pyramid.

ists, large or small. As producers, private entrepreneurs may retain an important role, but priorities of production, prices, distribution, and much else will increasingly be determined by the state. Both as capitalists and as consumers, the private sector is going to see its opportunities diminish.

IMPERIALISM'S MANY FACES

On the eve of the third anniversary of Nicaragua's liberation from Somoza and the National Guard, sporadic military confrontations flared into heavy fighting in the northeastern corner of the country. Bands of well-armed and well-coordinated *"contras"*— as active opponents of the revolution are called in Nicaragua— were engaged by units of the Sandinista armed forces. In the first battles, more than three dozen Nicaraguan soldiers lost their lives. Subsequently, many more were killed and wounded.

The area in which these clashes took place extends eighty miles south of the border with Honduras and forms part of the traditional homeland of the Miskito Indians. Early in 1982, repeated raids by *contras* based in Honduras forced the Nicaraguan government to relocate almost 10,000 Miskitos from the Río Coco area into new settlements farther to the south. Other Miskitos moved north into Honduras. The relocation was, in essence, a military operation. Fear and hostility swept through the indigenous population, and an already difficult situation on the northern Atlantic coast became even more difficult.

For the Reagan administration, which had given aid and encouragement to the *contras* as well as support to dissident Miskito spokesmen, the forced relocation was heaven-sent. An avalanche of outright falsehoods followed. And on Feb. 28 Alexander Haig waived a picture of burning bodies before the television cameras to "prove" that the Sandinistas were slaughtering Miskitos.* An administration that supports a Guatemala military establishment that systematically destroys whole villages and assassinates hundreds of indigenous persons suddenly transformed itself into the defender of Indian rights in Nicaragua.

---

*This photograph was later revealed to be a picture of victims of Somoza's National Guard, taken four years earlier. On March 1st, the State Department admitted to the error.

As in the northeast with the Miskito, so too in the cities and countryside of the rest of Nicaragua, as well as in Honduras, Costa Rica, Washington, New York, Florida, and elsewhere. The battle against the Sandinistas is waged in Congress, in multilateral lending agencies, in international organizations, in the press, in European and Latin capitals, and in the training camps for *contras*. In fact, wherever the many difficulties and vulnerabilities of the Nicaraguan revolution present an opportunity, some arm or mouthpiece of the U.S. government is sure to be found on the offensive, with words, pats on the back, blows to the abdomen, dollars, or equipment designed to do as much damage to the Sandinistas as possible.

When asked why this policy is being pursued, officials of the Reagan administration give a variety of answers. But when pressed, at least the embassy in Managua answers in a single vein: U.S. hostility derives from the aid and comfort that the Sandinistas are giving to the guerrilla movement in El Salvador. Without doubt, some aid and comfort do flow from Nicaragua to opponents of the El Salvadoran regime. How much and in what form remains an open question, since the original evidence offered by the U.S. government, in 1981, was extremely flimsy and since no additional evidence has been forthcoming (the embassy says that such evidence exists but cannot be made public, because to do so would jeopardize intelligence sources).

It is difficult to believe, however, that the El Salvador question is the driving force behind the imperialist assault on the Nicaraguan revolution. The hostility is too deep, too consistent, manifested in too many ways, and pursued too aggressively for this to be true. At least from the vantage point of Nicaragua, it seems clear that this administration, no matter what Nicaragua's relation to El Salvador, is seeking nothing less than the overthrow of the Sandinista government. If this can be accomplished "peacefully," through destablization in the context of severe economic difficulties, so much the better. But if military measures are necessary, Washington finds that acceptable too, for the fighting and dying will be done by Nicaraguans and others from the region, not by North Americans.

A visit to Nicaragua confirms both the futility and the criminality of U.S. policy toward the Sandinista revolution. Not only are the Nicaraguan armed forces and militia growing stronger every day,but with each Nicaraguan killed by the *contras* one can feel the spreading of the determination to resist outside pressures. Of course, if the country is subjected to an extended period of severe military threat and aggression, important changes will undoubtedly take place. The space allowed to opposition voices would shrink and perhaps disappear altogether. The economy would go on a war footing. But none of this would mean the end of the Sandinista revolution; it would mean only its transformation.

If the futility of this approach to the revolution is obvious, its immorality is even more evident. With all of its faults and problems, the current government of Nicaragua is the first in the country's entire history that is genuinely attempting to improve the living and working conditions of the majority of citizens. Housed in shacks, poorly fed, often without electricity, running water, and health or educational facilities, most Nicaraguans have no future outside the revolution, and certainly no future under renewed American hegemony. As a peasant receiving the land title for a newly organized cooperative said, "Neither the imperialists nor the Somocistas ever gave us land, and we aren't going to give it back or let any of them return."

In sum, for most Nicaraguans the Reagan administration promises not "liberation" from Sandinista rule but more hardship, more strife, and possibly a great deal of bloodshed. And all of this for a people who have already had more than their share of hardship, strife, and bloodshed. Little wonder that even Nicaraguans highly critical of the Sandinistas fear Washington's policies. They, too, understand that if their country is again consumed in war, they and their sons and daughters will be the ultimate losers. They, too, understand the bankruptcy of U.S. policy toward Nicaragua. Nevertheless, yet again a U.S. administration is desperately trying to make the history of another nation conform to its own interests and prejudices. The fact that the Nicaraguan people will be forced to pay for Washington's arrogance evidently does not matter to President Reagan and his advisers.

State

Violence and

Agrarian Crisis

in Guatemala

THE ROOTS OF THE INDIAN-PEASANT REBELLION

Shelton H. Davis

n January 1982 the *New York Times* carried an editorial entitled "Guatemala Amok." It referred to a diplomat who claimed that "Guatemala was a bloodbath waiting to happen." It noted that over the past fifteen years more than 30,000 lives had been taken in the "unceasing war between Guatemala's left and right." What it found especially horrifying, however, was how the pace of the killing had increased in recent months and how little pressure the Reagan administration was placing on the Guatemalan government to end the bloodbath.[1]

By 1982 not only had the killing intensified, but the Reagan administration had stepped up its efforts to depict the current regime in Guatemala as reformist and improving. Today, the social forces that are pitted against one another are increasingly polarizing the society, with the military and their industrial and agrarian elite allies on one side and the rural population, mostly Indian peasants, on the other. The massive involvement of Indian peasants in this war is unique in Guatemalan history. In the past, there were many interpreters of Indian behavior. But now the indigenous communities of Guatemala are speaking for themselves and expressing their opposition to the conditions that have created their misery.

Before turning to my main argument, I would like to discuss briefly some of the conventional ideas in North America about the reasons for the bloodbath in Guatemala. Many journalists and officials in this country explain the current violence as the result of some sort of "holy war" between left- and right-wing fanatics in that country. On the one side, there is supposed to be a number of well-organized bands of Marxist guerrillas, Cuban trained and supported, intent upon seeing the coming of a political revolution at any social and human costs. On the other side, there is an array of mysterious right-wing "death squads," seemingly outside of the control of the government but feared by the general population. Finally, in the middle, there is Guatemala's large peasantry, mainly Indian in its ethnic heritage and just awakening from centuries of political slumber.

A fall 1981 article by Flora Lewis in the *New York Times* is typical of the national discourse concerning violence in Guatemala. Lewis, who viewed the Guatemalan situation as being hopeless, wrote that people were being killed by the hundreds but that, "often, nobody knows why." According to her, the only way to explain the Guatemalan situation is to recognize that it is a war without reason between the fanatical, anti-Communist Right and the equally zealous guerrillas of the Left. "There is a sinister war going on," she wrote, "between two cold-blooded groups seeking to dominate by terror. There are no white hats. The great bulk of the people are caught between, and if they turn to one side for protection, they know they are marking themselves as targets for the other."[2]

The U.S. State Department attributes the violence to leftist efforts to polarize the country that are responded to by the Right. Although the Right is credited with a certain amount of violence, the State Department argues that it is the Left that foments violence as a conscious policy.[3] Other journalistic and official accounts could be cited which espouse this theory of a "holy war" between right- and left-wing extremists in Guatemala, with the country's large peasantry stuck in the middle.

For at least three reasons, however, I find this view of political violence in Guatemala deficient. First, even a cursory reading of the sociological literature on violence in Guatemala shows that most of the victims are innocent peasants and rural workers rather than urban-based, political ideologues. Studies on the victims of political violence for the years 1966 through 1976, for example, indicate that although all sectors of the Guatemalan population (political party leaders, students, professionals, clerics, trade unionists, and the like) were represented among the victims of kidnappings, torture, and assassinations, more than 65 percent were peasants and rural workers.[4]

The class-based nature of political violence in Guatemala was recognized by the Reverend William L. Wipfler of the National

Council of Churches in testimony that he presented before a congressional subcommittee in 1976. "It is clear from the documentation provided by a number of reliable sources," he stated, "that peasant smallholders, tenant farmers, members of agricultural cooperatives and landless peasants make up the great majority of victims. In almost every country the rural sector is particularly vulnerable to the problem of the violation of their rights and security, but in Guatemala where such a high percentage of the peasantry is indigenous, this is particularly true."[5]

Second, the large amount of evidence collected by human-rights organizations over the past decade indicates that the supposedly independent "death squads" in Guatemala are actually coordinated by the government and composed of government security forces. Amnesty International has made what is perhaps the most persuasive case for government complicity in extrajudicial violence in Guatemala, but a similar conclusion has also been reached by the Inter-American Commission on Human Rights, the International Commission of Jurists, the International Labor Organization, and the United Nations Human Rights Commission. What is often reported as "right-wing violence" in Guatemala is really state terrorism in disguise.[6]

Finally, the conventional wisdom about the nature and causes of political violence in Guatemala breaks down when one considers the recent growth of activism and popular appeal of the guerrilla movement in the country. Although some commentators see the rural population as being stuck between the insurgents and the army, others have reported a growing recruitment of Indian peasants into the guerrilla movement. State Department sources indicates that there has been a growth in the strength of the guerrilla movement in recent months. In July 1981 the State Department reported that military clashes between the army and the guerrillas averaged ten a month and that selective bombings and other acts of sabotage averaged approximately thirty-five a month. Analyses of guerrilla actions based on their own communiqués indicate figures two to three times as large. Obviously, any adequate interpretation of the current civil strife in Guatemala needs to explain the guerrilla movement's increasing appeal among Indian peasants as well as its recent militancy and growth.[7]

I would like to suggest that Guatemala, rather than being the scene of a "holy war" between left- and right-wing fanatics, is actually in the throes of the first stages of a process that the anthropologist Eric Wolf has called a modern "peasant war." The current violence in Guatemala is a logical outcome of recent social processes and not an aberrant political phenomenon. Specifically, the nature of and the recent changes in the agrarian structure explain a great deal about the present struggle. This peasant war, at least in its origins, has many similarities with others analyzed by Wolf. Wolf cites four preconditions necessary for active peasant participation in revolutionary movements: (1) traditional peasants are dislocated by the expansion of modern capitalist relations of production, (2) population growth increases the problems of peasant agricultural production, (3) the state loses its control over the peasantry, and (4) peasants form links with urban social classes and with revolutionary political parties. Although Central America has its own, unique history and although this process is more advanced in neighboring El Salvador, there are good reasons for regarding recent events in Guatemala as the initial stage in a modern "peasant war."[8]

To understand why peasants are assuming such an important role in national politics, it is necessary to discuss several important changes that have taken place in Guatemalan rural society. For decades, anthropologists and economists have been aware of how seasonal labor migration connects the coffee-export economy of the Guatemalan Pacific coast with the Indian peasant economy of the western highlands.[9] This seasonal migration represents government-supported efforts to force highland Indians to leave their villages periodically to work as laborers on the cotton and sugar plantations of the coast. Although this has generated enormous wealth for the agro-export economy, it has only deepened the poverty of the Indian peasantry. Most of the studies by rural sociologists that discuss the social and economic significance of the pattern of *latifundio-minifundio* land tenure in Guatemala mention the fact that 2 percent of the farmers own more than 53 percent of the cultivable land, while another 77 percent of the farmers do not have enough land to subsist.[10] The changes that have occurred in the Guatemalan agricultural economy over the past few decades have affected peasants' political attitudes and behavior.

In the 1950s a major process of crop diversification took place in the export sector of the Guatemalan agricultural economy. Between 1952 and 1962 the area cultivated in cotton along the southern coast of Guatemala increased from 18,997 to 176,154 acres; production increased from 2,100 to 65,000 tons; and export earnings increased from less than $3 million to over $30 million. By 1965 cotton surpassed bananas as Guatemala's second-major agricultural export crop, after coffee, and it accounted for nearly 20 percent of the country's export earnings.[11]

This boom in agricultural exports continued throughout the 1960s and into the early 1970s. Between 1960 and 1974, for example, the export value of coffee increased from $74.6 million to $172.9 million; that of cotton, from $5.8 million to $71 million; that of sugar, from $0.1 million to $49.6 million; and that of meat, from $0.2 million to $21.5 million. Overall, the value of Guatemala's five major agricultural export crops increased from $105.3 million to $367.5 million. During this period, Guatemala's export agricultural sector—as measured by average annual increases in production—outperformed twenty-two other countries in Latin America, including Mexico, Colombia, and Brazil.[12]

On the peasant side of the Guatemalan agricultural economy, the picture was not quite as optimistic. Between 1950 and 1973 Guatemala's population increased from 3 million to 5.6 million people, at an average growth rate of approximately 3 percent per year. During this same period, however, domestic food production did not keep pace with population growth. Between 1961 and 1973, for instance, the annual increase in the production of corn averaged only 1.6 percent, that of wheat only 2.3 percent, and that of beans only 4.8 percent, compared with an overall average annual growth rate of 5 percent for the country's five major export crops. A chief reason for the poor performance of the food-production sector relative to the export sector was that the amount of arable land devoted to export crops expanded by 6.5 percent per year, while arable land for food production increased by only 1.7 to 2.0 percent per year. By the early 1970s, when Guatemala's earnings from export agriculture were booming, the country had to import record amounts of corn, wheat, and beans.[13]

At the same time, population growth eroded the already minuscule parcels of land possessed by peasant farmers. Between 1950 and 1970, for example, the number of farm families possessing plots that were too small for subsistence increased from 308,070 to 421,100. During this same period, the average size of farms in Guatemala dropped from 8.1 to 5.6 hectares, and the number of landless peasants increased to about one-quarter of the rural work force.[14] Land problems were particularly severe in the western and central highlands, where the majority of Guatemala's Indian population lives and where the average size of farm units decreased from 1.3 hectares per person in 1950 to less than 0.85 in 1975.

Numerous studies indicate a general deterioration of the social and economic conditions of Guatemala's peasant population in the years from 1960 to 1975. Whether one considers rural unemployment, family income, nutritional status, access to health and educational services, or any one of a dozen other measures of social welfare, Guatemala's immense peasantry is one of the poorest in Latin America.[15]

Despite warnings by the U.S. Agency for International Development (AID) and by the Inter-American Committee on Agricultural Development, the Guatemalan government did nothing to alleviate the misery of its peasantry in the period from the Castillo Armas takeover in 1954 until about 1975. In 1955 and again in 1963, the government introduced special legislation calling for the distribution of national *fincas* (plantations) and unused lands to peasants, but almost every independent assessment of these colonization programs found them to be wanting. In the fifteen years from 1955 to 1970, for example, government land-reform programs benefited only 31,000 families, compared with over 100,000 families who received land parcels under the pre-1954 Arbenz agrarian-reform program and an average annual increase in population of about 90,000 people.[16]

By the early 1970s, when the unemployment rate was at 42 percent in the countryside and when the cost of living in Guatemala City was going up by nearly 50 percent, Guatemalan peasants and workers began to organize to demand a greater share of the nation's wealth. One of the major forms that such collective action took in rural areas was the development of the cooperative movement. Although some attempts at cooperative organization had been made during the Arévalo regime, these came to a halt after the Arbenz agrarian-reform program was introduced in 1952. In the late 1950s and early 1960s, however, Roman Catholic missionaries began to promote cooperatives in rural areas. By 1967 there were 145 agricultural, consumer, and credit cooperatives functioning in Guatemala, with a membership of over 27,000 people.

During the late 1960s and early 1970s. AID provided several million dollars for the further development of the cooperative movement. By March 1976 there were 510 cooperatives in Guatemala, organized into eight large federations and having a combined membership of more than 132,000. Fifty-seven percent of these cooperatives were located in the Indian highlands, where, according to reports written at the time, they were having a major impact on Indian political attitudes, marketing strategies, and agricultural techniques.[17]

While the cooperative movement was taking root in the countryside, an independent and democratic labor movement was beginning to flex its muscles in Guatemala City. Although Guatemala is basically an agricultural country, it has seen a significant increase in the number of its urban workers in recent years. When the Guatemalan labor code was passed in 1946, only 19,447 persons were classified as belonging to the industrial labor force. By 1973, following more than a decade of manufacturing growth and foreign investment, over 212,000 people were engaged in manufacturing; a similar number were involved in construction, commerce, transportation, communications, and other urban-based industries. Many of these people were first-generation urban workers, who had migrated to Guatemala City only in the preceding decade and who maintained strong kinship and other ties with people in rural areas.[18] Despite a hostile political environment, marked by periodic attacks on groups critical of the government, the increase in the size of the urban work force, and a 1973 teachers' strike, led to a growing trade-union movement. Although this movement never reached the degree of organization experienced by labor under the Arbenz government, it is estimated that more than 85,000 workers—or between 5 and 6 percent of the economically active population—belonged to labor unions in 1975.[19]

In 1976 eight of Guatemala's largest unions and labor federations joined together to form the National Committee of Trade Union Unity (CNUS). From its inception, CNUS members were interested in forming links of solidarity with peasants and rural workers as well as in representing the interests of urban workers. One of the original member unions of CNUS was the powerful United Sugar Workers Federation (FETULIA), which in 1976 led a major strike against the large Pantaleón sugar mill on the south coast. Lawyers from CNUS also assisted peasant cooperatives in frontier areas that were encountering difficulties in obtaining land titles from the government, and federation members joined mine workers who were striking in such distant areas as Huehuetenango and Alta Verapaz.[20]

For a brief period, from 1974 to 1976, it was uncertain how the Guatemalan military would respond to the growth of the cooperative and labor movements. Upon assuming the presidency of Guatemala in 1974, General Kjell Laugerud took the unprecedented step of providing official support for the cooperative movement. José Miguel Gaitan, a strong supporter of cooperatives, was named deputy director of the national agricultural credit bank, and the government promised several million dollars for cooperative development. A number of cooperative leaders were even invited to the Presidential Palace to discuss what the role of their organizations might be in the government's five-year development plan and how cooperatives might be used in the settlement of the far-northern part of the country.[21]

At the same time, in response to the growing repression, a new organization, the recently formed Guerrilla Army of the Poor (EGP), made its presence known in the northern part of the country. The EGP adopted a more militant strategy, calling for a "prolonged popular war." Its successes were very limited, but its zone of operation was in the heavily Indian areas, where it began to develop techniques for reaching local populations using the native languages spoken in the communities.

The government's inability to control the cooperative movement became clear following the tragic earthquake that struck Guatemala in February 1976. This earthquake, as many observers have noted, was as much a "class phenomenon" as it was a "natural disaster." Most of the damage occurred in the slum areas of Guatemala City and in the department of Chimaltenango, where the cooperative movement had its greatest strength. In the aftermath of the earthquake, the government proved entirely incapable of directing the national reconstruction effort. Hence, cooperative members and slum-dweller associations sought independent aid from international relief agencies and began the process of local reconstruction on their own.[22]

For the Guatemalan government, the chaos created by the earthquake presented a military rather than a social problem. Using the suppression of the guerrilla movement as a pretext, the Guatemalan army began military operations in the department of El Quiché just two weeks after the earthquake. In a swift attack on the towns of Chajul, Cotzal, and Nebaj, several people were killed, including the head of the local Catholic Action committee, five sacristans in the local Catholic churches, and four bilingual schoolteachers. Members of the cooperative movement especially felt the blows of the government's terror campaign in the Quiché area. Between February 1976 and the end of 1977, sixty-eight cooperative members were killed in the Ixcán region, forty in Chajul, twenty-eight in Cotzal, and thirty-two in Nebaj.[23]

During this period, the army also began a full-scale military effort in the northern-frontier-strip area, where a number of international petroleum companies had been given exploration permits and where, for the past several years, the government had promised peasant colonists titles to land. The scope of this militarization of rural areas came to world attention in May 1978 when members of a special-forces unit of the Guatemalan army killed over one hundred Kekchi Indian peasants seeking land titles from the government in the town of Panzós, Alta Verapaz. Many people hoped that the international attention that focused on the Panzós massacre would bring an end to government terrorism and violence. In fact, Panzós was only the beginning of a more systematic campaign of terror against the Indian and peasant peoples of Guatemala.[24]

Throughout 1978 and 1979 the military continued to occupy towns in El Quiché, kidnapping catechists and cooperative members on the pretext that they were assisting guerrilla forces in the

area. Finally, in January 1980, a group of Quiché peasants—
outraged by the disappearance and killing of seven catechists from
the town of Uspantán—went to Guatemala City to protest the
military occupation of their communities. After taking their case
to the Guatemalan congress and several radio stations, the Indians
went to the Spanish embassy to seek the assistance of the ambassador in obtaining an investigation of the deaths of their countrymen. The Guatemalan government responded to the peasants by
surrounding the embassy with security police and then burning it
to the ground. Thirty-nine people were killed in this incident,
including thirty peasants from El Quiché, seven embassy staff
members, and a former vice-president and foreign minister of
Guatemala.[25]

After the Spanish-embassy massacre, it became clear that only
a well-organized and clandestine movement would be able to
counter the violence of the government. In 1978 a new organization called the Committee for Peasant Unity (CUC) was formed
to defend the rights of farmworkers in Guatemala. The CUC is
the first labor organization in the history of Guatemala to link
highland Indian peasants with poor *ladino* workers. Although the
organization has been forced to function in secrecy and has seen
many of its leaders killed, it has the support of thousands of
seasonal and permanent farmworkers.

In February 1980 the CUC called a strike of 70,000 cane cutters
and 40,000 cotton workers, forcing the government to raise the
legal minimum wage of farmworkers from $1.12 to $3.20 per day.
The following September, a CUC strike of 10,000 coffee pickers
almost led to the abandonment of the coffee harvest on fifteen
plantations in the municipality of Colomba. The coffee strike was
particularly important, because it occurred in an economic sector
that employs more workers, provides more tax revenues, and
accounts for a greater proportion of export earnings than any other
part of the Guatemalan economy. By establishing a firm base
among both peasants and plantation workers, the CUC has the
potential of dismantling the entire Guatemalan agricultural economy.[26]

Currently, there are four guerrilla organizations in Guatemala,
numbering between 2,000 and 4,000 combatants and occupying

large areas of territory in the western and central highlands, the Pacific coast, and the northern lowlands. Two of these organizations—the Guerrilla Army of the Poor (EGP) and the Revolutionary Organization of the People in Arms (ORPA)—are particularly active in Indian areas of Guatemala. The EGP, which was organized in 1975, functions in the far-northern departments of Huehuetenango, El Quiché, and Alta Verapaz, as well as along the southern coast around Escuintla. In the northern departments, it has ambushed a number of army patrols, dynamited municipal buildings and electricity towers, occupied towns such as Chichicastenango and Sololá, and perfected a tactic of "armed propaganda" meetings. The EGP is reported to have established, during the past two years, a firm base among the local indigenous population of this region. The EGP Ernesto "Che" Guevara guerrilla front, which was established in Huehuetenango in 1979, is said to be made up almost entirely of Mam-, Jacaltec-, and Kanjobal-speaking Indians.[27]

ORPA has had similar successes among Indian peoples in the central and western parts of the country. In September 1980 ORPA occupied several Indian towns around Lake Atitlán, conducting propaganda meetings among local residents and forcing many tourists to leave the area. In response to the ORPA actions, the Guatemalan army set up a base in Santiago Atitlán and began to terrorize the local population. Gaspar Culán, the director of the Indian-language radio station—"La Voz de Atitlán"—and several other Indian leaders were murdered by the army in one of its antiguerrilla raids. When the people protested this incident and other acts of violence by the army to the mayor of Sololá, they were told they could expect no help from the government as long as ORPA continued to function in the area.[28]

The Guatemalan army's counterinsurgency campaign against the guerrillas is aimed at physically and psychologically terrorizing the rural population. This campaign, which appears to be modeled after tactics first developed by the French in Algeria, has gone through four stages. In the first, government security forces chose selected community leaders for kidnapping, torture, and assassination. In the second, the government threatened and killed religious leaders, because it believed that they served as the major link between the peasants and the guerrillas. In the third, the army bombed and harassed key villages, on the pretext that these villages served as strategic support populations for the guerrillas. Finally, in the most recent stage—which began with an army offensive in Chimaltenango in November 1981—thousands of troops swept across an area, killing suspected leaders, burning fields, and attempting to drive a wedge between the peasantry and the guerrillas.[29]

Wolf has suggested that the more a state terrorizes an economically dislocated and politically aware peasantry, the more likely it is that this peasantry will reach out and join a revolutionary movement. This appears to be what happened in Guatemala in 1980 and 1981. Before this time the four guerrilla organizations that existed in Guatemala had been relatively weak forces in the overall political picture of the country. As the Guatemalan army increased its terror campaign in the countryside, however, Indians began to join with the guerrilla movement as a means of community defense and self-protection. At the same time, the guerrilla movement itself began to define a more central role for the Indian population in the popular struggle, and in February 1982 the four guerrilla armies announced the establishment of a single command structure.[30]

The Indian population of Guatemala, once marginal in the political affairs of the country, is now a crucial actor in the civil war. Having found organizational expressions for their age-old discontent, it will most likely not cease its activism, no matter what the outcome of the present struggle. Two important conclusions flow from this. First, the peasant war that reached such a high level of intensity in 1980–81 is the direct product of Guatemalan history, caused by policies of developing agricultural export industries at the expense of the rural indigenous population. No amount of strident East-West rhetoric can alter this fact. Second, the Reagan administration's policy of granting legitimacy to the military regimes of Guatemala can only lead to more misguided and militaristic measures that will not solve the problem but merely drown it in more blood. Sooner or later, the popular demand for justice will have to be satisfied.

NOTES

This essay is based on a paper delivered at the panel discussion "Land Reform in Central America," held at the Latin American Studies Association Annual Meeting in Washington, D.C., on 5 March 1982. Since the writing of the paper, two new governments, headed by Gen. Efraín Ríos Montt and Gen. Oscar Humberto Mejía Victores, have assumed power in Guatemala. Although some aspects of the situation, such as the balance of forces between the guerrilla movement and the army, have changed radically, it appears to me that the argument presented in the essay is essentially correct as it stands. For this reason, I have made only minor changes in the text presented at the meeting.

1. "Guatemala Amok," *New York Times,* 13 January 1982.
2. Flora Lewis, "Despair in Guatemala," *New York Times,* 2 October 1981.
3. Testimony by Stephen W. Bosworth, principal deputy assistant secretary of state for inter-American affairs, before the House Committee on Foreign Affairs, Subcommittees on Human Rights and on International Organizations and Inter-American Affairs, *Human Rights in Guatemala: Hearing,* 97th Cong., 1st sess., 30 July 1981. When asked to explain the escalating political violence in Guatemala, Bosworth said that it "stems from both endemic social and economic factors and from the willful efforts by both the right and left to polarize the country." Although he did not elucidate on the social and economic causes involved, he did assert that the most recent wave of violence began in October 1978 when the "left opposition exploited an economic issue [the rise in bus fares in Guatemala City] to lead street riots in which 30 people were killed." According to Bosworth, the "country's rightist elements" reacted to the left-wing "disruption of public order" by escalating the scope of violence in which "centrist groups," such as the Christian Democrats, have been the major victims. Although the right wing causes many casualties, it is the left wing, Bosworth maintained, that "pursues a calculated policy of increasing armed violence" and that carries out "atrocities such as kidnapping children, murdering business managers, and plundering property."
4. Gabriel Aguilera Peralta, "Efectos cuantitativos de la política de terror del estado guatemalteco en relación al movimiento popular," *Estudios Sociales Centroamericanos,* no. 27 (1980): 217–49.
5. Testimony by the Reverend William L. Wipfler, director of the Committee on Latin America and the Caribbean, National Council of Churches, before the House Committee on International Relations, Subcommittee on International Organizations, *Human Rights in Nicaragua, Guatemala, and El Salvador: Implications for U.S. Policy: Hearings,* 94th Cong., 2d sess., 8 and 9 June 1976.
6. Amnesty International, *Guatemala: A Government Program of Political Murder* (London, 1981).
7. U.S. State Department figures on the clashes between the Guatemalan army

and the guerrilla organizations are cited in the July 1981 hearings before the Subcommittees on Human Rights and on International Organizations and Inter-American Affairs of the House Committee on Foreign Affairs. Guerrilla communiqués regularly appear in *Noticias de Guatemala,* published in San José, Costa Rica. For recent U.S. press accounts of the "civil war" in Guatemala, see Raymond Bonner, "Guatemalan Army and Leftist Rebels Are Locked in a Growing Civil War," *New York Times,* 4 December 1981; and Christopher Dickey, "Rich Guatemala Plunders Itself with Warfare," *Washington Post,* 22 January 1982.

8. Eric R. Wolf, *Peasant Wars of the Twentieth Century* (New York: Harper & Row, 1969).

9. See, e.g., Sanford Mosk, "Indigenous Economy in Latin America," *Inter-American Economic Affairs* 8, no. 3 (1954): 3–25; and idem, "The Coffee Economy of Guatemala, 1850–1918: Development and Signs of Instability," *Inter-American Economic Affairs* 9, no. 3 (1955): 6–20.

10. The most complete study of land-tenure patterns in Guatemala remains the Inter-American Committee on Agricultural Development report *Guatemala: Land Tenure and Socio-Economic Development of the Agricultural Sector* (Washington, D.C.: Pan American Union, 1965).

11. The rise of cotton production in Guatemala is discussed in Richard Newbold Adams, *Crucifixion by Power: Essays on Guatemalan National Social Structure, 1944–1966* (Austin: University of Texas Press, 1970), chap. 7.

12. Data on the performance of the Guatemalan agricultural export economy are taken from Inter-American Development Bank/International Bank for Reconstruction and Development/U.S. Agency for International Development, *General Report on the Agricultural and Rural Development of Guatemala* (Washington, D.C., 30 April 1976). For a comparison with the agricultural performance of other Latin American countries during the same time period, see Alain de Janvry, *The Agrarian Question and Reformism in Latin America* (Baltimore: Johns Hopkins University Press, 1981), table 2.1, p. 69.

13. The relation between the rise of agricultural export production and the decline of domestic food production is discussed in Lehman B. Fletcher, Eric Graber, William C. Merrill, and Eric Thorbecke, *Guatemala's Economic Development: The Role of Agriculture* (Ames: Iowa State University Press, 1970). See also Inter-American Development Bank, *General Report.*

14. An analysis of the relation between population growth and land scarcity is contained in William C. Merrill, *The Long-Run Prospects for Increasing Income Levels in Guatemala's Highlands* (Guatemala: National Council of Economic Planning, 1974).

15. A general description of the state of misery of Guatemala's rural population is contained in the World Bank Country Study Report *Guatemala: Economic and Social Position and Prospects* (Washington, D.C., 1978).

16. For a discussion of recent land-reform programs in Guatemala, see Thomas

Melville and Marjorie Melville, *Guatemala: The Politics of Land Ownership* (New York: Free Press, 1971); and Rokael Cardona, "La legislación agraria y el problema de la tierra en Guatemala," in *Estudios Sociales Centroamericanos,* no. 25 (1980): 319–53. On the Arbenz agrarian reform program, the best source remains José Luis Paredes Moreira, *Reforma agraria: Una experiencia en Guatemala* (Guatemala: Editora Universitaria, 1963).

17. An overview of the growth of the cooperative movement in rural Guatemala is contained in William H. Rusch, Fred L. Mann, and Eugene Braun, *Rural Cooperatives in Guatemala: A Study of Their Development and Evaluation of A.I.D. Programs in Their Support* (McLean, Va.: American Technical Assistance Corporation, 1976). For a more personal account of the early development of the cooperative movement by two persons who participated in it, see Thomas Melville and Marjorie Melville, *Whose Heaven, Whose Earth?* (New York: Knopf, 1971). For a description of the effects of both religious conversion and cooperatives on the social ideology of a local Indian community, see Kay B. Warren, *The Symbolism of Subordination: Indian Identity in a Guatemalan Town* (Austin: University of Texas Press, 1978).

18. A general overview of rural-to-rural and rural-to-urban migration patterns in Guatemala is contained in René Arturo Orellana, Virginia Pineda de Gracias, and Andrés Opazo Bernales, "Migraciones internas y estructura agraria: El caso de Guatemala," *Estudios Sociales Centroamericanos,* no. 11 (1975): 41–90. On *ladino* migrants in Guatemala City, see Bryan R. Roberts, *Organizing Strangers: Poor Families in Guatemala City* (Austin: University of Texas Press, 1973). On Indian migrants, see William J. Demarest and Benjamin D. Paul, "Mayan Migrants in Guatemala City," in James Loucky and Margo-Lea Hurwicz, eds., *Mayan Studies: The Midwestern Highlands of Guatemala,* in *Anthropology UCLA* 11, nos. 1 and 2 (1981).

19. One of the best English-language discussions of the recent revitalization of the labor movement in Guatemala is Roger Plant's *Guatemala: Unnatural Disaster* (London: Latin America Bureau, 1978). Plant bases much of his account of the Guatemalan labor movement on a manuscript by Mario Lopez Larrave, which was published as *Breve historia del movimiento sindical guatemalteco* by Editorial Universitaria in Guatemala City in 1979.

20. A good discussion of the role of the CNUS in the contemporary labor struggle in Guatemala is CIDAMO, "The Workers Movement in Guatemala," *NACLA Report on the Americas* 14, no. 1 (1980): 28–33. On worker-peasant alliances, see Carlos Felipe Castro Torres, "Crecimiento de las luchas campesinas en Guatemala, Febrero 1976–Mayo 1978," *Estudios Centroamericanos* 33 (1978): 462–77.

21. The government's plan for promoting cooperative development is discussed in Secretaria General del Consejo Nacional de Planificación Económica, *Estudio/programa del movimiento cooperativo de Guatemala* (Guatemala, September 1976).

22. Some of the social and political implications of the 1976 earthquake and the politics surrounding the national reconstruction effort are discussed in Plant, *Guatemala.*

23. A detailed description of events in the department of El Quiché is contained in an anonymous MS entitled "La iglesia en El Quiché: Martirio y esperanza de un pueblo" (Guatemala, 1980). For one of the only accounts of the Guatemalan army's attack on the church and peasants in the Ixcán area, see Ron Chernow, "The Strange Death of Bill Woods: Did He Fly Too Far in the Zone of the Generals?" *Mother Jones,* May 1979.

24. A number of protest documents describing the Panzós massacre are contained in the International Work Group for Indigenous Affairs report *The Massacre at Panzós* (Copenhagen, 1978). For a more analytic account of the causes of the massacre, see Gabriel Aguilera Peralta, "The Massacre at Panzós and Capitalist Development in Guatemala," *Monthly Review* 31, no. 7 (1979): pp. 13–23.

25. To my knowledge, the only detailed description of the Spanish-embassy massacre and the events leading up to it is contained in a report released by the Guatemalan Democratic Front against Repression (FDCR) soon after it occurred. The FDCR account is corroborated by the report of the Inter-American Commission on Human Rights on human-rights violations in Guatemala, published in October 1981.

26. For a description of the Committee for Peasant Unity (CUC) and the 1980 strike actions in the plantation area, see "Guatemala: Major Breakthrough in Campesino Struggle," *Sugar World Special Report,* April 1980.

27. For a journalistic account of the Guerrilla Army of the Poor's Ernesto "Che" Guevara front in Huehuetenango, see the articles by Mario Menéndez in the Mexican journal *Por Esto,* July–August 1981. A participant's account of the early history of the recent guerrilla movement is contained in Mario Payeras, *Los Dias de la selva* (Mexico: Editorial Nuestro Tiempo, 1981).

28. "Guerrillas Put the Military in a Sweat," *Latin America Regional Reports: Mexico and Central America,* 9 January 1981, 5.

29. For an account of the army offensive against the guerillas that began in November 1981, see "Guatemala: Army Shifts Strategy," *El Salvador Bulletin* 1, no. 3 (1982), published by the U.S.–El Salvador Research and Information Center, P.O. Box 4797, Berkeley, Calif. 94704.

30. In February 1982 the four guerrilla organizations in Guatemala signed a unity proclamation. See "Proclama unitaria de las organizaciones revolucionarias EGP, FAR, ORPA y PGT al pueblo Guatemala" (Guatemala, February 1982).

Guatemala

SOCIAL CHANGE
AND POLITICAL CONFLICT

Lars Schöultz

INTRODUCTION

U.S. policymakers seem to believe there are only three basic alternatives in Latin American political struggles: democratic reformist regimes, right-wing tyrannies supportive of the United States, and Communist dictatorships supportive of Soviet-Cuban expansionism. Although policymakers have made a verbal commitment to encouraging the first alternative, they have been reluctant to dissociate the United States from the second for fear of encouraging the third.

The current unrest in Guatemala reflects a classic problem of social change: how to adjust to the gradual but inexorable political awakening of previously passive social groups. This awakening is a function of economic changes in recent decades, especially the development of large-scale commercial agriculture on the Pacific coast, which requires considerable amounts of migrant wage labor, and the development of mineral resources in the northern transversal strip, which involves the displacement and disruption of Indian communities. These changes have occurred recently, with considerable speed. Nearly all scholars argue that thus far the change has been largely for the worse, because local support systems have been destroyed while nothing has replaced the void other than wages.

If the problem in Guatemala were only the lack of a social-security system to pick up the slack created by the destruction of traditional institutions, there might be an easier solution. Modernization, however, has created not only the need for basic social services but also the desire to participate in political life. Traditional people have come to recognize quite quickly that the political system is the means modern people use to address their needs. Newly mobilized social groups now want a share of political power, yet the existing political system has refused to yield. Instead it has attempted to eliminate physically any political group that advocates a more pluralistic political system. This is the cause of contemporary unrest in Guatemala.

Historically, a society with sharp internal cleavages, Guatemala is currently experiencing a period of increasingly rapid disintegration. It is unfortunate that this accelerating change and the traumatic changes in Nicaragua and El Salvador are occurring simultaneously, for it encourages analysts and policymakers to think in terms of regional instability—"the turmoil in Central America"—despite nearly universal agreement among persons familiar with the country that local conditions and forces in Guatemala are responsible for what is happening there.[1] Given the events of the past few years in Central America, however, the situation in Guatemala readily conjures up in the minds of security-conscious policy makers in the United States, an image of falling dominoes. With the "loss" of Nicaragua, they perceive the need to protect Guatemala and El Salvador. They feel as they do despite the fact that it is impossible to identify for whom and from what the two countries should be saved unless, of course, we decide to resort to the archaic jargon of the cold war and insist upon saving a part of the free world from Marxist communism. Moreover, their analysis is concluded without any understanding of the truly monumental costs such a salvage job would entail.

Not the least of these costs would be an opportunity cost—a lost chance to encourage a transition to some form of genuine democracy and long-term stability in Guatemala. Despite Guatemala's long history of political violence, the present condition of near barbarism cannot continue indefinitely; the question is not whether but how the situation will be resolved. That is a question for Guatemalans to answer. Nonetheless, it would be disingenuous to suggest that the United States has no role to play in Guatemala; we have played a major role in Guatemalan politics for decades.

Most U.S. citizens would like that role to include an effort to encourage political and social reform leading to a more pluralistic society.[2] Most U.S. policymakers share this desire, for they recognize that throughout Central America the social stability based upon repression has eroded and been replaced by active opposition movements. Ironically, some form of change is now a prerequisite for the stability that U.S. policymakers have always prized in Central America. The question now, therefore, is not how to hold back the clock, for it has already moved ahead, but how to ease the trauma that inevitably accompanies the transition to a more modern society.

THE ECONOMIC ROOTS
OF CONTEMPORARY GUATEMALA

It is not possible to approach the topic of democracy in Guatemala without first discussing the Guatemalan political economy. Like many other Latin American countries, postcolonial Guatemala had a society that was highly stratified, its economy was export oriented, and its politics were dominated by repeated clashes between liberals and conservatives. But unlike the others, Guatemala had been the base of a regional merchant monopoly and the seat of Spanish power during the colonial period. Guatemala's Creole merchant elite grew strong as a result of the monopoly trade, especially after the establishment of the Consulado, in 1793.

Following independence, in 1823, the power of the merchant class was challenged by landed interests that had opposed Spanish mercantilism and that now wanted to establish new relations with the rest of Europe, primarily with Great Britain. The precarious balance between these two important groups allowed a series of *caudillos* to exercise much greater influence and to control the government longer than was possible in the rest of Central America. Four men played this role during the first century of independence: Rafael Carrera (1839–48 and 1851–65), Justo Rufino Barrios (1873–85), Manuel Estrada Cabrera (1898–1920), and Jorge Ubico (1931–44). Each held power in alliance with liberal or conservative elites.

Given the differing policy preferences of liberals and conservatives, the most pressing task in Guatemala was not to establish a national government to exercise effective control but rather to determine the purpose for which power would be used. In the immediate postcolonial period, the primary goal was to hold together the Central American Confederation in the face of resistance by the "provinces." Underlying this goal was another: the need to reconcile the interests of "conservatives" (*latifundistas,* some merchants, and church elites), who favored centralized government, continued mercantilism, and little change in the structure of privilege, with those of "liberals" (market-oriented landowners, intellectuals, liberal professionals, and middle-income groups), who stood for decentralization, free trade, and liberal economic reforms. These rival coalitions were relatively typical of the entire region, but the cleavages were particularly sharp in Guatemala because of the relatively advanced Guatemalan economic development and hence divisive functional specialization.

The liberals eventually emerged victorious thanks to an important change in Guatemala's export economy: they became the new economic elite whose power rested upon a developing coffee export market. By 1870 coffee exports represented 44 percent of the country's total exports, giving the sector a prominence it has not yet relinquished. Like their Salvadoran counterparts, the Guatemalan planters were impressed by the example of Costa Rica. According to Woodward, these liberals saw themselves as practical men, believers in at least the superficial aspects of positivism, especially the theory of comparative advantage.[3] Less-sympathetic observers suggest that their liberalism was more self-serving, since in practice it meant "a more active role for the state in protecting and subsidizing, but never regulating or restricting, private enterprise, and an open door to foreign interests."[4] What is certain is that liberals understood the need to defeat powerful interests opposed to the restructuring of the agricultural sector (the Consulado de Comercio, the Sociedad Económica de Amigos del País, and the church). If they wanted to take advantage of the expanding international demand for coffee, they would have to implement policies that would produce reorganization. Specifically, they needed land, credit, infrastructure, and labor.

The land came from the church and communal Indian holdings, which in turn "liberated" an abundant source of labor. As the process of land concentration proceeded, enormous pressure was placed on small landholders to turn over their lands. Foreign investors were encouraged to provide the needed capital for the development of infrastructure and, increasingly, to provide credit for the production and marketing of coffee. According to Torres-Rivas, the Guatemalan liberal revolution brought about a modernization without parallel at any other time in Central American history.[5] But the liberal victory did not produce the complete destruction of all traditional forces, and it fell considerably short of laying the foundation for a modern state. The church, small landowners, and municipal and Indian *ejidos* suffered the brunt of the land redistribution. Medium-size cultivators were able to retain and expand their holdings, however, and the *latifundio* gave way to the hacienda (plantation) and the *minifundio* (small holding). Thus, a rural proletariat emerged without the disappearance of the *campesino*.

At the same time, the Creole oligarchy that constituted Guatemala's governing class was expanded to include the predominantly rural *ladino* (non-Indian) upper middle class, a group that was rapidly accumulating capital through coffee production. In addition, a further process of elite assimilation occurred as merchants made wealthy during the colonial era gradually moved into agricultural production through foreclosures, while the larger planters established their own banking institutions (six of these were in operation by 1895). As the original rationale behind the societal division into liberal and conservative groups disappeared, the Guatemalan elite became an integrated liberal oligarchy. By the twentieth century, Guatemala's planters, bankers, owners of commercial houses, and representatives of foreign corporations made up a fairly small, well-established elite.

What kind of an economy did these liberal elites produce? It was, first, agricultural and they have persistently emphasized that agricultural production is the heart of the economy. All macroeconomic data from Guatemala are highly unreliable, but it is believed that agriculture constitutes at least 25 percent of the nation's GDP, at least one-half (and perhaps as much as two-thirds) of the economically active population being employed in agriculture. Moreover, the relative importance of agriculture has declined only slightly during the past two decades. In the meantime, manufacturing increased its share of the GDP by less than 4 percent in the years 1960–79, to the present 16 percent of the GDP. The national development plan for 1979–83 continued the long-term strategy of rural development.[6]

Second, they created a dual agricultural sector, one part oriented toward subsistence farming and the other toward agricultural exports. For more than a century, coffee has been the primary agricultural export, but its share of total agricultural exports declined from a high of 82 percent in the early 1950s to about 44 percent today. Cotton, the second-most-important export, is a relative newcomer that accounts for more than 20 percent of Guatemala's agricultural exports. Farmed by modern methods on plantations in the Pacific region, cotton has boomed while bananas have declined. Sugar received a major boost in the 1960s following the reassignment by the United States of the Cuban sugar quota, and nontraditional agricultural exports, particularly meat and cardamon ($50 million in exports in 1979), are making further inroads into the export shares of Guatemala's traditional agricultural exports. In the late 1970s many analysts predicted that exports of nickel and petroleum would change the basic position of Guatemala's foreign trade, but these predictions now appear to have been too optimistic.

Third, Guatemala developed a stable economy with steady but very modest growth. Between the end of World War II and 1966, the GDP increased an average of 4.4 percent per year, or about 1.0 percent per year per capita. From the mid-1960s to the late 1970s, the annual rate of growth in Guatemala's GDP was about 5.8 percent. At first this growth was accompanied by mild inflation— among the lowest in Latin America in the years 1960–75, and *the* lowest (at 0.1 percent) during the period 1961–65—but in recent years Guatemala's inflation rate has been about the average for Latin America. Nearly all of Guatemala's inflation is caused by factors beyond its control, particularly the rise in petroleum prices. The nation's balance of trade is often favorable.

Fourth, the economy was opened to foreign investors and creditors. According to Herrera, the book value of foreign investment in Guatemala is 27 percent of the total investment, the highest percentage in Central America.[7] The old Compañía Agrícola de Guatemala (United Fruit) is now gone, but the list of foreign investors in Guatemala is impressive in its scope, covering virtually every economic activity except subsistence agriculture.

Fifth, the liberal oligarchy produced an inequitable economy. In a predominantly agricultural society, land ownership is the primary source of wealth. There are currently about 600,000 *fincas* in Guatemala, but 166,000 of these are smaller than 1.4 hectares (3.5 acres) and occupy only 2.3 percent of the land. One-fifth of the *fincas* occupy 70 percent of the land.[8] As a result, the distribution of income is highly skewed: 5 percent of the population receives 34 percent of the national income, while 70 percent of the population subsists on an average annual income of $74.

In summarizing these features of the Guatemalan economy, one finds it hard to disagree with AID researchers who wrote more than a decade ago that "Guatemala's recent performance can be described as one of economic stability—internally and externally—with modest output growth. It would not be unfair to say that Guatemala's economic and social development record has been poor. There is little doubt that the absolute standard of living of a large part of the population has declined. Since the size of the population and the labor force increased, the number of unemployed and disguised unemployed must have risen considerably."[9] More recently, Torres-Rivas indicated that "in Guatemala, perhaps more than in any other country, . . . economic growth by itself does not resolve any social problem."[10]

Modest industrialization, new mineral exploitation, and, especially, the modernization of export agriculture have dramatically changed the social stratification of Guatemala, forming a large migrating rural proletariat and creating an "informal" sector in the urban centers, the members of which live near the fringe of human existence.

These new sectors live so poorly that Guatemala's social statistics are among the worst in the hemisphere: the infant-mortality rate is 89 per 1,000 live births (160 in rural areas), life expectancy is fifty-eight years (fifty years for Indians, sixty years for *ladinos*), and at least 60 percent of the adult population is illiterate. And these official statistics are probably optimistic, grossly underestimating the deprivation among the rural Indian population, which constitutes about 40 percent of the population of 7 million. Indians have found that data reporting is a prelude to taxation and military service.

U.S. policymakers, indifferent to the implication of this evidence of human deprivation, maintain an attitude of optimism. The 1979 State Department human-rights report on Guatemala chose to emphasize plans for the near future, accepting as reasonable the hopelessly optimistic 1979–83 development plan designed to provide free health and education services through the ninth grade. Although the 1980 report was far more pessimistic (noting, for example, that the government official in charge of the development plan had been assassinated), it, too, continued the naïve practice of accepting government plans and official statistics as an indicator of government intentions. The 1981 report provided an impressive array of positive statistics but failed to interpret them accurately. For example, though it is true that the Lucas García government was "spending 25 percent of its agricultural budget for colonization of the northern transversal belt," it is also true that very little of the land in question was being distributed to peasants —AID calls the Guatemalan agrarian reform "a drop in the bucket." The land in the transversal strip has fallen largely into the hands of military officers. There is a quite widely accepted norm in Guatemala that the general in charge of the government should assist in improving the life-styles of his colleagues who remain in the barracks.[11] In any event, it is important to recognize that the Guatemalan public sector is small in terms of personnel, expenditures, and services, and there is little to indicate any significant change can occur without large-scale international financial assistance.

However, there is clearly no commitment on the part of the current Guatemalan government to even the most modest socioeconomic reform programs. A large literature now exists to indicate that external development assistance will have little impact upon the poor so long as the nation's economic and political elites remain indifferent to their plight. After considerable effort, including interviews with officials of the State Department's Office of Central American Affairs, I was unable to identify the empirical basis for the State Department's 1979 claim that "there are significant elements within Guatemalan society and the Government who propose an expanded role for government in promoting equitable economic and social development." As a minor concession to candor, the State Department removed the adjective "significant" from its 1980 report, but it reinserted the word in 1981.[12] The Reagan State Department refuses to recognize that the Guatemalan economy is controlled by Manchester-school liberals committed to the trickle-down theory of socioeconomic development. Unfortunately, that theory has not worked well in the Third World. In Guatemala, it has not worked at all.

THE STATUS QUO AND POLITICAL DEMOBILIZATION

The dominant political ideology in Guatemala since 1954 has been based upon two pillars: the defense of the existing structure of socioeconomic privilege and the demobilization of emerging social sectors. At first this was accomplished by the dismantlement of the programs inaugurated during the Arévalo-Arbenz decade (1945–54). A 1954 decree repealed the Land Reform Act of 1952, and the government thereafter returned 99.6 percent of the land that had been expropriated. Nearly all beneficiaries of the aborted land reform were dispossessed, and all peasant cooperatives were dissolved. The nationwide literacy program was halted. If implemented, it would have doubled the number of citizens capable of reading, thereby dramatically increasing the pool of potential political participants.[13]

These efforts to halt mobilization before it could develop have been supplemented by the very direct policy of physically attempting to exterminate any organization exhibiting even mild anti–status quo attitudes. It was to be expected that the guerrilla insurgency of the mid-1960s would arouse violent opposition from the government, but in its counterinsurgency program the government apparently decided that indiscriminate terror was an appropriate policy. To eliminate a few hundred guerrillas, the government killed perhaps 10,000 Guatemalan peasants. Reflecting the Vietnam mentality of his time, Col. John Webber, a U.S. military attaché, felt inclined to agree with the government's position: "The Communists are using everything they have, including terror. And it must be met."[14]

For three decades the Guatemalan government has used terrorism to demobilize the population. Long before the term became common in the southern cone, *desaparecido* was a household word in Guatemala. In the early 1970s there was even a human-rights group, the Comité de Familiares de Personas Desaparecidas, engaged in documenting this form of demobilization: 15,325 cases were reported in the period 1970–75, some 75 percent involving government agents or government-sponsored paramilitary groups. As a reward for his efforts, the apolitical leader of the committee, Edmundo Guerra Theilheimer, was murdered by a right-wing terrorist group in March 1974. Simply stated, murder is the government's preferred method of controlling those citizens who encourage reform and democracy in Guatemala. Particularly favored is the selective assassination of emerging political leaders: Manuel Colom Argueta (March 1979) and Alberto Fuentes Mohr (January 1978) are only among the most notable of thousands of political leaders whose lives have been ended by the government or government-sponsored death squads in the effort to deter political mobilization. The inescapable conclusion to be drawn from the enormous documentation on government-sponsored violence is that the forces supporting the status quo are implementing a long-term, persistent policy of demobilization through death and intimidation.

Which are these forces? It is difficult to answer this question with precision, for the names of leaders and organizations change with frustrating frequency. The military as an institution has not changed, however, and by all accounts it has been responsible for much of the terror. But the difficulty in assessing the role of the military is in determining its level of independence from civilian elites. One can spend a lifetime discussing the question of whether the civilian dog is wagging its military tail. Certainly the military enjoys considerable autonomy, and in recent years all major civilian political parties have offered military officers as their presidential candidates, but military actions have been closely related to the protection of civilian elites—the 1978 Panzos massacre of Indians engaged in a land dispute is an excellent example, as is the military's involvement in the union breaking at the Pantaleón sugar plantation. Perhaps it is simply advisable to assert that there appears to be a mutual accommodation based upon a community of interests among the military and the nation's civilian oligarchy. In any event, they are closely interlocked politically.

Several political parties have developed to support the status quo through demobilization. This gives the military the opportunity to pick among several groups of civilian elites who themselves differ but little on ideology or policy. The military does not have a party; it has candidates. In 1970 the favored candidate was Col. Carlos Arana Osorio, who associated himself with the ultraconservative National Liberation Movement (MLN), a party founded by Col. Carlos Castillo Armas and directed by Mario Sandoval Alarcón, who also counts among his organizational credits the founding of *Mano Blanca,* the right-wing death squad. In 1974 the army's candidate was Gen. Kjell Laugerud García, who stood for election with the Nationalist Coalition of the MLN and the Democratic Institutional party (PID). After Laugerud broke with the MLN, the army selected a new coalition to carry its banner in 1978—the PID and the inaptly named Revolutionary party (PR). Thus, in 1978 the electorate was given a choice between the ultraconservative MLN candidate, the ex-president general Enrique Peralta Azurdia, who was called out of retirement in Miami to head the party's ticket, and Laugerud's choice, Gen. Romeo Lucas García. (A third candidate, the Christian Democrats' Gen. Ricardo Peralta Méndez, was considered a moderate.) In the late 1970s the rightwing portion of the political party spectrum was completed by the Authentic Nationalist party (originally the Central Aranista Organizada), which reflected the ideas of the ex-president Carlos Arana Osorio, another general who had reached national prominence by directing the devastating counterinsurgency campaign in Zacapa in 1966–68. In 1976, Arana Osorio formed a coalition with the MLN and the PR in a successful effort to gain control of congress.

In 1982, voters were offered the choice of four right-wing candidates. The military's choice was Gen. Angel Aníbal Guevara, General Lucas García's former defense minister. He was challenged by the MLN's Mario Sandoval, the Authentic Nationalists' Gustavo Anzueto Vielman, and Alejandro Maldonado Aguirre, who was nominated by a coalition of the National Renovation party and the Christian Democrats. The least radical of the four, Maldonado Aguirre was characterized by the *New York Times* as "a moderate right-winger."[15] Although Guevara emerged victorious from the contest, he was never to assume office. Two weeks after the 7 March election, army officers ousted General Lucas García and installed the retired general Efraín Ríos Montt as chieftain of a military junta. Ríos Montt initially appeared inclined to greater moderation, but it soon became apparent that the change involved only the cast of characters, not the script of Guatemalan politics.

In response to the Sandinista victory in nearby Nicaragua, the Lucas García government had adopted a siege mentality that accelerated both the undeclared guerrilla warfare between Left and Right and the horrifyingly effective crusade by paramilitary death squads. Until 1980 the U.S. State Department explained the rising levels of human-rights abuses by issuing a "violence as usual" commentary on Guatemalan political culture. Then, in its 1980 annual report on human-rights practices, the State Department conceded that Guatemala was undergoing an uncommonly violent period, marked by widespread government violations of fundamental human rights:

> In 1980, kidnapping and assassinations reached higher levels than in 1972. Deaths which appeared to be politically motivated averaged about 75 to 100 each month. Reportedly these acts were carried out by armed extremists of the left and right and by elements of the official security forces. The government has not taken effective steps to halt abuses or carry out serious investigations. The high incidence of political and personal violence continued to seriously effect the exercise of most fundamental liberties. Abductions and assassinations have the effect of rendering habeas corpus and fair trial meaningless even though they are constitutionally guaranteed. In an open letter to the Guatemalan Catholic hierarchy made public November 2, the Pope deplored the wave of violence and pleaded with those responsible to bring it to an end.[16]

A number of nongovernmental human-rights organizations have argued that violations in Guatemala increased alarmingly in the late 1970s and have remained high in the initial years of the 1980s. In May 1979 the Commission on Human Rights of the World Peace Council issued a condemnation of the Guatemalan government, calling on the Lucas administration "to cease repression and to dissolve the paramilitary groups." In November 1979 thirty-five representatives from eight Western European countries met in Antwerp for the Conference on Solidarity of the Human Rights Committees for Guatemala. Conference members lamented in particular that "the active leaders and members of the trade unions, student bodies, peasant organizations, religious groups and democratic parties are suffering repression, house searches, kidnappings, persecutions, death threats, torture and assassination by the army, police, and paramilitary groups maintained and led by the military dictatorship." International opinion has continued to denounce state terror in Guatemala, pointing in particular to the systematic murder, kidnapping, threats, and torture of union members, peasants, students, religious workers, and members of political parties.

In October 1982 AI released a report stating that the Guatemalan military government had "massacred more than 2,600 Indians and peasant farmers in a new counterinsurgency program launched after General Efraín Ríos Montt came to power in March." According to AI, the government had "destroyed entire villages, tortured and mutilated local people and carried out mass executions in at least 112 separate incidents between March and July." On 5 April 1982, for example, troops entered a village in Quiché, "forced all the inhabitants into the courthouse, raped the women and beheaded the men, and then battered the children to death against rocks in a nearby river."[17]

These reports should disabuse anyone of the notion that the Guatemalan government is willing to permit moderate reforms. The Ríos Montt government is engaged in implementing policies very similar to those of previous administrations.

MODERATE CHANGE AND LIMITED PLURALISM

In Guatemala today there simply is no moderate economic, military, or political center. The forces defending the status quo have been able to maintain undisputed control over the armed forces and the electoral machinery of the central government, so that only the most eternally optimistic moderate political actor has been willing to make the sacrifices (potential and real) to take a stand in the Guatemalan political center. Until early 1981 that actor was the Carter administration.

The Carter administration's policy of encouraging moderation represented a significant departure from the previous position of the U.S. government. U.S. complicity in the ultraconservative coup that overthrew the Arbenz government in 1954, the major U.S. aid program to Guatemala in the mid- and late-1950s, and the military counterinsurgency program in the 1960s that facilitated the government-sponsored reign of terror in the countryside that continues to this day suggested the dominant direction of U.S. policy toward Guatemala. Not surprisingly, a problem of credibility appeared not only among Guatemalans but also among U.S. citizens who in the past had been highly critical of the alliance between their government and the forces of reaction and repression in Guatemala.

Beginning in 1977, the Guatemalan government rejected U.S. military aid following the publication of the 1977 State Department human-rights reports. Congress promptly prohibited FMS credits to Guatemala in the foreign-assistance appropriations act for fiscal year 1978, but the *deliveries* never ceased and other types of economic and military aid continued, as Tables 1 and 2 indicate. In October 1979 and again in May 1980, the United States decided not to support multilateral development bank loans to Guatemala, but here again the signals were weak: during the Carter administration five other loans received an affirmative U.S. vote, with the explanation that the loans were for projects that directly benefited needy people. In any event, the cool reception that the assistant secretary of state William Bowdler received during his visit to Guatemala in September 1979 indicated only that the Guatemalans were getting the message, not that they were willing to consider reforms. The government balked at accepting the relatively liberal George Landau as U.S. ambassador, betting instead on a change in U.S. policy. As the London periodical *Latin America* noted in late 1979, "the best the Guatemalan government can hope for is a victory at next year's US presidential polls for a Republican."[18]

What, specifically, was the Carter administration attempting to accomplish? Discussions with State Department personnel suggest that the goal was a stable, progressive government selected through open, competitive elections. U.S. officials apparently believed that a *procedural* change—an honest election—would have led to a resolution of several fundamental issues. First, it would have discouraged leftist extremism by destroying the growing coalition between Marxist guerrillas and more-moderate civilians who had been forced into the radical camp for lack of an acceptable alternative. Second, it would have encouraged the silenced majority in the center to re-enter the political arena. And, third, it would have

TABLE 1: *U.S. Military Aid Deliveries to Guatemala*
(Thousands of Dollars)

Fiscal Year	Total	FMS[a]	MAP	EDA	IMET	Commercial Exports
1950–59	1,278	496	531	0	251	
1960	227	44	76	11	96	
1961	480	66	29	41	344	
1962	1,473	16	518	132	807	
1963	3,710	31	2,151	1,063	465	
1964	1,774	238	1,307	149	80	
1965	2,595	488	1,068	643	396	
1966	1,662	391	802	113	356	
1967	2,039	207	1,202	384	246	
1968	2,783	363	1,524	371	525	
1969	1,306	144	877	44	241	
1970	2,530	278	1,358	264	630	
1971	2,270	846	635	354	435	556
1972	7,665	6,229	458	724	254	513
1973	4,220	1,820	1,401	500	499	142
1974	4,500	1,484	1,539	1,021	456	209
1975	4,846	3,378	260	788	420	471
1976	3,847	3,041	280	42	484	345
1977	2,803	2,169	104	67	463	1,020
1978	2,456	2,410	46	0	0	550
1979	3,634	3,627	1	0	6	868
1980	2,366	2,254	71	0	41	417
1950–80	60,462	30,020	16,237	6,711	7,494	5,090

SOURCE: Defense Security Assistance Agency.
[a]Includes FMS financial guarantee program.

forced the Right out of office—no one claims that it could win
a fair election—the essential first step in implementing significant
structural reforms to defuse an explosive social situation.

Even if the Carter administration had not been voted out of
office, history suggests, this democracy-oriented electoral policy
would have failed in Guatemala. The electoral transition to democracy was attempted in Guatemala, in 1945–54, and it failed.
If it had been attempted again, it would almost certainly have
failed once more, for in the ensuing decades nothing happened to
suggest that any outcome other than failure was possible.

Since 1954 the Guatemalan electorate has become accustomed to
an extraordinarily high level of electoral fraud. In 1954 Carlos
Castillo Armas won a Ubico-style plebiscite with 99 percent of the
vote. In 1957 the election was so fraudulent that it had to be

TABLE 2: *U.S. Economic Aid to Guatemala*
(Millions of Dollars)

Year	Total	AID	PL480	Other
1962–65	45.5	21.0	5.8	18.7
1966	9.0	4.1	.9	4.0
1967	14.1	11.5	1.9	.7
1968	16.5	11.2	1.0	3.4
1969	9.1	6.1	2.2	.8
1970	32.2	29.1	2.5	.6
1971	16.7	14.2	2.0	.5
1972	16.6	12.5	3.4	.7
1973	12.0	9.5	1.7	.8
1974	4.7	2.5	1.2	1.0
1975	14.1	9.5	3.4	1.3
1976	43.5	29.0	12.5	2.0
197T*	4.4	3.7	.3	.4
1977	20.8	14.3	4.5	2.0
1978	10.6	4.5	4.6	1.5
1979	24.7	17.4	5.3	2.0
1980	13.0	7.8	3.3	1.9
1981	19.0	9.1	7.5	2.4
1962–81	326.5	216.9	64.9	44.7

SOURCE: Agency for International Development.
*197T = Transitional Quarter

annulled. In 1958 Guatemalans had to choose between Gen. Miguel Ydígoras Fuentes and the even-more-conservative Cruz Salazar. In 1963 the scheduled presidential election was preempted by Colonel Peralta Azurdia. In 1966 Méndez Montenegro won in a fairly honest contest, but before he could assume office he was forced to sign a pact with the army, guaranteeing a continuation of the status quo. In 1970 the votes for Arana Osorio were counted fairly, but in an environment of extreme terror. In 1974 the election was won by Ríos Montt, but the MLN-dominated electoral commission decided that its candidate, General Laugerud, had achieved a plurality. In 1978 the Lucas victory was extraordinarily fraudulent, even by Guatemalan standards, prompting a *Washington Post* correspondent to report that "the fraud perpetrated here is so transparent that nobody could expect to get away with it."[19] Only 36 percent of the registered voters appeared at the polls, and one-fifth of them cast spoiled ballots. After the 1982 elections the government's candidate, General Guevara, told a press conference that "we have won these elections freely and cleanly through hard work," but protest demonstrations were called by two of the three opposition candidates—Sandoval and Maldonado—who accused the government of widespread fraud. Recovering from an operation for throat cancer, Sandoval asked his running mate to declare the election of Guevara "the most scandalous fraud in Guatemala's history."[20]

In the 1960s the guerrilla leader Marco Antonio Yon Sosa remarked that "the electoral path is barred in Guatemala, not only because the bourgeoisie cannot provide democratic elections and continue to remain in power. It is also barred because the workers do not believe in elections."[21] The existence of competition among parties, the holding of elections, and even the honest tally of votes should not be permitted to obscure the facts that the electorate is given little or no choice among competing candidates and that much of the electorate is regularly terrorized and intimidated during the electoral process. If a new, attractive candidate is permitted to campaign—in 1979, at U.S. insistence, the Lucas government permitted four new parties to register, the first new additions to the party list since 1968—then the government simply kills the new party leadership—the "final solution" à la Guatemala.

Not surprisingly, therefore, the Guatemalan electorate simply ignores as best it can the entire process of elections and voting, as Table 3 clearly demonstrates. Guatemalan citizens may not be able to select their leaders through elections, but they can communicate a message that merits consideration. The message is, in Sloan's words, that "the power structure manipulates the electoral laws in such a way that no party which threatens the interests of the military, the landowners, or the capitalists is allowed to partici- pate."[22] If during the Carter administration a Guatemalan were to have been asked what had changed in recent years to make voting more meaningful, the only possible response would have been that the United States had for a brief period moved slightly toward supporting the political center. But while the Carter administra- tion refused to provide *unquestioning* support for the forces of repression, it did supply substantial support: $8.5 million in mili- tary aid and $1.8 million in commercial arms sales during fiscal year 1978 through fiscal year 1980. There will have to be several rows of zeros in Table 1 before even the most optimistic Guatema- lan will accept the personal risks that accompany active political participation in contemporary Guatemala. Until then, politically active Guatemalans will continue to shun the center.

SIGNIFICANT STRUCTURAL CHANGE AND DEMOCRATIZATION

The day after the election of 3 March 1974, the government trucked thousands of machete-wielding peasants into Guatemala City. Their task was to keep the supporters of General Ríos Montt off the streets while the government-controlled electoral commis- sion adjusted the election results to produce a victory for General Laugerud. As the fraud became apparent, angry students began to demonstrate, asking Ríos Montt for arms to defend their victory. General Laugerud's running mate, the MLN's Mario Sandoval, challenged Ríos Montt's supporters to a street fight: "We will be waiting to meet them to show them that we will not tolerate blackmail and threats." On 14 March, Ríos Montt conceded. Shortly thereafter, he accepted a diplomatic post in Europe.

During the years since 1974 the Guatemalan political forces that

TABLE 3: Participation and Abstention in Seven Guatemalan Elections

Year	Adult Population	Registered Voters	Percentage of Adult Population Registered	Voters	Percentage of Abstention	Votes for Winner	Percentage of Adult Population Selecting Winning Candidate
1945	NA	310,000	NA	296,214	4.5	255,660	NA
1951	NA	583,300	NA	407,453	31.2	266,778	NA
1958	1,500,000	736,400	49.1	492,274	33.2	190,972	12.7
1966	2,100,000	944,170	44.9	531,270	43.7	209,204	10.0
1970	2,400,000	1,190,449	49.6	640,684	46.2	251,135	10.5
1974	2,492,306	1,568,724	62.9	659,229[a]	58.0	209,964	8.4
				727,174[b]	53.6	298,953	12.0
1978	3,150,000	1,785,764	56.6	652,073	63.5	262,960	8.3

SOURCE: Adapted from Instituto de Investigaciones Politicas y Sociales, "Los partidos politicos y el estado guatemalteco desde 1944 hasta nuestros días," *Estudios Centroamericanos* 33 (1978): 428.

NA = not available.

[a] Data from the Frente Nacional de Oposición.

[b] Data from the Registro Electoral.

champion significant structural change took a number of major steps toward effective organization, a remarkable effort in an environment of extreme repression, where emerging progressive leaders are regularly—almost inevitably—assassinated. Several of the emerging groups have been forced to move further to the left on the political spectrum than their ideological positions would suggest it appropriate. To these groups, "significant change" means an end to governmental terror and repression, an open political system, and a major attack upon the nation's social problems—agrarian and other redistributive reforms, plus the establishment of an effective social-service infrastructure to meet the population's basic needs.

In terms of their political organization, these new groups are still quite weak. In the late 1970s the principal component was the social democratic Frente Unido de la Revolución (FUR), but its leadership was decimated—at least six major leaders were killed in the three months leading up to the March 1980 municipal elections —and many remaining leaders left the country or went underground. This left two major opposition political organizations seeking goals similar to those of the FUR: the Frente Democrático contra la Represión (FDCR) and the Frente Patriótico 31 de Enero. Together, these two organizations speak for perhaps a hundred labor, peasant, student, and church groups, plus a number of small political parties. Both organizations were formed in early 1980; each is linked to a separate guerrilla organization. The FDCR is associated with the Guerrilla Army of the Poor, while the Frente Patriótico 31 de Enero is closely linked to the Rebel Armed Forces.

Their weakness should not last much longer, for the level of political mobilization is rising quite rapidly in contemporary Guatemala, and functional groups are quickly filling the organizational void. The development of organized labor has been particularly noteworthy in light of the antilabor policies of he post-1954 period. After the fall of the Arbenz government, the Castillo Armas regime canceled the registration of 533 unions and changed the national labor code to make effective unionization impossible. The number of organized workers fell from 100,000 in 1954 to fewer than 27,000 in 1955. Throughout the past decades the level of repression of labor has remained high. In 1966 twenty-eight trade unionists were arrested while attending a clandestine meeting, tortured, and then thrown out of a plane flying over the Pacific. In 1973 the government broke a teachers' strike by injuring 300 peaceful demonstrators; President Arana called the strike "a cover for a Communist plan to overthrow the government."[23]

Nonetheless, labor organizations continue to sprout and develop. In past years these organizations coalesced as the Frente Nacional Sindical (1968), the Consejo Nacional de Consulta Sindical (1973), and more recently the Comité Nacional de Unidad Sindical (CNUS). Parenthetically, we may note that another CNUS existed briefly in the mid-1940s, but merged with nonaffiliated labor groups to form the now-defunct Confederación General de Trabajadores de Guatemala (CGTG). The besieged CNUS was founded by seventy-two labor groups in March 1976, at the beginning of the labor dispute at Embotelladora Guatemalteca—the U.S.–owned and operated Coca-Cola franchise in Guatemala. After that, CNUS became a central force not only in labor struggles but in antigovernment activity as well. Its leadership felt the full pressure of repression by the Lucas García and Ríos Montt governments.

A related rural labor organization is the Comité de Unidad Campesina (CUC), today perhaps the most militant part of Guatemalan organized labor. The CUC reached national prominence in 1980, when it organized a successful two-week strike by 50,000 Pacific plantation workers. Formed with the assistance of guerrilla leaders, the CUC is believed to be expanding from its highland base in Quiché and Chimaltenango into the Pacific plantation region. In the face of massive repression, nearly all labor leaders have now gone underground. The CNUS, the CUC, and the Central Nacional de Trabajadores (CNT) represent social forces that msut be part of any attempt to restructure Guatemalan political life.

The Indians are a second emerging group in contemporary Guatemala. In 1959 Monteforte Toledo wrote that "until now, no political group has made the effort to fully understand the peasant Indians as a new, independent political factor. One can be sure that this significant part of the Guatemalan population is increasingly inclined to enter the political arena, encouraged not by outside persons or by momentary issues, but in positive response to practical programs that will address their needs."[24] These needs are absolutely basic. A decade ago an AID-sponsored team noted that "all the data that have been reviewed on production, yields, farm size, income and employment indicate that the income position of small farmers has deteriorated considerably since 1950. . . . Over large areas of the central region per capita production is surely falling, and total production may be declining as well."[25]

The Guatemalan Indian population is now in the process of shaking off centuries of lack of interest in *ladino* politics. In 1974, for the first time, two Indians were elected to congress as Indians rather than as *ladinos,* and in the following year one of them gave a speech in Cakchiquel—another first for congress—complaining about the takeover of Indian lands by outsiders. Today, the Indian population finds itself in increasingly precarious living conditions, deprived of much of its land and forced to sell its labor as migrant farmhands on coastal plantations in order to survive. In the face of this deprivation, there are increasing reports of Indian membership in guerrilla groups, as well as growing overt political militancy. The January 1980 occupation of the Spanish embassy by Quiché- and Ixil-speaking Indians who had come to Guatemala City to protest army atrocities is only the most spectacular example of this militancy. Land invasions and self-defense committees are the initial indicators of a mobilization that will undoubtedly grow as the *ladino* population continues to encroach upon the Indian life-style. As a result of this awakening, however, it is the Indian population of the western highlands that has borne the brunt of the Ríos Montt program of repression. At the time of this writing (late 1982), U.S. newspapers carry daily accounts of Indian massacres by government troops.

Two remaining groups—part of the church and the universities —also belong to the antigovernment opposition. The Asociación de Estudiantes Universitarios can be expected to spearhead any antigovernment movement, and its members will be joined by their professors. This last group is truly an endangered species— twenty-five San Carlos University faculty were murdered in the first half of 1980—and remaining militants have probably gone underground and/or joined the guerrillas.

The church hierarchy has yet to demonstrate the social concern found among bishops in Nicaragua and El Salvador, probably in part because the church has been favored by post-1954 governments. The Castillo Armas government restored to the church virtually all of the privileges it had lost in the 1870s, for which the archbishop praised Castillo Armas as "a martyr of authentic anti-Communism," an evaluation probably shared by much of the current hierarchy. At lower levels, however, church authorities have been involved in a variety of antigovernment activities, and many parish priests, missionaries, and lay workers have been assassinated by right-wing paramilitary forces. There is some indication that the church is unifying in the face of this violence. On 27 May 1982 the traditionally conservative Guatemalan Conference of Bishops issued a statement against violence that condemned by implication the Ríos Montt government: "never in our history have such extremes been reached, with the assassinations now falling into the category of genocide."[26]

Finally, there are the guerrillas. At first, the groups from the 1960s—the Fuerzas Armadas Rebeldes (FAR) and the MR13— disappeared and gave way to two newer organizations, the Ejército Guerrillero de los Pobres (EGP) and the Organización del Pueblo en Armas (ORPA), but by 1980 the FAR had begun operations once again. The EGP is by far the largest of the three groups. It was formed in 1974 by a group whose leaders included the former FAR militant César Montes, who disagreed with other FAR leaders over the role of the Indian population in armed struggle. Operating in at least four (and perhaps seven) independent commands, the EGP has had success in recruiting Indians, especially in northern Quiché, Huehuetenango, Chimaltenango, and Alta and Baja Verapaz. It has also been active in coastal plantations, where its deeds included the daring kidnapping of Roberto Herrera Ibarguen, the owner of Pantaleón, the nation's largest sugar plantation, and a former minister of interior and foreign relations. The EGP works closely with what is left of the Comité de Unidad Campesina and the Frente Patriótico 31 de Enero.

Little is known about ORPA except that it, too, sprang from

the FAR in the early 1970s after disagreements over the role of the Indian population. Although ORPA has been active in the highlands since 1979 and had sufficient strength to occupy Santiago Atitlán in early 1980, it has been hard hit by government attacks. The FAR was originally a military wing of the Guatemalan Communist party (Partido Guatemalteco de Trabajo). Following a period of inactivity after its defeat in the late 1960s, the FAR developed considerable strength in the Guatemalan trade-union movement—it helped form the CNUS—but its military capabilities are minor. FAR guerrillas operate in Guatemala City, Chimaltenango, and in the remote Petén. In general, the guerrillas have made life miserable for the security forces in rural Guatemala, but they have yet to launch a major attack that would indicate the existence of a significant threat to the government. Under Ríos Montt, the government has seized the initiative in rural warfare, and all the guerrilla groups are preoccupied with defending themselves and local Indian communities.

THE REAGAN ADMINISTRATION

It is no secret which of the three alternative paths mentioned at the beginning of this essay in Guatemalan politics the Reagan administration prefers. On 5 May 1981 the State Department announced that "the Administration would like to establish a more constructive relationship with the Guatemalan Government. Our previous policy clearly failed to contribute to an improvement of the situation inside Guatemala, while Cuban-supported Marxist guerrillas have gained in strength. We hope changes in the situation in Guatemala will soon permit a closer cooperative relationship. We want to help the Guatemalans to defend themselves against the guerrillas and to work with them to control indiscriminate violence of all kinds." Within days the Secretary of State's special emissary, Vernon Walters, visited Guatemala. After meeting with officials of the Lucas government, he told reporters that the United States would help to defend "peace and liberty" and "the constitutional institutions of this country against the ideologies that want to finish off those institutions." This promise was converted into concrete action in early June, when the Department of Commerce approved a $3.1 million cash sale of military vehicles to Guatemala: one hundred jeeps, fifty 2.5 ton cargo trucks, and a variety of vehicle parts. Since then, the Reagan administration has played a cat-and-mouse game with members of the U.S. Congress—particularly those in the House—who are opposed to further U.S. support of right-wing governments in Central America. At the present time there is a stalemate in the U.S. government. Obviously, however, the Reagan administration wishes to adopt a policy of support for the existing government in Guatemala because, in its view, Guatemala "is facing a Cuban-supported Marxist insurgency."[27] In the view of many members of Congress, this is a policy that is patently devoid of positive long-term consequences because the premise—communist insurgency—is wrong.

As these opposition groups increase their demands to participate in political life, Guatemala's political system must change. There can be moderate change or there can be significant change, but the preservation of the status quo is clearly out of the question. The social forces at work today in Guatemala can be halted temporarily by infusions of U.S. military aid, but the era of nineteenth-century oligarchic politics is at an end in Central America.

Why, then, would the Reagan administration, whose pragmatism has been demonstrated repeatedly on domestic issues, decide to stand and fight on the side of the dinosaurs in Guatemala?

In this century, new popular demands are being heard; these are, by all but the most traditional standards, demands for rights rather than for privileges. And they are rights—to shelter, food, literacy —that the majority of Guatemalans are systematically denied not because they are poor but because the human and financial resources of their society are controlled by groups that are no more concerned about the moral implications of malnutrition than about those of political murder. Yet, as we have seen, these are the groups that all recent U.S. administrations have traditionally supported in Guatemala, not because we stand for either malnutrition or murder, but because our policymakers believe that support for the status quo in Guatemala is essential to our national security.

The twentieth century has finally invaded Guatemala, yet U.S.

policymakers are unwilling to accept the demonstrated fact that turmoil is caused by people who now, for the first time, are claiming the right to the satisfaction of basic needs. Instead, they have interpreted instability as an indicator of Cuban and Soviet expansionism. U.S. policymakers thereby convert unfamiliar social unrest in Guatemala into the cold-war language with which they are comfortable. But if social science can be of any service to policymakers, it is to point out when changing circumstances have made familiar formulas obsolete. The process of mobilization has gone beyond a critical point in Guatemala, and *that country will enjoy neither peace nor stability until the basic needs of the people are met by a fundamental restructuring of privilege.* That is the new reality. U.S. policymakers must accept it as *the* fundamental premise of an effective policy toward Guatemala and, indeed, toward all of Central America. There is no alternative.

All recent U.S. administrations have been unable to create and implement a policy toward Latin America that is based upon this new reality. Some have come close, but none has been successful. As John Kennedy said of the Dominican Republic following the assassination of the tyrant Rafael Trujillo, in 1960, "there are three possibilities in descending order of preference: a decent democratic regime, a continuation of the Trujillo regime or a Castro regime. We ought to aim at the first, but we really can't renounce the second until we are sure we can avoid the third."[28] A similar calculus obviously governed the Carter administration's policy toward Guatemala. The Reagan administration has simply reduced the options to the last two and decided that the third is avoidable only if the United States concentrates upon supporting the second.

That there are not two or three but probably an infinite number of forms of political change apparently never occurred to the Carter or Reagan or Kennedy policymakers. Instead they snapped on their cold-war blinders, reducing the field of vision to two or three polar possibilities, and plunged ahead in the race with an imaginary opponent—communism. That they did so with the best of all intentions—the desire to protect U.S. security—does not make less tragic the fact that they failed first to determine whether and by whom our security was being threatened in Guatemala.

NOTES

1. In preparing this essay, I found the following published works particularly valuable: Richard Newbold Adams, *Crucifixion by Power: Essays on Guatemalan National Social Structure, 1944–1966* (Austin: University of Texas Press, 1970); Shelton Davis, "Land of Our Ancestors: A Study of Land Tenure and Inheritance in the Highlands of Guatemala" (Ph.D. diss., Harvard University, 1970); Don T. Etchison, *The United States and Militarism in Central America* (New York: Praeger, 1976); Lehman B. Fletcher et al., *Guatemala's Economic Development: The Role of Agriculture* (Ames: Iowa State University Press, 1970); "Guatemala: Drama y conflicto social," *Estudios Centroamericanos* 33, número especial (1978); Carlos Guzmán Bockler, *Colonialismo y revolución* (Mexico: Siglo Veintiuno, 1975); Carlos Guzmán Bockler and Jean-Loup Herbert, *Guatemala: Una interpretación histórico-social* (Mexico: Siglo Veintiuno, 1970); Robert E. Hinshaw, *Panajachel: A Guatemalan Town in Thirty Year Perspective* (Pittsburgh: University of Pittsburgh Press, 1975); Susanne Jonas, "Guatemala: Land of Eternal Struggle," in *Latin America: The Struggle with Dependency and Beyond,* ed. Ronald H. Chilcote and Joel C. Edelstein (New York: Wiley, 1974), 89–219; Susanne Jonas and David Tobis, *Guatemala: Una historia inmediata* (Mexico: Siglo Veintiuno, 1976); Charles David Kepner, Jr., *Social Aspects of the Banana Industry* (New York: Columbia University Press, 1936); Thomas Melville and Marjorie Melville, *Guatemala: Another Vietnam?* (London: Penguin Books, 1971); Mario Monteforte Toledo, *Centro America: Subdesarrollo y dependencia* (Mexico: Universidad Nacional Autónoma de México, 1972); idem, *Guatemala: Monografía sociológica* (Mexico: Universidad Nacional Autónoma de México, 1959); Franklin D. Parker, *The Central American Republics* (New York: Oxford University Press, 1964); Neale J. Pearson, "Guatemala: The Peasant Union Movement, 1944–1954," in *Latin American Peasant Movements,* ed. Henry A. Landsberger (Ithaca: Cornell University Press, 1969); Roger Plant, *Guatemala: Unnatural Disaster* (London: Latin American Bureau, 1977); John W. Sloan, "Electoral Frauds and Social Change: The Guatemalan Example," *Science and Society* 34 (Spring 1970): 78–91; Edelberto Torres-Rivas, *Interpretación del desarrollo social centroamericano: Procesos y estructuras de una sociedad dependiente* (San José, Costa Rica: EDUCA, 1971); idem, "Vida y muerte en Guatemala: Reflexiones sobre la crisis y la violencia política," *Foro Internacional* 20 (1980): 549–74; Joel L. Verner, "El Congreso Nacional Guatemalteco de 1966–1970: Análisis de una élite," *Foro Internacional* 11 (1971): 569–87; Jerry L. Weaver, "Political Style of the Guatemalan Military Elite," *Studies in Comparative International Development* 5 (1969–70): 63–81; Ralph Lee Woodward, Jr., *Central America: A Nation Divided* (New York: Oxford University Press, 1976).

2. John E. Reilly, ed., *American Public Opinion and U.S. Foreign Policy* (Chicago: Chicago Council on Foreign Relations, 1975).

3. Woodward, *Central America,* 150–51.

4. Jonas, "Guatemala," 134.

5. Torres-Rivas, *Interpretación del desarrollo social,* 65, 79.

6. Inter-American Development Bank, *Economic and Social Progress in Latin America, 1979 Report* (Washington, D.C.: IDB, 1980), 15, 21.

7. René Herrera Zúniga, "Nicaragua: El desarrollo capitalista dependiente y la crisis de la dominación burguesa, 1950–1980," *Foro Internacional* 20 (1980): 621.

8. Jeremiah O'Sullivan-Ryan, "El rol de la información en la vida del agricultor de subsistencia: Un estudio en el altiplano de Guatemala," *Estudios Centroamericanos* 33 (1978): 508; Monteforte Toledo, *Guatemala,* 641.

9. Fletcher, *Guatemala's Economic Development,* 25–26.

10. Torres-Rivas, "Vida y muerte en Guatemala," 557.

11. U.S. Congress, House Committee on Foreign Affairs and Senate Committee on Foreign Relations, *Country Reports on Human Rights Practices for 1979,* 96th Cong., 2d sess., 1980, 329–30; U.S. Congress, House Committee on Foreign Affairs and Senate Committee on Foreign Relations, *Country Reports on Human Rights Practices* [1980], 97th Cong., 1st sess., 1981, 444–45; U.S. Congress, House Committee on Foreign Affairs and Senate Committee on Foreign Relations, *Country Reports on Human Rights Practices for 1981,* 97th Cong., 2d sess., 1982, 441–49; the quotation on colonization is on 448. The quotation by an AID official is in U.S. Congress, Senate Committee on Appropriations, *Foreign Assistance and Related Programs Appropriations, Fiscal Year 1982,* 97th Cong., 1st sess., 1981, pot. 1, p. 269.

12. *Country Reports for 1979,* 329; *Country Reports* [for 1980], 445; *Country Reports for 1981,* 447.

13. The role of the U.S. government in these reforms and counterreforms is analyzed in two recent studies of major importance: Richard H. Immerman, *The CIA in Guatemala: The Foreign Policy of Intervention* (Austin: University of Texas Press, 1982); and Stephen Kinzer and Stephen Schlesinger, *Bitter Fruit: The Untold Story of the American Coup in Guatemala* (Garden City, N.Y.: Doubleday, 1981). Immerman's volume contains an unusually helpful bibliography.

14. *Time,* 26 January 1968.

15. *New York Times,* 28 January 1982, 23.

16. *Country Reports* [for 1980], 441.

17. *Amnesty International Report, 1979* (London: AI Publications, 1979), 63–66; *Human Rights Internet Newsletter* 5 (1979–1980): 55–60; Amnesty International, *Guatemala: A Government Program of Political Murder* (London: AI Publications, 1981); Amnesty International news release, 11 October 1982.

18. *Latin America Regional Report,* 16 November 1979, 5.

19. *Washington Post,* 6 March 1978.

20. *New York Times,* 9 March 1982, 4; 10 March 1982, 4.

21. Quoted in Adolfo Gelly, "The Guerrilla Movement in Guatemala," *Monthly Review* 17 (May 1965): 12.

22. Sloan, "Electoral Frauds and Social Change," 81.

23. See Miguel Angel Albizures, "Luchas y experiencias del movimiento sindical, período 1976–junio 1978," *Estudios Centroamericanos* 33 (1978): 478–93.

24. Monteforte Toledo, *Guatemala,* 303–4.

25. Fletcher, *Guatemala's Economic Development,* 196.

26. *New York Times,* 12 September 1982.

27. U.S. Department of State, *Congressional Presentation, Security Assistance Programs, FY1983* (Washington, D.C.: Department of State, 1982), 461.

28. Arthur M. Schlesinger, Jr., *A Thousand Days: John F. Kennedy in the White House* (Boston: Houghton Mifflin, 1965), 769.

Honduras

ON THE BORDER OF WAR

Steven Volk with Anne Nelson

Yes, We Have Some Bananas

The Fruit Company, Inc.
reserved for itself the most succulent,
the central coast of my own land,
the delicate waist of America.
It rechristened its territories
as the "Banana Republics"
and over the sleeping dead,
over the restless heroes
who brought about the greatness,
the liberty and the flags,
it established the comic opera.
—PABLO NERUDA, "THE UNITED FRUIT CO."

Banana republics: an easy epithet, connoting backwardness, unworthiness as nations, mere appendages of the United States. Many apply the term loosely to Latin America as a whole, collapsing the region into a single, contemptible image.

For others—writers such as Pablo Neruda—the term describes those territories of Central America which are run as private plantations by giant, U.S.–based fruit companies. When these writers think of banana republics, they think first of Honduras.

In 1950 the United Fruit Company (since renamed United Brands) and the Standard Fruit and Steamship Company (now a subsidiary of Castle & Cooke) owned or leased over 630,000 acres of Honduras's most verdant flatlands. Their plantations first spread along the "succulent" northern Caribbean coast and later dropped south to the Gulf of Fonseca. The fruit companies also owned the railroad and the ports, the congresses and the presidents.

In the late 1940s William Krehm,* a reporter for *Time* magazine covering Central America, described how the fruit companies maneuvered their conquest. "Bananas are a wonderful fruit," Krehm wrote:

> Sliced and added to cold cereals, they make a savory breakfast dish. . . . But to Hondurans in the hopeful year of 1911, they promised an interoceanic railway . . . that would span the isthmus and bring to the scattered settlements the blessings of civilization. . . . Between 1867 and 1870 the Government contracted four British loans totalling six million pounds to build the railway. The money stuck to the fingers of politicians and bankers, and to top it all Honduras made the grievous mistake of paying the contractor by the mile. The railway wriggled imaginatively in the easy lowlands, and got winded before it had penetrated too far inland. By the time 50 miles had been built, the funds had evaporated in the tropical heat. But the debts contracted, with accumulated interest, amounted to $125 million in 1916, and proved a millstone around the neck of the tiny country.

The Customs Receivership

Krehm's report continued:

> That staggering indebtedness had its sequel. Under President Taft the U.S. State Department had evolved a special formula for bringing the Carib lands under its sway: loans for the liquidation of their European debts, guaranteed by an American customs receivership—much as a dentist fits a golden crown upon an enervated molar.

Made in 1910 with the liberal regime of Miguel Dávila, the customs-receivership agreement barred tariff exemptions until the loan was paid off. This posed a serious handicap for adventurers like the colorful Samuel Zemurray, who had no desire to pay taxes for the bananas his Cuyamel Fruit Company exported from Honduras. Zemurray supplied arms and the ship *Hornet* to launch the conservative leader Manuel Bonilla's overthrow of Dávila.

---

*Published in Spanish, Krehm's manuscript was never issued in its original English. The State Department saw to that, as well as to Krehm's expulsion from Mexico and from *Time*. (Personal correspondence from William Krehm.)

Brought around to see the force of Zemurray's logic, the State Department stepped in to negotiate Dávila's surrender. On October 1, 1911, Bonilla was elected president and Honduras became a banana republic.

The railway will o' the wisp had the Hondurans bemused again, and Zemurray exploited it to the fullest. With an understandable influence over the Bonilla regime, he not only obtained princely concessions for his own Cuyamel Fruit Co., but also for United Fruit Co. . . . [which had] agreed to build a railway to Juticalpa, half way from the north coast to the capital, and eventually to the capital itself. The Cuyamel Co. made similar promises. Yet the milage that was laid was little more than what was strictly necessary for the operation of the banana industry. It tended, therefore, to run parallel to the sea instead of climbing into the highlands. For each kilometer of railway built, the companies received from 550 to 1,100 acres in lots of 10,000 to 12,000 acres which were to alternate with similar lots reserved for peasant farmers. But the companies, through intermediaries, went in for homesteading too. Illegally and at a nominal price, they acquired these "alternative lots" so that their plantations might stretch in vast unbroken domains.

The Absentee Oligarchy

The fruit companies' stranglehold on the Honduran state points up one of the most significant differences between this country and its Central American neighbors—a difference that wins for Honduras the definitive title of a true banana republic. In most of the other Central American nations, a native oligarchy had arisen in the late 1800s or, at the latest, by the first third of the 1900s. In coordination with the foreign firms that were by then beginning to invest in the region, these oligarchies ruled for the benefit of themselves and the firms.

Honduras, on the other hand, had no local economic oligarchy until the late 1950s; foreign agro-exporting firms remained predominant, and precapitalist forms of land tenure persisted.[1]

What accounts for this different development, which Honduras shares in large measure with prerevolutionary Nicaragua? Clearly the ever-more preponderant role of foreign firms in Honduras discouraged the emergence of a local economic elite. But this is not a chicken-and-egg question. The fundamental explanation resides in the particular agrarian structure in Honduras, a structure strongly influenced by Honduras's very low population density.

Throughout the nineteenth century, Honduras was one of the most sparsely populated countries in Central America. In 1895 it was estimated to have a population of slightly less than 400,000 compared with El Salvador's 700,000. Thus, even though only 20 to 30 percent of the Honduran landmass is suitable for any kind of agriculture, the population density was still much lower than in El Salvador, a country five and one-half times smaller.[2]

With little pressure on the land, there was little motivation to destroy older communal forms of landowning (the *ejido*) during the so-called liberal reform period in the nineteenth century. The survival of the *ejido* is one of the reasons why a coffee oligarchy never arose in Honduras. Another reason was the remoteness of the coffee-producing areas. More important, there was neither the pressure to use land more productively nor a large landless work force to be harnessed to capitalist agricultural production.

The local landed power groups remained content to rent out their holdings to peasant farmers, limiting their role to more of a political than an economic alliance with the foreign companies. They saw as their main activity the creation and maintenance of the legal and political conditions necessary for the functioning of the foreign capitalists.

If the landed elite were not inclined to convert their landholdings into capitalist enterprises, the foreign fruit companies most certainly were. They imported large numbers of black workers from the Caribbean to work on their plantations, and they gathered for themselves not only the bulk of the land but also the best lands. By 1910, 80 percent of all banana lands were under the control of U.S. firms. Four years later the five principal concessionaires held more than one million acres of coastal land, much of it the most fertile soil in the country.[3]

Although the banana companies returned some of this land to the state over the years, they continued to own vast tracts of the best land in the country. This became a serious problem in the second half of the twentieth century, when the population expanded rapidly. People were increasingly forced to move to the already crowded west and south, since the companies occupied the rich coastal lands.

Land to the Landowners

As late as 1950 only 48 percent of the country's land was in private hands. The rest belonged to the state (31 percent), *ejidos* (17 percent), or other forms of communal holdings. In that 48 percent, however, property ownership was very unevenly divided. According to the 1952 agricultural census, the top 4 percent of the farms spread over 57 percent of the territory while the smallest 65 percent of the farms occupied only 15 percent of the land.[4] Concentration, nevertheless, did not imply a greater capitalization of the land. Huge tracts, both on plantations and on the smaller farms, were either left idle or underutilized. In 1946, for example, the Tela Railroad Company (United Fruit's Honduran subsidiary) owned or leased 410,000 acres. Of these, only 20 percent were in production. The rest were held in reserve, used for flood fallowing, or given over to pasture or the cultivation of some small-scale crops so that the company would not be threatened by peasant invasions.[5]

The Strike of 1954

In May 1954 the United Fruit Company was shaken by a strike destined to change the course of both labor and capital in Honduras. Although Honduran workers had been organizing and striking since the 1920s, only after the 1954 strike did the government and private enterprise legally recognize trade-union organizations, making Honduras virtually the last country in the hemisphere to accept unionization.[6]

Workers at the Tela Railroad Company's north coast installations marched out on 1 May, demanding a 50 percent wage hike, better working conditions, and, most important, legal recognition. This elicited an entirely novel approach to labor militancy from U.S. multinationals and Latin American governments. Galvez sent troops to the northern plantations but agreed to listen to a new voice from the United States. Leaders of the American Federation of Labor (the following year it merged with the CIO) and of its Latin American spin-off, the Inter-American Regional Organization of Labor (ORIT), sent advisers to Honduras to mediate the crisis.[7] The negotiators managed to remove the most militant leaders on the central strike committee and to replace them with known anti-Communists.[8] On 9, July the AFL and the CIO pressured United Fruit to settle the strike; after a firm basis was laid for the creation of a conservative, anti-Communist, "free democratic" trade union in Honduras, the company agreed. Wages went up 10 to 15 percent, some working conditions were improved, and the Workers Union of the Tela Railroad Company (SITRATERCO) was recognized, complete with the most conservative members of the central strike committee on its executive board. Within a year, ORIT had sponsored the organization of an additional fifteen unions in Honduras.

By forcing the fruit companies to recognize trade-union organizations in 1954, the Honduran workers won an important victory. But it was clearly conditional. From the United Fruit strike of 1954 until the present day, conservative forces in the U.S. labor movement (using ORIT and, after 1962, the American Institute for Free Labor Development, AIFLD) continue to play a very active role in the Honduran workers' movement, both among industrial workers and among the peasantry, as we will see.

The impact of productivity increases and of employing labor-saving devices was nothing short of disastrous for the worker. Within three years, from 1954 to 1957, employment at the Tela Railroad Company declined from 26,456 to 13,284.[9] By 1959 Standard Fruit had also fired almost 50 percent of the workers it had employed in 1954.[10] These changes begun in the post-1954 period were the first in a series of major reorganizations that ultimately led the fruit companies to rely increasingly on local producers for the direct production of bananas, reserving for themselves the task of commercializing.

A First Attempt at Reform

Scarcely out of the frying pan of the United Fruit strike, the government found itself slowly roasting in the fires of social conflict created by the fruit companies' massive dismissal of workers. A reformer, Ramón Villeda Morales, of the Liberal party, had slipped through the split in the National party to be elected president in 1954, but his assumption of office was blocked by the National party, and only the passage of time, plus a helpful military intervention to force a new election, put him in power in 1957. As just compensation for its generosity, the military wrote into the new Honduran constitution the right of the chief of the armed forces to contest the president's orders, thus giving itself a more formalized role in the political affairs of the nation.

Villeda set up a public-works program to provide the nation with some basic infrastructure (as of 1950 the capital city had no paved roads) and to employ some of the thousands of dismissed banana workers. He also ordered a number of land-colonization plans, distributing lands in regions of low population density to peasant families *(lotes de familia)* and creating new areas of colonization *(colonias agricolas)*. [11] More important, in September 1962 Villeda pushed through the country's first agrarian-reform law.

In part an attempt to systematize informal land tenancies and generally to increase productivity in the rural sector, the agrarian-reform law was also designed to quiet an increasingly militant rural population. The anger of the landless and the peasant *minifundistas* soared in the post–World War II period, as population growth put a real pressure on the land. More rural dwellers were without land, and the size of small plots decreased. In 1952, 75 percent of Honduran farms were under 10 hectares (24.7 acres), and most averaged under 4 hectares (9.9 acres). These small plots were clustered on land that is generally poor, rugged, remote, and subject to the severest erosion, particularly as cattle ranchers were expanding their holdings by destroying nearby forests.

The 1962 agrarian-reform law met quite few of its goals. As was to be expected, it immediately drew howls of protest from the large fruit companies and local ranchers. The National Agrarian Institute (INA), created in 1961 to oversee the new colonization projects and given authority over the reform process, was hamstrung by a lack of funds and the relative sympathy of many of its directors for the large landowners.

The Peasant Movement and U.S. Labor

President Villeda did not rely on the agrarian reform alone to silence peasant militancy, however. In October 1961 a radical organization known as the National Federation of Honduran Peasants (FENACH) had begun organizing in the northern part of the country. FENACH concentrated its efforts on mobilizing renters and other marginal tenants living on the lands of the Tela Railroad Company. The government employed the same tactic against FENACH that it had used against the striking United Fruit workers in 1954: it fostered the creation of a parallel peasant association to challenge it. And, as before, it got a little help from its friends, the AFL-CIO and ORIT.

A year after the appearance of FENACH, a Honduran Labor federation created the National Association of Honduran Peasants (ANACH), again with the aid of the AFL-CIO and ORIT. Similar to other ORIT-inspired unions, ANACH began its life by raiding members from the more combative FENACH.[12] As a 1968 Senate investigation of U.S. influences in the Latin American labor movement noted, "ORIT has never quite solved the problem of emphasis as between fighting communism and strengthening democratic trade unions."[13]

When the American Institute for Free Labor Development (AIFLD) was founded by the AFL-CIO, in 1962, it established a close and influential relation with ANACH, which has continued to this day.[14] During the early 1960s ANACH served to provide the government with a conservative base of support in the countryside.

The agrarian-reform process begun in 1962 was abruptly halted on 3 October 1963, when the air force colonel Oswaldo López Arellano seized power and deposed the Villeda government. Over the next ten years, López Arellano would act first as a conservative and then as a reformist, championing the cause of the more progressive sectors of the Honduran bourgeoisie in 1972. For the moment, however, he chose the most direct path to weaken the reform process in the countryside. He unleashed a furious repression against the combative FENACH, which led to its destruction. The moderate ANACH was a lesser victim of López Arellano's wrath; it survived to inherit some of the militant members of the peasantry from FENACH. These later helped shape its more progressive stands.

New Crops and New Problems

The forces that inspired the 1963 coup sought to destroy the impetus for change from below. They nevertheless favored the modernization of the Honduran productive system, and this implied important changes in both the city and the countryside.

Some important changes had already been occurring in the rural sector since the end of World War II. Bananas, which accounted for 88 percent of the value of Honduran exports in the period 1925–39, declined to 70 percent of the total value in 1950 and to 45 percent in 1960.[15] Pushed by international demand and supported by the state's credit mechanisms and technical aid, the production of coffee, cattle, cotton, and timber grew impressively after the war. Coffee, still grown by small producers even though marketed by a handful of exporters, more than doubled its production between 1945 and 1960. The acreage sown to cotton shot up almost twenty-six-fold between 1950 and 1965, creating a demand for nearly 30,000 seasonal laborers. Cattle exports also rose during this period. In the 1940s and 1950s most Honduran cattle were shipped on the hoof to neighboring Central American countries. But in the 1960s Honduras began to export beef, mainly to the United States, thanks to the installation of the country's first meat-packing plants.

This was also the period of significant industrial growth in Honduras. Typical of industrialization programs throughout Latin America in the late 1950s and 1960s, the process was designed to allow the local manufacture of some commodities previously imported. Typically again, the Honduran industrialization plan brought no lessening of imports, but rather an increasing penetration of foreign, particularly U.S., capital and capital-goods imports into the manufacturing sector.

The vehicle in which U.S. capital drove into Honduras was the Central American Common Market. Planners at the United Nations' Economic Commission for Latin America (ECLA) first sponsored the notion of a free zone for the movement of labor and capital among the five Central American countries in the late 1950s. Their aim was to equalize development and investment among the five countries. Had it been achieved, this would have benefited chiefly Honduras and Nicaragua, the region's most underdeveloped countries.[16]

By the time the Central American Common Market (CACM) was officially created, however, the United States had taken over the process, seeing it as an excellent opportunity for U.S. investments. ECLA's vision was never realized. Under U.S. influence, foreign investors were guaranteed freedom of investment, without any regard for regional balance. Furthermore, foreign capital was allowed to acquire local firms, dominate new areas of investment, and employ local credit facilities without restriction.[17] Between 1960 and 1968 the book value of U.S. investment alone in Central America had tripled, to more than $500 million.

The result was disastrous for the sectors of Honduran capital that were counting on the CACM for equal access to the region's markets. Honduras was flooded with products made in El Salvador and Guatemala, and its own industries were increasingly branded "owned by the U.S.A."

Over 70 percent of Honduras's largest firms were founded between 1950 and 1968, and U.S. capital played a dominant role in most of them. U.S. multinationals controlled 100 percent of the production of Honduras's five largest firms, 88.7 percent of the twenty largest, and 82 percent of the fifty largest companies.[18] By 1969, U.S. investments in Honduras totaled more than $200 million, in a country whose entire GNP was only slightly more than $500 million.[19]

The myth of the Central American Common Market, a fairy tale that featured Honduras as Cinderella equaling her more powerful siblings in the region, exploded in 1969 with the outbreak of hostilities with El Salvador. Honduras was not Cinderella, and if anyone was enjoying the largess of Prince Charming, it was the corrupt politicians and military officers and those local groups most tied to foreign investment. The war with El Salvador would make this quite clear.

The "Soccer War"
It is quite possible that many people in the United States first learned about Honduras and El Salvador when, settling down with

their evening papers sometime in early July 1969, they read about Central America's "Soccer War." Yet the brief war between Honduras and El Salvador had much less to do with soccer than with the decades of tensions produced by the uneven demographic and economic status of the two countries.

El Salvador was by far the more developed. Its coffers brimming with profits from record coffee sales in the period 1945–50, the country industrialized rapidly in the 1950s and 1960s. Although the urban-industrial sector changed dramatically in that period, the countryside did not. In 1950, 38.5 percent of the Salvadorans classified as agriculturally active could be considered either landless or land poor. By 1971 that figure had climbed to 50.8 percent.[20] Unable to own or rent land, rural Salvadorans had two options: they could migrate to the cities, or they could go to Honduras, where land was more abundant and rents were lower. By the end of the 1960s, some 600,000 rural Salvadorans had acted, half of them going to the cities and half crossing into Honduras, most without the benefit of immigration papers. It is estimated that by 1969 the Salvadorans made up nearly 20 percent of all agriculturalists in Honduras and owned over 500,000 acres of land.[21]

In the first half of this century, it was not hard for Salvadorans to settle in Honduras. Although only about 20 percent of its lands were suitable for any kind of agriculture, its population was still small in relation to the land available. An increase in the rate of population growth coupled with worsening inequality in landholding changed this in the post–World War II period. By the early 1970s, a decade after the passage of the first agrarian-reform law, land ownership remained as concentrated as it had been in 1952. A total of 120,000 *minifundistas,* constituting 67 percent of the farming population, occupied only 12 percent of the rural farmland, whereas 667 large landowning families held 27 percent of the land.[22] Meanwhile, in the period 1950–74, the Honduran population doubled.[23]

Smallholders and renters in El Salvador, Guatemala, and Honduras maintained an equally precarious grip on their lands. But only in Honduras did the commercialization of agriculture disrupt communal forms of property ownership so late in the twentieth century. Many analysts see in this the reason why, in the 1960s, Honduras gave birth to the most militant and, before long, the best-organized peasant movement in Central America.[24]

The peasant movement was split into two main organizations. Larger, less militant, and tied to the AFL-CIO through ORIT, ANACH was nonetheless pushed by its members to get active in the land invasions of the later 1960s. The other, the National Peasant Union (UNC), was a major organizer of land seizures. Founded in 1963 and based on Christian peasant leagues, the UNC was linked to Christian Democracy through the Latin American Confederation of Workers (CLAT).[25]

Land seizures placed the government in an unusual position. Its neglect of the 1962 agrarian-reform law had spurred the radicalization of the peasant movement. At the same time, López Arellano, who had halted the reform in 1963, now sought its revival to help him forge himself a new political base. No revolutionary, he tried to satisfy peasants' demands for land without alienating the interests of landowners or banana companies, by reviving the National Agrarian Institute (INA).

Unfunded almost since its creation, in 1961, the INA in 1967 was granted an adequate budget and an activist director, Rigoberto Sandoval Corea.[26] For the next five years INA was a useful but limited ally of the peasants. It initiated no actions on their behalf, but its support of land seizures spelled the difference between failure and success. Success, however, could happen only while INA had cash and when it dealt with owners willing to part with (often idle) land in return for capital.

The harshest opposition to the land seizures and to INA policy in general came from the National Federation of Farmers and Ranchers (FENAGH), an association of large landowners founded in 1966. In a 1967 petition to the Honduran president, FENAGH argued, "It is foreigners who are usurping rural properties, especially foreigners of Salvadoran nationality."[27]

Although there exists no evidence to support FENAGH's claim that the Salvadorans instigated the land invasions, there was now pressure on the Honduran government to expel the Salvadorans as "troublemakers" and "land usurpers." Furthermore, a massive deportation of rural dwellers would relieve pressure on the land in southern and western areas, opening new opportunities for Honduran peasants to settle there.

In the final analysis, the war between Honduras and El Salvador was a logical consequence of the inability of the rulers in each country to deal with their most pressing internal social and economic problems: for El Salvador, the rigid control by a few families of the nation's land; for Honduras, the predominance of the banana companies and the ranchers in the rural sector, and an absolute inability to develop an industrially based economy with a requisite productive infrastructure. Rather than solve their countries' internal problems, they sent their soldiers to fight one another.

On 30 April 1969 Honduran authorities gave Salvadoran settlers thirty days to get out.[28] By late May over 11,000 refugees had re-entered El Salvador, propelled by Honduran government edicts and the vigilante tactics of the Mancha Brava goon squad, organized by the National party. By June, when the two national soccer teams met in San Salvador, tensions were extreme. A Honduran loss led to the expulsion of thousands more Salvadorans. The Salvadoran government sealed its border, hoping that Honduras would have to resettle the migrant Salvadorans. In early July, Salvadoran troops crossed into Honduras to "defend the human rights of their countrymen," peasants who went to Honduras primarily because they had no human rights at home.

Salvadoran troops pushed to Nueva Ocotepeque and threatened to isolate the country by cutting off the roads to Guatemala and Nicaragua. Although it had the best air force in the region and, in theory, the capacity to mobilize 60,000 men, Honduras nevertheless faced a rout. The OAS threatened an economic boycott against El Salvador, which then agreed to withdraw, content with its psychological victory. Honduras closed its borders to Salvadoran traffic, and a demilitarized zone was established, pending a final truce (not reached until 1980). El Salvador eventually had to repatriate some 60,000 migrants.

For Honduras, the war was nothing short of monumental. Defeat revealed a command structure that was inefficient, backward, and corrupt. And defeat paved the way for reform in

Honduras. The Honduran officer corps became increasingly influenced by younger officers who drew their inspiration from the military reformers in Peru and Panama. Many of the older, corruption-tainted officers were purged.

The war also furthered a realignment in the nation's social elite. Broadly speaking, we can identify two wings of the upper class. One, composed of traditional oligarchs whose wealth was tied up in the land, had the most connections with other foreign capitalists, since both backed an economic system that protected landholding and favored exports. Smaller and less well articulated, the other wing comprised the new industrialists centered in San Pedro Sula and Tegucigalpa who produced for the domestic market. This sector had benefited from government credits during the 1960s, and ironically, it was strengthened when Honduras pulled out of the Common Market, for it no longer had to compete with a huge influx of consumer goods from El Salvador and Guatemala.

Although momentary circumstances and a policy of alliances with the workers and peasants propelled this new bourgeoisie into a position of state control, it remained fundamentally weak, given the underdevelopment of Honduran industry. Agriculture dominated the economy, contributing 40 percent of the GNP in 1965, compared with 29 percent for El Salvador and 23 percent for Brazil.[29] In the same year, industry contributed 12 percent of the GNP in Honduras, compared with 16 percent and 22 percent in El Salvador and Brazil, respectively. As late as 1970 nearly 70 percent of Honduran industrial production was in traditional areas: food production, clothing, and other consumer items, as opposed to the production of means of production (machinery) or intermediary goods (chemicals, etc.).[30]

This structure was reflected in the work force. In 1971, 76 percent of the economically active population (EAP) was engaged in agriculture while only 8 percent was in industry, a scant 67,000 workers. Banana-plantation workers remained the most thoroughly unionized sector of labor. The industrial work force tended to be organized along craft lines (tailors, shoemakers, butchers) or in small industrial groupings (food workers, construction trades, metalworkers, miners).[31]

The Plan for National Unity

Political forces shifted rapidly in Honduras after the war with El Salvador. Common opposition to continued conservative rule allowed a reform movement to coalesce. At the end of 1970 a formal alliance brought together the Private Enterprise Council of Honduras (COHEP), with its ties to the new bourgeoisie; the Workers Confederation of Honduras (CHT), a 45,000-member ORIT-linked labor-peasant confederation formed in 1964; and the armed forces, represented by their commander in chief, General López Arellano, who entered the coalition last. Having over-thrown Villeda Morales in 1963 and "constitutionalized" his presidency in a bogus 1965 procedure, he now toyed with contriving a "re-election" in 1971.[32]

López Arellano's passage through the halls of Honduran power surely is a source of wonder. In 1963 he deposed a liberal reformer, led the attack on peasant unions, and smothered agrarian reform. Allied with reformers by the decade's end, he retook power in 1972, drawing peasant-union support, and revived agrarian reform. In part his behavior was mere opportunism, yet a certain coherence runs through his actions. In classic Latin American populist fashion, López sought an elusive middle path, lashing out against the Left whenever it got too strong, striking the Right when it was too stubborn.

Important changes between 1963 and the early 1970s facilitated this strategy. López first worked through the aging alliance between the armed forces and the National party, but by the 1970s both traditional parties were so discredited that he sought to base his power on new forces: the new bourgeoisie joined by the reformist labor and peasant movements. López, COHEP, and the CHT drafted the "Political Plan for National Unity," calling for a single, nonpartisan candidate for president in the June 1971 elections, and for a program of reforms, albeit minimal.

Fearful of losing political ground, the Liberal and National parties accepted the unity proposal while rejecting the single-candidate idea. Wanting partisan presidential elections, plus an automatic one-seat majority in congress for the winning party, they could still muster influence—and the reformers compromised.

Ramón Ernesto Cruz, an old lawyer from the National party, was elected president in 1971.

The reformers had hoped that the crisis following the 1969 war would force the Liberals and Nationals to change their ways. But no: even before the elections, the two parties divvied up the major government posts.[33] With Cruz in office, conservatives felt firmly back in the saddle. This is evident enough in agrarian policy; Cruz made Horacio Moya Posas the head of the INA, thereby halting any late-1960s momentum still left in the agrarian-reform process.[34] The government stopped expropriating illegally held lands, corporate and private, and started jailing peasants caught in land seizures. Much to FENAGH's delight, INA now turned against any effort to legitimize peasant land seizures, often violently.

The Political Plan Disintegrates

On 18 February 1972, police killed six peasants inhabiting an unused part of a large estate.[35] Often brutal, peasant-landowner relations in Honduras have seldom involved the murderous violence typical of those in El Salvador and Guatemala. Yet, escalating repression sapped what little legitimacy remained for the Cruz government, especially in the eyes of workers.

The workers' outrage also reflected their growing alienation from the established party system. At the same time, their unions were taking on the characteristics of a political pressure group. This political rather than purely economic role does not mean that the unions had become more radical—to the contrary, ORIT- and AIFLD-linked organizations dominated Honduran labor, sometimes even helping the state to break the more combative sectors of the movement.[36] The Liberal and National parties both represent landowners, and they are comparably conservative despite their rhetorical differences;[37] the ORIT-led movement saw worker interests served by an alliance with the new industrialists.

On 4 December 1972, as thousands of peasants approached Tegucigalpa on a "hunger march," López Arellano dismissed President Cruz, and again assumed the presidency himself. He quickly enacted several reforms, including an agrarian reform, which he saw as the regime's "fundamental task." Decree Law 8 gave peasants immediate, if temporary, access to national and *ejido* lands held by INA; more important, it forced private owners to rent idle land to peasants on demand. More than 600 peasant settlements were established in the next two years,[38] but without much impact on private landholding, since only 19 percent of the lands adjudicated to peasants under Decree 8 were private property, more than 70 percent being national lands.[39]

Decree 8 regulations expired in late 1974 and were replaced in early 1975 by a new agrarian reform law written with the advice of specialists from the University of Wisconsin. The new legislation had a dual purpose—replacing traditional low-productivity properties with modern capitalist enterprises while containing the militant land seizures that had become epidemic after Hurricane Fifi destroyed nearly 60 percent of the country's agricultural production in September 1974. To this end, the law promoted peasant cooperatives, and outlawed land seizures, threatening to exclude any peasant who took part in such takeovers from all benefits of the agrarian reform.

The Cooperatives and the Fruit Companies

Aside from what seems to have been an honest concern for the increasingly desperate state of the peasantry, the government's eager promotion of peasant cooperatives was consistent with the evolving production strategy of the U.S.–based fruit companies. United Fruit and Standard Fruit, anticipating serious political problems, began to return land. By 1972 United Fruit had already returned approximately 135,000 acres.[40] Much of the land turned over to the Honduran government became peasant cooperatives, growing bananas for sale to the fruit companies. In other words, the companies began to move away from their traditional role as direct producers of the fruit in favor of a more advantageous role as marketer.

Under this new arrangement, the multinationals were no longer directly vulnerable to labor disputes or to the natural disasters that annually punished Honduras's banana plantations. They could also indirectly benefit from the government credits and the international aid that were funneled into the cooperatives. Finally, they were able to clean up their image by returning land to the government.

For their part, the cooperatives can only be seen as a limited victory for the peasants. A well-run cooperative could result in better housing and social services for its members. But the very success of some cooperatives depended on reproducing exploitative relations, on members' "exploiting" themselves and their families by working long hours for low pay. Going some steps further, a cooperative called "Guanchias Ltd." began to hire wage laborers in the early 1970s. The members were soon fighting these workers' unionization plans and firing the principal activists who worked on the plantation.[41] To many, it became obvious that positive change would remain limited as long as control over the prices and marketing of the commodities they produced remained in the corporate boardrooms of the banana companies in the United States.

Bananagate

On 3 February 1975 Eli Black, United Brands' chairman, tossed his briefcase through his sealed skyscraper window and followed it down forty-four floors to the street below. His suicide piqued the curiosity of the Securities and Exchange Commission, which opened an investigation into the company's affairs.

On 9 April it reported that United Brands had paid a $1.25 million bribe to an official of the Honduran government in exchange for relief from an export tax on bananas.[42] The new tax of fifty cents a box had been levied by Honduras a year earlier as part of a plan by the Union of Banana Exporting Countries to recoup some of their losses caused by escalating fuel costs. Soon after announcing it, the Honduran government halved the tax, thereby saving United Brands an estimated $7.5 million that year alone.[43] Who pocketed the payoff? A Honduran commission concluded that the economic minister Abraham Bennaton Ramos did, at a secret meeting in Switzerland.

But it was López Arellano who paid the price for the "Bananagate" affair.

The Honduran military was no stranger to charges of corruption. Top-level officers were charged with having stolen relief goods that poured in after Hurricane Fifi. Younger, lower-ranking officers untainted by the charges took control of the Supreme Council of the Armed Forces in February 1975, forcing López to retire as chief of the military a month later.[44] On 22 April, López lost the presidency as well, a casualty of United Brands' bribes.

With the ouster of López Arellano, in a bloodless coup by Col. Juan Alberto Melgar Castro, conservatives had finally rid themselves of an old nemesis, and the country swung sharply to the right. The reform program ground to a halt. By now experienced in dealing with governments that changed direction rapidly, the peasant movement did not wait to see its victories swept away. On 18 May 1975 the 38,000-member National Peasant Union (UNC) seized land on 128 farms throughout the country, withdrawing only when the government threatened to remove them by force.[45] Then, on June 25, the UNC led a nationwide "hunger march" that was to converge on the capital from five directions. One column had just reached Juticalpa, a town in Olancho, when the army moved in to stop it.

Aided by some local ranchers, the soldiers attacked while the marchers were meeting at a training center. Five peasants were shot to death. Nine others—students, priests, and peasant leaders—disappeared. Their mutilated bodies were found a week later in a dynamited well on the Horcones ranch.

The killings shocked the nation, which, unlike El Salvador, did not have the 1932 *matanza* on its conscience. But local ranchers were serving notice that, from then on, they were playing for keeps. This situation strengthened the peasant movement, forcing both the 80,000-member ANACH and the FECORAH, the agrarian co-op federation, to approach the UNC's more militant position lest they be abandoned by their members.

On 9 October 1975 the three organizations joined in the National Front of Peasant Unity and gave Melgar Castro two weeks in which to distribute over 300,000 acres of land to 30,000 landless peasants. At the same time, the leaders of El Salvador, Guatemala, and Nicaragua were prodding him to crush the movement before its influence infected "their" peasants. Melgar Castro's solution was to move in both directions at once.

In October 1975 he created the Agrarian Policy Commission with the power to override INA decisions, and he replaced the INA's progressive director, effectively crippling the agrarian-reform agency. On the other hand, he expropriated 57,000 acres from United Brands and 84,000 from Standard Fruit. And in 1976 he caved in to the peasants' demands and reappointed Rigoberto Sandoval Corea to lead the INA. Given this turn of events, Sandoval ordered additional expropriations, including 58,000 acres from domestic owners.

Enter the Agrarian Policy Commission. It blocked the action against national owners, starting a series of heated controversies, which led to Sandoval's resignation in early 1977, thereby laying to rest the 1975 agrarian-reform law. This rightist victory encouraged reactionary actions in other areas—progressive officers were pushed from the Supreme Council of the Armed Forces and progressive union leaders outmaneuvered by the new regime with the help of AIFLD.

Las Isletas

Las Isletas, however, was to serve as the centerpiece of the military's turn to the right: an example of a marriage of interests between multinational corporations, corrupt officers, and a reactionary government. The Las Isletas Peasants Enterprise* was begun as a workers' collective on lands abandoned by Standard Fruit after Hurricane Fifi destroyed their plantations in 1974. The new enterprise was run by a board of management selected by a general assembly of the work force and continued to sell its bananas to Standard.** But the collective actually refused to accept bribes or be intimidated when it came to setting a price on the fruit.[46] And, in early 1977 Las Isletas contemplated exporting its produce through COMUNBANA, the marketing arm of the Union of Banana Exporting Countries, instead of through Standard.[47]

Enough was enough. In February, goaded by Standard Fruit, encouraged by the government, and supported by troops of the Fourth Army Battalion under Lt. Col. Gustavo Alvarez, a small group of Las Isletas members called a "special convention" to elect

---

*A peasant enterprise *(empresa asociativa campesina)* is a productive unit in which all means of production are held collectively, the land is worked collectively, and the workers' management decides on the generation, accumulation, and distribution of any surplus.

**In 1968 Standard Fruit and Steamship became a wholly owned subsidiary of Castle & Cooke. Castle & Cooke continued to operate in Honduras under the name Standard Fruit.

a new leadership. The army moved in, arresting some 200 militant members of the cooperative and guarding the 35 workers who declared themselves the new leaders.[48]

In those days, Lt. Col. Gustavo Alvarez was on the payroll of Castle & Cooke, "much as you might hire an off-duty policeman," Donald J. Kirchhoff, the company's chairman, rationalized.[49] Far from being an "off-duty policeman," however, Gustavo Alvarez was an all-too-active military officer.

Its leaders languishing in jail, Las Isletas signed a long-term contract with Castle & Cooke through Standard Fruit for the marketing of their produce, agreeing to pay freight costs and accepting a per-box price of $1.46, $1.19 *less* than the price offered through COMUNBANA. The new management also began to siphon off funds to continue the services of its military protectors. The local military, the government, and Castle & Cooke were driving a once-prosperous worker-managed enterprise into the ground.

Elections on the Agenda

As the government of Melgar Castro struck out against the peasants' and workers' movements, it announced that general elections would be held in 1979. The Nationals and the conservative wing of the Liberals fully expected that elections would be their means for returning the country to the old mechanisms of political domination that had been shaken by the reformist attempt. Thus, elections were one way to give a democratic facade to a conservative regime, a move seen as highly desirable by the U.S. government.

Yet, on 7 August 1978, weakened by continual charges of corruption as well as by an ongoing struggle for power in the military, General Melgar Castro was overthrown in a bloodless coup. He was replaced by a junta led by Gen. Policarpo Paz García, the chief of the armed forces and head of the junta; Lt. Col. José Domingo Alvarez, the air force commander; and Lt. Col. Amílcar Zelaya Rodríguez, the chief of military security. The conservative junta immediately promised that elections would be held in 1980, a move which, according to many observers, was dictated by the Carter administration in return for aid.

INTO THE CENTRAL AMERICAN MAELSTROM

In a region where the fires of revolution burn white hot, Honduras has been a model of stability, a bizarre anomaly. Although Honduras's wealthy landowners, ranchers, and industrialists have not been loath to use violence to maintain their privileges, neither have they unleashed a war of genocide against their own people. Similarly, although the Honduran military has been repressive in the past, it has also led reform movements. Not only did the ruling military junta allow constituent-assembly elections in April 1980 and presidential elections in November 1981, but, to general surprise, these were honest and well attended. Furthermore, while the Honduran Left has spawned at least four guerrilla organizations* as well as many popular movements, these cannot compare to the revolutionary armies of Guatemala, the FMLN-FDR of El Salvador, or the victorious FSLN in Nicaragua. Above all, the Hondurans seemed genuinely anxious to stay out of the regional conflicts. In short, Honduras was one country *fewer* for U.S. policymakers to worry about in a region filled with seemingly insoluble problems.

Yet, ironically, it is U.S. policy itself that presents the greatest threat to Honduras's relative stability today. Not content to let well enough alone, U.S. policymakers are attempting to build Honduras into a regional reactionary powerhouse and a staging base for counterrevolutionary activities in Central America. And, if this policy carries any guarantees at all, it is that, before long, Honduras too will be sucked into the regional conflagration.

Writing in *Foreign Affairs* shortly after Ronald Reagan's election, Viron Vaky, President Carter's assistant secretary of state for inter-American affairs from 1978 to 1980, predicted that "Latin America will be the sector of foreign policy in which there are the largest differences in perceptions and premises between the old and new Administrations."[50]

On the level of "perceptions and premises," Vaky was quite correct; Carter and Reagan have grounded their policies in differ-

---

*These are the Cinchoneros Popular Liberation Movement, the Padre Ivan Betancourt Popular Revolutionary Command, the Morazanista Liberation Front of Honduras, and the Lorenzo Zelaya Popular Revolutionary Command.

ent assumptions. Carter's advisers, for example, were much more likely to see the context of Central America's struggles as "that of authoritarian systems eroding under the pressures of demands for reform which they cannot or will not accommodate."[51] Those vying for Reagan's attention, by contrast, discount internal factors and, instead, blame the Soviet Union.

Though the premises are different, policy nevertheless has often been the same. Nowhere is this as evident as in the case of Honduras.

Under President Carter, the Honduran military leaders were courted, cajoled, and showered with loans and grants. Levels of aid to the country were the highest in Central America, except for Panama, in 1978, and second to none in 1979. In September 1979 Carter dispatched a special envoy, William Bowdler, to Tegucigalpa to meet with Gen. Policarpo Paz García, who headed that country's governing military junta.

Their talks were obviously positive. A few days later, Assistant Secretary Vaky, in a policy address on the region, noted that the administration was "impressed" by democratic progress in Honduras.[52] The U.S. diplomats, it seems, preferred to overlook what Honduran labor unions called a "wave of repression" that had swept the country since Paz García assumed power.[53]

Carter's envoy had emphasized two themes with Honduran leaders. First, he put strong pressure on General Paz to keep his pledge of holding elections. Second, Carter's policy demanded that the Hondurans no longer stand apart from the regional crisis. Honduras, according to Vaky's 1979 policy statement, must play a key role in preventing "regional conflicts and [the] potential infiltration" of supplies and guerrillas to other struggles.

Aid and Elections

Paz García kept his part of the agreement when he returned to Honduras. On 23 April 1980, elections were held for a seventy-one-member constituent assembly, which would pave the way for a return to civilian rule. To nearly universal amazement, the Liberal party won a slim victory over the National party in very heavy voting, an indication both of popular repudiation of military rule and of U.S. pressure for clean elections.[54] But it was not necessarily to be taken as a mandate for progressive government, for the Liberals were often as conservative as their traditional rivals.

Indirectly rebuffed at the polls, Paz García was not so easily turned out of office. The military junta formally handed over power to the newly elected constituent assembly, but the Liberals, lacking an absolute majority, were stymied in their attempts to form a government. As a way out of this crisis—which many observers claim was engineered by Paz—they asked the general to stay on as interim president until the installation of a new elected leader in early 1982. Paz, who in the meantime had dismissed some twenty-five high-ranking officers, mostly reformers, agreed.[55]

Satisfied that Paz García had kept his part of the bargain, Carter actively lobbied for the increased aid for Honduras that he had requested. On 23 March 1980, when Paz García was still touring the United States, the columnist Jack Anderson had written, "The President seems determined to add still another sorry chapter to the chronicle of Yankee imperialism in Central America. The Administration apparently has chosen Honduras to be our new 'Nicaragua'—a dependable satellite bought and paid for by American military and economic largess."[56] In fact, in 1980 the country received $53.1 million in economic aid and $3.9 million in military aid. This meant that during the important 1978–80 period, Honduras received more U.S. aid than any other Central American country.

Two days after the appearance of the Anderson column, the assistant secretary of state John Bushnell argued before Congress that if Honduras was to play a key geopolitical role in the region by halting the flow of arms into El Salvador, it had to be well equipped. He asked that Congress approve a one-year loan of ten UH-1H (Huey) gunship helicopters to Honduras to patrol the border with El Salvador. "We predict that the conflict with El Salvador will diminish quickly," he added, blinded by the light at the end of the tunnel, "and that, when this happens, the helicopters will be returned to the United States."[57] History sometimes repeats itself as tragedy; the loan has been extended to five years, and the conflict "with" El Salvador is far from a resolution.

The Hueys were just one part of the significant arms buildup that began in the late 1970s and continued into the 1980s. Between 1975 and 1979 Honduras was the fourth-largest arms importer in the entire Central American–Caribbean region (after Cuba, Mexico, and the Bahamas) and the largest importer in Central America proper.[58] Its air force, long referred to as the best in Central America, boasted Israeli-modified French Super-Mystère jets, Yugoslav-modified Canadian F–86 Sabre jet fighters, A–37 combat planes from the United States, as well as training and reconnaissance planes from Britain and the United States.[59] It had British tanks, Israeli patrol boats, and U.S. trucks and jeeps. The United States provided smaller equipment as well, sending M-16 and M-14 rifles, side arms, grenade launchers, mortars, recoilless rifles, and communications equipment.[60]

The United States also played a leading role in the training of Honduran officers. Between 1971 and 1980 the United States trained 2,259 military personnel in Honduran and U.S. facilities, nearly double the number of Hondurans trained in the period 1951–70.[61] Higher-level Honduran officers received special attention. Nearly 100 Honduran officers attended the "Command and General Staff" courses at the U.S. Army School of the Americas in the Canal Zone from 1976 to 1980, three times more than from any other Latin American country.[62]

And then there were the military advisers. In early 1982 ninety-seven U.S. military advisers and support personnel—nearly all from the U.S. Special Forces (Green Berets)—were in Honduras. This was almost twice as many as in neighboring El Salvador. Unlike the first thirty-seven advisers sent in 1980, the U.S. soldiers sent in 1982 patrolled the border with El Salvador, carried M-16s, and dressed in camouflage. By mid-1983, the number of advisers had surged to 162

Under the care and oversight of the United States, Honduras had been prepared for the Central American wars.

Into the Fray

Honduran soldiers patrolling the border with El Salvador in early 1980 would often share a drink and some small talk with Salvadoran guerrillas who had crossed the border. After all, since the 1969 war, Honduran soldiers and their counterparts in El

Salvador shared nothing but enmity. Yet, shortly after Paz García's return from Washington, this decade-old open wound was suddenly sutured. On 14 May 1980, in a joint action with Salvadoran troops, Honduran soldiers prevented hundreds of Salvadoran refugees from crossing the Río Sumpul into Honduras. Approximately 600 refugees were killed, trapped between the Hondurans who wouldn't let them step onshore and the Salvadorans who shot them down as they struggled back.[63] The Río Sumpul massacre was only the first in a string of grisly mass murders of Salvadoran refugees trying to flee to Honduras.

Then, on 30 October after eleven years of bickering, Honduras and El Salvador penned their acceptance of a peace treaty, formally ending the 1969 war. That the two countries should want to settle an old conflict was not surprising. What was remarkable about the treaty was the fact that El Salvador dictated the terms at a moment in which it was exceptionally weak in relation to Honduras. The treaty actually resolved few of the outstanding problems between the two countries. But it did give the Salvadorans full access to the *bolsones territoriales,* demilitarized zones along the border, which had been patrolled by the OAS since the end of the war. The Carter administration had been pressing hard for a resolution of the conflict that would give Salvadorans access to the *bolsones* so that they could pursue the guerrillas.[64] Instead of breaking bread with guerrillas, Honduran border troops were now instructed to cooperate with Salvadoran troops in attacking them.

While the Honduran military moved against Salvadoran guerrillas on their southwestern border, they cast a blind eye on the activities of Somoza's former national guardsmen who were camped on their southeastern border. In late 1980 and early 1981 the Nicaraguans reported ninety-six incursions by Nicaraguan exiles and others based in Honduras.[65] As a *Washington Post* reporter wrote, former national guardsmen "regularly cross from Honduras into Nicaragua to stage small-scale attacks on Nicaraguan farms and, occasionally the army of the Sandinistas."[66]

As Honduras became more involved in the Central American struggles, its military officials increasingly discussed and developed strategy with the military leaders of El Salvador and Guatemala. According to a number of reliable sources, top brass from the three countries met secretly in Honduras twice in early 1980.[67]

Thus, by the time the Reagan entourage encamped in Washington, Honduras was already guided by a policy that would lead it both to elections and (presumably) legitimation and to increasing military participation in the Central American conflicts. True to form, Reagan seemed more concerned with the latter goal. He reduced the level of economic aid to Honduras from fiscal year 1980 levels, but sharply increased military aid, arms sales, and the use of military advisers.

If the Carter-Reagan objective of building Honduras into a regional contender carried with it the danger of drawing that country headlong into neighboring wars, by strengthening the Honduran military the United States also ran the risk of undermining its goal of returning civilian rule to that country. For now, the military would be content to exercise its prerogatives from the sidelines. But if the men in olive drab didn't fancy the results of the November 1981 elections, one could be sure that they were equipped to do something about it.

ELECTIONS AND BEYOND

The Honduran press called it "election fever," and it was certain that what the populace lacked by way of practice in the electoral process, it made up for in enthusiasm. The excitement had been building for weeks before the 29 November 1981 polling date, and Hondurans were deeply aware that the elections gave them a rare moment in the world spotlight. Moreover, as everyone from politicians to sportscasters stressed, Honduras was earning the attention it deserved as the obedient child in a region of troublesome, if not barbaric, juvenile delinquents.

Although the military government of Gen. Policarpo Paz García had officially acquiesced in the idea of elections by the end of the Carter administration, there were increasing indications that he was getting cold feet as the date approached. The constituent-assembly elections of April 1980 indicated that the Liberal party had a clear edge on the National party, which was traditionally identified with the country's military. By September 1981 the Nationals were pushing for another postponement of the elections (already moved back from their original date of 23 August), while Paz was entertaining proposals for a new civilian-military government that would allow him to retain a central role. The opposition, linked to the Liberals, moved in for a quick checkmate: news of a land scam involving the finance minister, Valentín Mendoza, a close associate of Paz, was leaked to the press with the strong suggestion that the scandal could be extended to the Presidential Palace if need be. It was a classic move. Paz, knowing when he was beaten, slunk off to his offices to wait out his term, and elections proceeded.

Economic Basket Case

Honduras's business community, unlike that of El Salvador and Guatemala, was disgusted with the cupidity and mismanagement on the part of the military, which had brought the country to the brink of financial ruin. By 1980 the Honduran economy was something of a basket case. After nearly twenty years in power, the military had not been able to shake Honduras's reliance on agricultural exports, which still represented 75 percent of all exported goods (principally bananas and coffee and, to a lesser extent, refrigerated meat, wood, and cotton). As the international terms of trade continued to favor petroleum and manufactured goods over agricultural commodities, this meant that, each year, the Hondurans could afford fewer imports from the same level of exports. For example, in 1972 Honduras could buy a barrel of oil with three pounds of exported coffee. By 1980 it needed twenty-four pounds.[68] To pay for this growing deficit, Honduras turned to foreign loans. Long-term financing totaled $257 million in 1980, bringing the foreign debt to $1.2 billion.

The government brought in the International Monetary Fund in early 1981 as a condition demanded by foreign lenders for the granting of future loans. But IMF policies, above all a 10 percent tax on most imports, created even more havoc. Given Honduras's reliance on a variety of foreign imputs, the tax resulted in a lowering of Honduran production, less income from exports, and a wave of insolvencies. According to one Honduran entrepreneur, only forty-five days after the economic plan was initiated, more than 200 industries were already on the edge of bankruptcy.[69]

The wretched state of the economy began to strain one constant of Honduran political life. No matter how many times power appeared to change hands in Honduras through the century, there was one symbiotic relation that didn't change: those who controlled the wealth of the country needed those with the guns to guarantee "political stability," while the military needed money-men—in the form of the traditional oligarchy, the financiers, or the new industrialists—to guarantee there would be an economy to skim. Given the abysmal performance of the Honduran economy, the relation was breaking down.

The military was in a state of flux as well. The combination of Honduras's internal stability and the surrounding turmoil of the region left a power vacuum in the military itself in the last months of Paz's reign. Old money was abandoning the country, frightened by the regional conflicts, and new money, in the form of huge infusions of economic and military aid, poured in. There was bound to be a shift in the balance of power, all the more so as the Superior Council of the Armed Forces and the Liberal party, among others, sought a new alliance.

Conservative Liberals, Liberal Liberals . . .

From the outset it was apparent that the Liberal and the National parties would smother the smaller opposition parties, the Liberals being the odds-on favorite to win the election. It was often hard to tell the Liberals from their National opponents. Cynics maintained that the Liberals had a "cleaner" reputation than the Nationals simply because it had been longer since they had had access to the public till. But even the party's supporters admitted that it failed to gather much steam through the 1970s under the lackluster leadership of Modesto Rodas Alvarado. Furthermore, it had a new faction of fiery young upstarts to contend with. ALIPO (Popular Liberal Alliance) was a wing of the party dating back to the 1950s with social-democratic sentiments, though it avoided affiliation with the Socialist International. Estimates of ALIPO strength within the Liberal party varied from 10 to 35 percent, but its unlikely mix of university leftists, mildly progressive business people, and a strong presence in the national press gave it an influence disproportionate to its size.

In the months before the elections, there was a bitter struggle between ALIPO and the party regulars, in which some of the ALIPO threatened to bolt the party and work toward a swing-vote coalition of Christian Democrats and the PINU (National Innovation and Unity party) in the Chamber of Deputies. In the end, the would-be renegades backed down, partly mollified by the promise of major cabinet positions if they agreed to lend their support, and partly sobered by the prospect of a National party victory if they chose to withhold it.

As it happened, Modesto Rodas did not live to see the triumph of his party over its archrivals. His followers in the party mainstream, still known as the Rodistas, chose a folksy small-town doctor, Roberto Suazo Córdova, as his successor. Suazo, fifty-five, hailing from a rural department on the Salvadoran border, was known as El Brujo de La Paz for his reputation for dabbling in *santeria.*

Suazo may have been an unlikely candidate, but his National opponent, Ricardo Zúñiga, was downright unsavory. U.S.–embassy officials referred to him in private as a "Mayor Daley" type. It was widely recognized that he had links with the Mancha Brava goon squad and with contraband operations out of Miami.

By the time of the 1980 constituent-assembly elections, the National party's only hope rested with blind obedience to tradition, or outright fraud. The Nationals' strongholds were in the underdeveloped south of the country, where the average literacy rate was 50 percent, the lowest in Honduras. In the farther reaches of the Honduran countryside, many voters would state that they were voting "blue" (National) or "red" (Liberal) without even being able to name the candidate in question.

The Limits of Electoral Freedom

With the Liberals favored to win, the best that the two minority parties, the Christian Democrats (PDCH) and PINU, could hope for was the lack of a simple majority in the eighty-five-seat Chamber of Deputies, which would allow them to put together a swing-vote coalition. PINU was a relatively new party based on middle-class professionals, while the Honduran Christian Democratic party began as a peasant-student movement in 1963, incorporated as a political party in 1968, and participated in its first election in 1981.

The PDCH had been barred from the 1980 election on the grounds that it was a "friend of violence" and that it received funds from outside sources (namely, the international Christian Democratic organization). These objections were put aside in 1981, and the party was allowed to participate.

The Honduran Christian Democrats tend to be more radical than most of their Latin American counterparts, largely because of their association with the militant peasant union, UNC, and their inroads into the labor movement, rivaled only by the Honduran Communist party (PCH). In 1980, the PDCH startled the Christian Democratic movement by issuing a statement at its national convention that was highly critical of its Salvadoran counterpart and that called for a political settlement of the Salvadoran conflict. The PDCH also played an interesting mediator role between the sector of the country's Left represented by the Patriotic Front (FPH), and the traditional electoral parties. It was a full-fledged member of the front, a legal coalition of three illegal parties, until it amicably parted and slid into electoral legality in 1981.[70]

For the Patriotic Front itself, the elections represented more of a dilemma than an opportunity. Before the April 1980 elections, the leaders of the parties that constituted the Patriotic Front—the pro-Moscow Honduran Communist party (PCH), the Maoist Marxist-Leninist Communist party of Honduras (PCMLH), and the Honduran Socialist party (PASOH)—called for an electoral boycott. Instead, more than 80 percent of the electorate turned out to vote, as opposed to less than 50 percent in 1971. The Patriotic Front had no choice other than to analyze the new appeal of the elections and find a way to fit in.

The coalition decided to avoid a gratuitous defeat in the presidential race and concentrated its efforts and resources on four candidates in its four strongest departments. They soon found that Honduran electoral freedoms pertained more to some than to others.

Marco Virgilio Carías, an FPH candidate from the Socialist party and a university professor, was kidnapped several days before the registration deadline. He was released two weeks later, shaken but unhurt—and out of the running. At the same time, the government began a wave of crackdowns on Salvadoran and Guatemalan exiles living in Honduras. Its statements intentionally clouded the distinction between foreign exiles and local activitists, and presented the impression that Honduras was on the brink of its own dread cycle of "subversion and repression."

Then, a week before the elections, Aníbal Delgado Fiallos of the PCH was violently seized by the Department of National Investigation (DNI), by far the most loathed and feared branch of the country's armed forces. As his wife and children looked on, the DNI searched Delgado and ransacked the union offices from which he was running his campaign, taking lists of party supporters, equipment, and campaign funds. Delgado was taken into custody, but soon released. "They questioned me for fifteen minutes, and then the *comandante* apologized and said they had made a 'terrible mistake,' " he reported the following day.[71] Yet those responsible were never disciplined, nor was the party compensated for its losses.[72]

Finally, the election was weighted toward the traditional parties because of a law that made campaign funds available on the basis of votes amassed in previous elections. While the Liberals received approximately $1.25 million, PINU got only $350,000. The Christian Democrats were promised $15,000 (of which they received only $5,000), and the FPH received nothing at all, being forced to rely on public appearances and local radio talk shows for exposure.[73]

The built-in biases of the Honduran electoral system supported the claims of the disaffected Left in Honduras, which tended to scorn the electoral efforts of the FPH and the Christian Democrats without offering a concrete alternative. They argued that the leadership of the leftist parties had little to do with grass-roots organizing, which they said was reflected in their meager vote. "The elections don't have any importance here," noted one defector from the PCH, who has since become a leader of the illegal Popular Revolutionary Union (URP). "What we need are structural changes. The elections are just a diversion. In the days of the Romans they had bread and circuses; the difference here is that they don't give out the bread, they just hold the circus."

The Liberal Victory

Despite a last-minute flurry of charges, the elections took place as scheduled on 29 November. By all accounts, the voting itself was honest.

By the time it was over, the Liberals had won a stunning victory, polling more than 640,000 votes to the Nationals' 490,000. This gave them not only the presidency but also a majority in the Chamber of Deputies. The minority parties were as shattered as the Nationals, particularly the PINU and PDCH, who had hoped that together they would draw 10 percent of the vote. The Christian Democrats garnered some 19,000 votes, PINU 30,000, and the Patriotic Front's independents a scant 4,000. This translated into one sure seat and one possible additional seat for PINU, one possible seat for the PDC, and nothing at all for the independents.[74]

How would life be different in Honduras following Suazo's 26 January inauguration? His campaign rhetoric had not been particularly impressive, proposing to combat endemic corruption by "making sure every public servant puts in an eight-hour day," to relieve the economic crisis "by increasing production and productivity," and responding to the U.S. presence in El Salvador with the bald statement, "We believe that the United States is the defender of democracy and liberty in the world."[75] Much would depend on who ended up in key cabinet and advisory positions.

Still, it seemed highly likely that the deals that the Liberals had struck with the military would outweigh any agreement they had with ALIPO, their own reform sector. Before the elections, Suazo and Zúñiga, accompanied by their advisers, were called in for meetings with military authorities at which they were told that the ongoing investigation of corruption by a civil commission only "played into the hands of the enemies of the country." If the elections were to proceed, the two majority-party candidates would be obliged to sanction the reconstitution of the commission. Shortly afterward, the aggressive minority-party investigators were removed from the commission. The other condition imposed by the military was that the armed forces would have access to certain cabinet posts and veto power over others.

Divisions in the Military

To speak of "the military" in Honduras has always been misleading, for the strains range from the traditional old officer corps to "modern" Yankee boosters and the "military youth," deeply influenced by the reformist officers of Peru. But there is no denying the hard-liners' rapid consolidation of power following Suazo's election. Paz García's abrupt dismissal of twenty-five liberal young officers in 1980 was a blow to the reformers. Further, the key position in the military, and so in the government, is that of the head of the Superior Council of the Armed Forces, and, in January 1982, Col. Gustavo Alvarez, Castle & Cooke's man at Las Isletas, was selected. Alvarez, who soon promoted himself to the rank of general, had been head of the Public Security Forces (FUSEP), which also encompassed the Department of National Investigation (DNI), giving him more access to damaging information than anyone else in the country. (This was the U.S. equivalent of heading the National Guard, FBI, CIA, and all local police forces simultaneously.)

The United States to the Rescue

Suazo and his military backers immediately faced a major financial crisis. Low-interest, long-term loans from international lending institutions had dried up, as they had for the rest of Central America and the Third World, forcing the country to forage for short-term, high-interest loans from reluctant private foreign banks. Capital flight and a huge trade deficit had cut Honduras's foreign reserves from $150 million in 1980 to under $40 million at the end of 1981, less than was necessary to cover two weeks' imports. As a final blow, there was the failure of the Banco Financiera Hondureña (Banfinan), the second-wealthiest bank in Honduras, which collapsed because of corruption and mismanagement in late 1980. This had led a group of U.S. banks to take punitive steps against Honduras, affecting more than half the country's foreign credit. "If you lose your lenders' confidence, you lose the lifeblood of the economy," noted one interested observer.[76]

Under such doleful circumstances, a few eyebrows were naturally raised when Práxedes Martinez, the finance minister, returned triumphantly from New York a few days before the November

1981 elections to announce a new $100-million-loan package from the United States—including a $50 million advance on the national coffee crop after a year of the lowest coffee prices in recent history.[77] Honduras, a country with less than 1 percent of Latin America's total population, was to reap more than 17 percent of all AID funds destined for the region. Between 1981 and 1983, Honduras would receive more than $170 million in economic aid from the United States.

The stakes, of course, were regional. And this was precisely the message sent to Washington in mid-1981 by the Honduran military high command. In a detailed report, it pointed out that Honduras, like Guatemala and El Salvador, was in the throes of an economic crisis "caused by the Sandinista revolution" and that massive infusions of U.S. aid would be necessary to avert a similar result. They added that Honduras was the *tapón natural*—the obvious plug—to "Soviet-Cuban expansionism" in Central America, but one that should not be taken for granted.

This message was carried by a strong sector within the Honduran military, led by Gen. Gustavo Alvarez, that is eager to play a role in the regional Central American drama, in full collaboration with the military regimes of Guatemala and El Salvador, acutely aware of the short-term and long-term personal benefits it could reap. An active commitment by the Hondurans would generate increased sums of U.S. aid—and the opportunities for graft that would open—as well as a likelihood that the military would again assume direct political power.

Nor did the plea fall on deaf ears. With frightening speed, the Reagan administration has made Honduras its forward base of military operations in the tense region. While the country will no doubt be used as an important base for rear-guard actions against the Salvadoran guerrillas in the future, now it serves as the key element in the administration's offensive against the Nicaraguan government. This offensive has both covert and overt aspects.

Honduras has become the primary staging point for the CIA-funded "covert" war against the Sandinistas. More than 6,000 *contras* (counterrevolutionaries), largely drawn from Somoza's former National Guard, occupy the Honduran border with Nicaragua. By 1983, their attacks across the border were so frequent and blatant that the term "covert war" had lost all meaning.

As the *contras* stepped up their attacks against Nicaragua, the Honduran army itself was drawn into the fighting—eagerly, it would seem. Numerous reports from Nicaraguan government officials and journalists working the region note a steady Honduran shelling of the Nicaraguan border towns of Jalapa and Teotecacinte.[78]

In return for his support, General Alvarez is expecting his pound of flesh. Military aid to Honduras increased to $31.3 million in fiscal year 1982, and Reagan requested $37 million for fiscal year 1983 (of which $20.3 million has been approved thus far by Congress). But in June 1983, General Alvarez told a startled U.S. Congress that he expected $400 million in military aid over the next three years as a "minimum."[79]

In July, the administration announced the beginning of Big Pine II, a joint U.S.–Honduran military exercise that will put as many as 4,000 marine and army combat troops in Honduras at any one time over the next eight months. As part of the exercise, the largest ever held in the region, the army will build an undisclosed number of air strips in Honduras and, perhaps, a naval facility on its northern coast.[80] The costs of the exercise, which will leave Honduras as the most militarily sophisticated country in the region, are to be borne by the Department of Defense, and therefore do not require congressional approval.

The sector of the military that is seeking more of a regional involvement for Honduras is quite aware of a number of sobering precedents. In 1954 Honduras served as the staging ground for the CIA-sponsored coup that overthrew the Guatemalan president, Jacobo Arbenz. In 1961 Honduras's Swan Island, off the Atlantic coast, was the communications center for the Bay of Pigs invasion of Cuba. (It is currently being refurbished for future use.) And, three years later, Policarpo Paz García, a major at the time, led a contingent of Honduran troops as part of the "Inter-American Peacekeeping Force" that invaded the Dominican Republic.

While dominant, General Alvarez is not without opposition inside the military. Many younger officers who came of age in the aftermath of the 1969 "soccer war" bitterly resent the fact that Salvadoran troops are now being trained by U.S. advisers on

Honduran territory. Others fear that Alvarez is playing fast and loose with the military in order to bolster his own power in the country. In late 1982, Col. Leónides Torres Arias, head of military intelligence from 1976 until he was sacked by Alvarez in January 1982, charged that the Honduran military chief was planning an "adventure of madness" that Honduras could not win.

For the moment, however, this is Alvarez's game: the U.S. policymakers have succeeded in pulling Honduras into the Central American frying pan. In doing so, they have undoubtedly strengthened their military hand in the region, but the political, social, and economic consequences are just beginning to emerge. President Suazo Córdova, one of the region's few democratically elected leaders, has been reduced to a pathetic figurehead. General Alvarez no longer makes a pretense of clueing him in on the decisions that the military has made for him. As the military strengthens its grip on the country, the nation's human-rights record continues to deteriorate. According to the head of the Honduran Human Rights Commission, "Now we have a religious war to save democracy in which clandestine jails, disappearances, and torture are tolerated."[81] And the economy experienced a serious recession even as the military embarked on an unprecedented buying spree. Unemployment almost doubled in 1982, and the foreign debt soared. President Reagan may have won the battle for Honduras, but the region's wars are far from over.

NOTES

1. Anthony Winston, "Class Structure and Agrarian Transition in Central America," *Latin American Perspectives,* no. 19 (1978): 27–48.
2. William H. Durham, *Scarcity & Survival in Central America: Ecological Origins of the Soccer War* (Stanford, Calif: Stanford University Press, 1979), 22, 106–7.
3. Ibid., 116.
4. Mario Posas, "Política estatal y estructura agraria en Honduras (1950–1978)," *Estudios Sociales Centroamericanos* [Costa Rica], no. 24 (1979): 38.
5. Daniel Slutzky and Esther Alonso, *Les transformations récentes de l'enclave bananière au Honduras* (Paris: CETRAL, 1979), 21.
6. Mario Posas, "Tendencias ideológicas actuales en el movimiento obrero hondureño," *Anuario de Estudios Centroamericanos* [Costa Rica], no. 6 (1980): 25. Other general studies of the Honduran labor movement include Mario

Posas, *Luchas del movimiento obrero hondureño* (San José, Costa Rica: EDUCA, 1981); idem, *Lucha ideológica y organización sindical en Honduras (1954–1965)* (Tegucigalpa: Guaymuras, 1980); and Victor Meza, *Historia del movimiento obrero hondureño* (Tegucigalpa: Guaymuras), 1980.

7. On ORIT, see Hobart Spalding, Jr., *Organized Labor in Latin America* (New York: Harper Torchbooks, 1977), 256ff.

8. Posas, *Lucha ideológica*, 6–7.

9. Posas, "Política estatal," 53.

10. Ibid.

11. Between 1958 and 1960 the government distributed nearly 75,000 acres of land. Most of the colonies were established on lands ceded back to the government by the Tela Railroad Company or in zones where land ownership was never clearly established. See Posas, "Política estatal," 54.

12. Posas, *Lucha ideológica*, 41.

13. Senate Committee on Foreign Relations, Subcommittee on American Republics, *Survey of the Alliance for Progress, Labor Policies and Programs*, 90th Cong., 2d sess., 15 July 1968, 9.

14. See AIFLD, "Country Labor Plans: Honduras, 1977–1981" (Unpublished ms., n.d.), 1–17.

15. Slutzky and Alonso, *Transformations*, table 4.

16. See Susanne Jonas, "Masterminding the Mini-Market: U.S. Aid to the Central American Common Market," *NACLA's Latin America & Empire Report* 7, no. 5 (1973): 3–19.

17. Ibid., 13

18. Antonio Murga Frassinetti, "Concentración industrial en Honduras," *Economía Política*, no. 9 (September–December 1974): 70, 85–86.

19. Victor Meza, "Crisis del reformismo militar y coyuntura política en Honduras," *ALAI* [Montreal] 5, no. 3 (1981): 41.

20. Durham, *Scarcity & Survival*, 50.

21. Ibid., 25.

22. Rafael del Cid, "Las clases sociales y su dinámica en el agro hondureño," *Estudios Sociales Centroamericanos*, no. 18 (1977): 145.

23. Durham, *Scarcity & Survival*, 108.

24. Del Cid, "Class sociales," 154.

25. Marta F. Sánchez Soler and James A. Morris, "Factores de poder en la evolución política del campesinado hondureño," *Estudios Sociales Centroamericanos*, no. 16 (1977): 92–93.

26. Posas, "Política estatal," 49–50.

27. Durham, *Scarcity & Survival*, 162.

28. Mary Jeanne Reid Martz, *The Central American Soccer War: Historical Patterns and Internal Dynamics of OAS Settlement Procedures* (Athens: Ohio University Center for International Studies, 1978), 90.

29. United Nations, *Estudio económico de América Latina, 1973* (Santiago, Chile: UN, 1974), 156, 203, 231.

30. Roberto Robleda, "Algunos problemas del desarrollo industrial de Honduras," *Economía Política*, no. 13 (1972): 32.
31. Posas, *Lucha ideológica*, 23–32.
32. See Guillermo Molina Chocano, "Honduras: El proceso electoral," *Le Monde Diplomatique*, August 1980, 27.
33. Guillermo Molina Chocano, *Honduras, de la guerra civil al reformismo militar* (San José, Costa Rica: Programa Centroamericano de Ciencias Sociales, n.d.), 47ff.
34. Posas, "Política estatal," 78.
35. *Latin America*, 3 March 1972.
36. See Posas, *Lucha ideológica*.
37. Thomas P. Anderson, *The War of the Dispossessed: Honduras and El Salvador, 1969* (Lincoln: University of Nebraska Press, 1981), 44.
38. *Los Angeles Times*, 8 February 1976.
39. Posas, "Política estatal," 84.
40. *New York Times*, 24 April 1972.
41. Posas, "Política estatal," 64.
42. *Wall Street Journal*, 9 April 1975.
43. *Wall Street Journal*, 10 April 1975.
44. *Miami Herald*, 15 June 1975.
45. *New York Times*, 22 July 1975.
46. *Diálogo* [Guatemala], December 1980.
47. Roger Burbach, "Union Busting: Castle & Cooke in Honduras," *NACLA Report on the Americas* 9, no. 8 (1977): 41.
48. Roger Burbach, "Honduras: Challenging Castle & Cooke," *NACLA Report on the Americas*, 12, no. 2 (1978): 43–45.
49. *Wall Street Journal*, 26 November 1975.
50. Viron P. Vaky, "Hemispheric Relations: 'Everything Is Part of Everything Else,' " *Foreign Affairs* 59 (1981): 645.
51. Ibid., 623–24.
52. *Latin America Political Report*, 14 September 1979.
53. *Miami Herald*, 13 April 1979.
54. *Latin America Weekly Report*, 25 April 1980.
55. *Latin America Weekly Report*, 22 August 1980.
56. *Washington Post*, 23 March 1980.
57. John A. Bushnell, "La política de los Estados Unidos en El Salvador y Honduras," *Relaciones Internacionales* [Costa Rica], 1, no. 1 (1980): 97.
58. Stockholm International Peace Research Institute (SIPRI), *World Armaments and Disarmament Yearbook, 1980* (London: Taylor & Francis, 1980), 97.
59. SIPRI, *Yearbooks 1980* and *1981*, and *Washington Post*, 5 May 1981.
60. *Miami Herald*, 2 April 1980, and Gregorio Selser, "Tambien a Honduras refuerza Carter con armas pesadas," *El Día* [Mexico], 4 December 1980.
61. Department of Defense, Security Assistance Agency, *Foreign Military Sales*

and Military Assistance Facts (Washington, D.C.: Government Printing Office, December 1980), 67–68.

62. Michael T. Klare and Cynthia Arnson, *Supplying Repression: U.S. Support for Authoritarian Regimes Abroad* (Washington, D.C.: IPS, 1981), 51.

63. Philip E. Wheaton, *The Iron Triangle: The Honduran Connection* (Washington, D.C.: EPICA, 1981), 2–3.

64. *Latin America Weekly Report,* 22 August 1980.

65. *Barricada* [Managua], 30 April 1981.

66. *Washington Post,* 5 May 1981. See also *Le Monde,* 7 May 1981; *Uno Más Uno* [Mexico], 30 June 1980; and *El Día* [Mexico], 16 and 17 April 1980.

67. *Proceso* [Mexico], 8 December 1980.

68. *Financial Times* [London], 18 April 1980.

69. *Central America Report,* 27 June 1981.

70. Interview with Hernán Corrales Padilla, the Christian Democratic presidential candidate, San Pedro Sula, November 1981.

71. Interview with Aníbal Delgado Fiallos, San Pedro Sula, November 1981.

72. Interview with Miguelangel Rodesno, Local Electoral Tribunal, San Pedro Sula, November 1981.

73. Interview with Hernán Corrales Padilla.

74. Exact but early figures from *Tiempo* (1 December 1981): Liberals, 633,365: Nationals, 486,092; PINU, 29, 133; Christian Democrats, 18,785; FPH, 3,938. Under the Honduran voting system, parliamentary seats are allocated on the basis of a complex formula.

75. Roberto Suazo Córdova, press conference, La Paz, Honduras, 28 November 1981.

76. *Wall Street Journal,* 23 November 1981.

77. *Tiempo,* 24 November 1981.

78. *New York Times,* 13 June 1983.

79. *New York Times,* 10 June 1983.

80. *Washington Post,* 26 July 1983

81. *New York Times,* 9 November 1982.

EPILOGUE: AMERICA'S BACKYARD
Günter Grass

"AMERICA'S BACKYARD" is the phrase by which the countries of Central America are known: hence the Mexican saying "Poor Mexico, so far from God, so near the United States." And the description applies as well to the five small "banana republics" of the region among which Nicaragua—bordered to the north by Honduras and to the south by Costa Rica—is to be found. I went there with only superficial impressions, but I returned with vastly different perceptions.

What did I know before I went? Only what I had read. My support for the Sandinista revolution, always imbued with skepticism, had been expressed with caution. I had doubts about its possibilities of success. How could twenty-five-year-old commanders, mere guerrillas until three years ago, have learned the difficult art of economics and civil government? How long would it be before this revolution—as the lessons of history seem to show—would begin to eat its children? And in any case Poland somehow seemed to affect me more.

I had no idea how similar the Polish trade-union movement Solidarity and the Nicaraguan Sandinistas actually are, or how the persistent and defiant dependence of Poland on the Soviet Union is mirrored by that of Central America—in particular Nicaragua—on the United States. Indeed, the constraints felt both by the Sandinistas and by members of Solidarity—in spite of the geographical distance between them—is a negative proof of the point. They know only untruths about each other. The power threatening the Sandinistas, for example, wishes to be seen as the protector of the Solidarity movement—and there are those in Poland who believe this.

Meanwhile, the invasion-ready power on Poland's eastern border believes itself to be the protector of all freedom movements in the Third World—and people are not lacking in Nicaragua who think that, too. There they repeat the false reports from the Tass news agency—that Solidarity is a counterrevolutionary movement. Meanwhile, in Poland they believe the reports of the Voice of America that Nicaragua will soon be the next country to fall into the Cuban-Soviet grip.

From their position of such menacingly close proximity, and from painful experiences of interventions and dismemberment, the oppressed can see the danger only from the nearest superpower. So the thinly disguised hatred of the Russians in Poland corresponds to the perceptible hatred of the Yankees in Nicaragua.

Hatred narrows the perspective. And where the hatred grows daily as a result of the arrogance of the superpowers, everything —even the desire on their part to exercise their power with greater moderation—becomes defined as U.S. imperialism or Soviet domination. And, of course, this hatred in both places is quite understandable.

Anyone who, like me, visited Poland last year and has just returned from Nicaragua, realizes how foolish the superpowers have been in trying to control their backyards. For this time they are faced by a new and unfamiliar kind of opposition—and it won't be crushed. Their tried and tested punishment lessons no longer attract students. Both movements are the same—socialist and Catholic—and each one is endowed with that pagan and early Christian fervor with which all forms of domination find it difficult to come to terms. Even skeptics have to admit that Rosa Luxemburg appeared in Poland in the guise of the Virgin Mary and that in Nicaragua the Mother of God has the look of Rosa Luxemburg.

We have been able to read that there are political prisoners in Nicaragua. What is meant, of course, are the members of the National Guard who perpetrated crimes against the people until the last phase of the revolutionary struggle against Somoza. We asked about them, and Tomás Borge, a minister of state and, at fifty-two, one of the least-old men in the cabinet, immediately proposed a visit to Tipitapa prison.

Appalling—like every prison, and every place where people believe they are allowed to lock each other up—it differs from Somoza's torture centers by the humane way in which sentences are carried out. This practice is to be found nowhere else in the Third World and only experimentally in Western Europe (following the Scandinavian example).

Several hundred former national guardsmen live here and, depending upon their degree of participation in murder and torture, have received sentences ranging from three to thirty years. There is no death penalty. Prisoners work from Monday to Friday, and they have built a hospital and two new prisons with larger cells. In Somoza's old buildings prisoners were crammed in rows of cages. Saturdays and Sundays are kept free for visitors who come each week and are allowed to stay for three or four hours. There exist rooms, albeit too few, for married couples who are permitted a so-called intimate visit. There were some complaints concerning that, but the prisoners were noticeably uninhibited about voicing them. They also said that they would like a radio in order to listen to music during work. Many complained that their wives and parents frequently did not have enough money to travel from the capital Managua or from farther afield in order to visit.

Tomás Borge himself raised questions and made proposals. He, too, had spent five years inside this prison; for nine months he had had to suffer the hood and the handcuffs and for three months continuous torture. While he was a prisoner in Tipitapa, his wife was murdered. As in all the famous revolutions, one might have supposed that revenge would demand injustice for injustice, but Tomás Borge answered this directly, reiterating his long-held belief: "If we take revenge, we destroy the purpose of the revolution. Our revolution represents the renunciation of revenge."

The French, the North American, and the Russian revolutions all resulted in vengeful violence, murder, and mass liquidation. Indeed, all known revolutions have wanted to appease their ideals and make their people happy with theories soaked in blood. Yet in this tiny, sparsely populated, powerless land, where Christ's words are taken literally, the Sandinista revolution provides a different example.

"But has it really not come to internment and torture?" we asked distrustfully. "Yes," said Tomás Borge, "over 700 Sandinistas have been sentenced for looting, torture, and, in some cases, even murder."

There is no discrimination between punishment for the Sandinistas and that for the former National Guard. The vast majority of the guardsmen managed to flee the country, and over 5,000 of them are now grouped in Honduras, on the northern border of Nicaragua. The United States finances them, equips them with weapons, and constantly strengthens their ranks with new units trained in Miami. They push over the border, burn down villages, and try to establish support points for the war they are hoping to unleash. If it breaks out, the whole of Central America will be involved—and President Reagan and his government will be held responsible.

During the stopover in Miami on our outward journey, we rented a car and, after asking about training camps for exiled Cubans and Somocistas, we found them at the southern end of Miami Beach: one was concealed behind household rubbish heaps and the other was a fenced-in barracks, designated an "FBI-Area" by a sign next to the entrance. It warned unauthorized visitors to expect ten years' imprisonment or a fine of $10,000.

The U.S. government simply was not entitled to react with boycotts and protest against Soviet aggression in Afghanistan and Soviet pressure on Poland, because it supported, supplied, and bolstered the thousandfold murderer Somoza (and his father before him) with credits and military support until the very last phase of the war. Even today it wants to turn back the revolution by denying the Sandinistas material help—parts for U.S. products like agricultural machinery—and is quite openly ready to start a second Vietnam War in Central America.

I knew all that before the trip, but it was not until I arrived in Nicaragua that I was to feel so ashamed of those that I, a German, have to be allied with. As far as it is possible for an individual, I hereby wish to terminate this association for the following reasons: because for a long time it has not fulfilled its obligation to protect Western democracies; because its members are required to be silent and tolerant of the crimes of their superpower ally, in order not to weaken the alliance; because, as from all superpowers, only aggression is forthcoming; because the aggression can no longer be excused as superpower stupidity or ignorance; because I support both the Polish Solidarity and the Sandinistas in Nicaragua; and, finally, because I do not want to be halfhearted in opposing this unrelenting injustice.

How impoverished, helpless, and beset by insoluble problems does a country have to be before it is no longer seen as a threat by the shortsighted governments in the United States and Western Europe? Two and a half million inhabitants are concentrated in Managua and a few small towns and are otherwise distributed over thinly populated land.

Somoza left the revolution a troubled inheritance: empty coffers and $1.5 billion worth of debts, accumulated since the earthquake in 1972, when the capital was devastated. The ample donations toward rebuilding were pocketed by Somoza's family; the slums of Managua contained over 300,000 people; a large area of the country was laid waste because Lake Nicaragua had been polluted by sewage; capital totaling more than $1 billion had left the country; and the economy was in tatters—exports worht $500 million against essential imports costing $850 million.

In addition, the world market prices for Nicaragua's main exports—coffee, cotton, sugar—fell to their lowest levels. Whereas before the revolution a hundredweight of coffee had sold for $200, today it would fetch only $80. Balanced against that, the prices for imported goods—from simple tools to agricultural machinery—have risen sharply. Fifty percent of the main foodstuffs—maize and beans—have to be imported, and high interest rates are charged on insufficient credit in excess of $100 billion. Despite an increase in production, the country can look forward to bankruptcy in 1985.

The minister for land reform, Jaime Wheelock, and the minister for internal trade, Dionisio Marenco, clearly explained things to us on the blackboard. They are two young men who, in a short space of time, have learned to perform their functions expertly without abandoning a single revolutionary ideal. They spoke of the Sandinistas' "mixed economy" program. On its completion, the state will own 20 percent of the land, 30 percent will remain private, and 50 percent will be owned by cooperatives.

Jaime Wheelock showed us two cooperatives at work. For the most part it has been former Somoza land that the peasants, landless for generations, have been given. So far 5,000 peasants hold title deeds, and to our question "What has changed for them since the revolution?" we heard answers that explained the need for the revolution better than any party manifesto or theoretical justification. "Before, we had nothing and had to work very hard. Today, we work on our own land more and know why."

In the peasants' huts one frequently finds a picture of Sandino, general of the peasants, hanging next to an emblem of Catholic art, usually the Virgin Mary. Faith gives to the poor (in Nicaragua as well as in Poland) both strength and hope. In Nicaragua the revolution has begun to fulfill some of these hopes and it has not weakened the strength of religion. Rather, in accord with liberation theology, it has reinforced it.

For that reason the Sandinistas and the church have not parted company, and many priests hold ministerial or other administrative posts. This renewed Christian confidence is spreading across Latin America, and even in Cuba, where the revolution is thought to have been completed and is itself a model for Nicaragua, the Sandinistas will effect changes.

Because the movement was organized not from above but by the common people, the Catholic establishment looks down on it and waits mistrustfully.

In Nicaragua it is the archbishop of Managua who currently opposes the church's involvement in the revolutionary movement. He threatens from the pulpit, hoping that the medieval instrument of excommunication will once again prove useful. He uses the tiniest conflict as an excuse to unleash divisions among the clergy, imposing a further burden on this already externally threatened country with its worsening economic situation. The Sandinista leadership either ignores these foolish provocations or sometimes reacts too sharply. The situation has deteriorated since a letter from the pope apparently reiterating the opinions of the conservative clergy became a subject for polemic.

But listen, Wojtyla, Polish pope and frequent traveler, who has seen the world and experienced its suffering. Forgive the familiarity. Is it not still possible to hope that you, who has demonstrated in Poland that you are close to the concerns of the poor, the suffering, and the persecuted, might also take up the struggle against the well-off and the powerful—including even some of your own bishops and cardinals—and against all those who support the repression of the people?

Are not even you able to understand that the Sandinistas and Solidarity have the same roots—something that those most affected, in Nicaragua and Poland, are least able to appreciate because, for the moment, they are oppressed by the weight of the opposing superpower ideologies?

Just imagine, Holy Father, a Polish union leader and a Sandinista —Lech Walesa and Ernesto Cardenal—the worker and the poet-priest sitting at your table and explaining to you the needs, the suffering, and the hopes of their peoples, their ideals and their defeats, their failures and mistakes, their companionship and their loneliness, their worries about their daily bread or their daily maize. Could it not be that suddenly, perhaps with the wily intervention of the Holy Ghost, Walesa and Cardenal would recognize each other as brothers and you as the protecting power?

Panic-stricken and bristling with weapons, the superpowers angrily oppose each other—and they oppress whoever falls in their shadows. But look here, Holy Father: it's not just Poland that stands in a giant's shadow, but Nicaragua too. If you fail to complain to the United States in the way you have frequently admonished the U.S.S.R., you too will be guilty if once again this small and wretched land is overtaken by war and the revolution is crushed.

This revolution is endangered by outside interference and internal economic constraint and even by the Sandinistas themselves, whose mistakes are seized upon by hungry enemies with appetites that are satisfied only when the dark side of the revolution comes to light.

Fortunately, in Nicaragua there are politically responsible people (thin on the ground elsewhere) who admit their errors. A good example of this is the resettlement of the Miskito Indians from the battle-torn frontier with Honduras to the interior. Daniel Ortega, the government coordinator, confessed, "We've made plenty of mistakes. We knew nothing of their religious culture, of their ethnic characteristics, hardly anything about their history or the problems of racism which the English and North American settlers had left behind."

The U.S. ambassador to the United Nations took it upon herself to call the Miskito resettlement "genocide." These lies reflect badly on a country whose recent history was founded on land robbery and genocide.

We visited the young commander Dora María Téllez, who had taken part in the occupation of Somoza's palace. Modestly she said little about it—when the need arose, heroism was not lacking. As vice-president of the privy council, her energies are directed toward making this agency more efficient. The country needs a constitution, an electoral law, and guidelines for establishing political parties. Tomás Borge, Sergio Ramírez, and Dora María Téllez all assured us that 1985 would see the first election. "We'll win, of course," they all said—perhaps rather too loudly and too confidently.

The country is in need of democratic experience, knowledge about constitutional rights, and understanding of pluralistic government. Is it not possible for the Dutch, the Germans, and the Scandinavians to help by sharing their experiences of day-to-day democracy, by giving careful advice, and by helping a tiny, virgin country to form a constitution? It would not cost much, but no help or merely smart-aleck advice could cost a lot.

When we came home, West Germany was much as we had expected. Yet its external hardness and internal banality provided a shocking contrast. It is a rich and, at first glance, abundantly well-off country, but in spite of its so-called sound economy, "solidarity" is somehow missing.

As it has been for months before, the main topic is supplementary contributions. The idea is that people with well-paid and secure jobs should contribute 1 to 2 percent of their income so that new employment and eventually new apprenticeships can be financed. The number of unemployed in Germany amounts to almost 2 million, including many graduates. Of course, the secure employees, or more accurately their unions, have refused to accept this obvious opportunity to practice solidarity. The main burden of the present economic crisis would have to be carried by the employed. This, with other institutional egoism, undermines the stable economy and paves the way for a class society.

Nicaragua needs help. It is trying to develop its agriculture, which in a few years will produce surpluses (maize and beans), and so will help meet the growing worldwide hunger problem. We (and why not we?) are equipped to help Nicaragua, so why do we not offer aid? Or must we always obey the wishes of our superpower and take out the "Cuba truncheon," with which to crush everything—not just the Sandinista revolution but even our own ideals?

When we returned home, the protest movement in Poland had already run against water cannon and tear gas. Yet the old-fashioned word *Solidarity* has been resurrected and can now be found in the front line and in the backyard of the superpowers. Perhaps we, too, in our own homes, should give it a new lease on life.

INDEX

ABOUT THE CONTRIBUTORS

ENRIQUE BALOYRA is a professor of political science at the University of North Carolina, Chapel Hill. Born in Cuba, he has published widely on revolutionary politics and political transition in democratic and authoritarian regimes. His most recent book is *El Salvador in Transition.*

SHELTON H. DAVIS is director of the Anthropology Resource Center in Boston and the author of *Victims of the Miracle: Development and the Indians of Brazil.*

MARTIN DISKIN, an anthropologist, has studied Mexico for the past twenty-five years and written specifically about peasant life in Oaxaca. His attention has turned to the recent struggles in Central America, with particular emphasis on the agrarian origins of revolutionary activity and on agrarian reform. Since 1981 he has visited Central America several times.

RICHARD R. FAGEN is Gildred Professor of Latin American Studies at Stanford University. He is a past president of the Latin American Studies Association. His most recent book is *Capitalism and the State in U.S.–Latin American Relations.*

GÜNTER GRASS is one of Germany's most prominent and outspoken novelists and social commentators.

LUIS MAIRA was active in the Allende government in Chile and since 1974 has resided in Mexico. He directs the Instituto de Estudios de Estados Unidos (Institute for the Study of the United States) of the Centro de Investigación y Docencia Económicas (Economic Center for Research and Teaching) in Mexico City.

TOMMIE SUE MONTGOMERY teaches in the Department of Politics at Ithaca College, Ithaca, New York. She has lived and worked in Latin America, most recently spending a year in Nicaragua, where she worked at the Centro de Investigación y Asesoria Socio-económica (Center for Socioeconomic Research and Evaluation). She has written *Revolution in El Salvador,* based on her study of and her years of residence in that country.

ANNE NELSON, a journalist and photographer, has covered Central America since 1980. Her articles have appeared, among other places, in the *Los Angeles Times* and *The Nation,* and she has reported for the Canadian and British Broadcasting Companies.

LARS SCHÖULTZ is a professor of political science at the University of North Carolina, Chapel Hill. He has written widely on politics in the Southern Cone, especially Argentina, and in recent years has directed his attention to Central America. His most recent book is *Human Rights and United States Policy Toward Latin America.*

EDELBERTO TORRES-RIVAS is one of Central America's most distinguished social scientists. He was born in Guatemala and now resides in Costa Rica. His innumerable publications cover all aspects of social and political reality in Central America. His most recent book is *La crisis política en Centroamérica (The Political Crisis in Central America).*

STEVEN S. VOLK is completing his doctorate in history at Columbia University. He has been research director and president of the North American Congress on Latin America (NACLA), for which he has written on Latin American industrialization, capital penetration, and labor issues.

JOHN WOMACK, JR. is chairman of the Department of History at Harvard and Robert Woods Bliss Professor of Latin American History and Economics. He is the author of the prize-winning book *Zapata and the Mexican Revolution,* and is now finishing a book on industrialization and labor organization in early-twentieth-century Mexico.